Australia, New Zealand, and the Pacific Islands
since the First World War

Australia, New Zealand, and the Pacific Islands since the First World War

Edited by William S. Livingston
and Wm. Roger Louis

University of Texas Press, Austin & London

Library of Congress Cataloging in Publication Data

Main entry under title:
Australia, New Zealand, and the Pacific Islands since the
    First World War.
    Includes index.
        1. Australia—History—20th century. 2. New Zea-
land—History—1870– 3. Islands of the Pacific—His-
tory. I. Livingston, William S. II. Louis, Wm. Roger.
DU116.A9 990 78-24094
ISBN 0-292-70344-9

Design by Nancy Whittington

Contents

Preface

This volume is an attempt to assess the significant historical developments in the Southwest Pacific since the First World War. Its scope encompasses Australia, New Zealand, and the islands in the adjacent seas. Its themes are social and humanistic rather than scientific or technical, but the problems with which it is concerned include complex issues and a variety of intellectual disciplines. Some of the essays deal with international relations, some with politics, some with changing social structures, and one with literary themes. More specifically the theme of the volume can be described as the evolution of a regional identity, along with the evolution of separate national identities, in Australia, New Zealand, and the Pacific islands. What ties the chapters together and gives the book as a whole a particular character is the consideration of these new and distinct identities against a background dominated by the simultaneous erosion of British power and expansion of American influence. It is the interaction among three forces—dwindling British power, rising American influence, and nationalism in a variety of forms—that has transformed the Southwest Pacific since the time of the First World War, a transformation seen most clearly in the decolonization of the islands.

The Southwest Pacific was—and perhaps in a sense still is—almost wholly a British area. Historically it has appeared as a British enclave set down in a distant and alien world. Australia and New Zealand saw themselves as outposts of Britain, dependent in many ways on the mother country. But, in the period treated in this book, the dominion and power of Britain have diminished, and the peoples of the Southwest Pacific have had to reexamine their position and reassess their policies. A recurring and insistent theme of the book is accordingly the gradual decline of British power and the ascendancy of other influences, above all the American. In the essays by Norman Harper and C. Hartley Grattan this theme is explicit, but it permeates many of the others as well.

Yet clearly it would be a mistake to evaluate the major events of the Southwest Pacific since the First World War with either the British Empire-Commonwealth or the United States—or both —as the sole points of reference. Australia and New Zealand have their own unique identities, as indeed do the island peoples of the Pacific, and it would be a mistake to underrate the importance of those identities in any interpretation of those events. The cardinal purpose of the present volume is to synthesize the various interpretations of the forces that have helped shape the character of the region. Collectively these essays thus attempt to understand, not only the ways in which a traditionally British area has come increasingly under American sway, but also the ways in which the peoples of the Southwest Pacific themselves are asserting their own distinctive national personalities.

It is no accident that the book emerges from America, or indeed from Texas. With two exceptions, the essayists are all Australians or New Zealanders. But the two exceptions—Joseph Jones and Hartley Grattan—together with both editors, are on the faculty of the University of Texas. The setting of the University of Texas has been particularly favorable for the development of the book. The Humanities Research Center is the home of the "Grattan Collection"—officially the University of Texas Collection of Southwest Pacificana. That collection of books, pamphlets, journals, magazines, and correspondence was assembled through the diligent effort of Hartley Grattan over a third of a century. It now constitutes the single most valuable collection in the United States of materials on Australia, New Zealand, and the Southwest Pacific in general. Another element of the university setting that has helped to shape this volume is the Faculty Seminar on British Studies. The seminar has produced extended discussions about the history and politics of the British Empire and Commonwealth and the changing nature of the Southwest Pacific. The present book has been much assisted by some of those discussions.

In particular the idea of this volume originated in conversations with Hartley Grattan, who assisted in the planning of the project and enlisted several of the contributors. In an important sense, this study stands as a tribute to the imprint of Grattan's work on the scholarship of the Southwest Pacific.

The organization of the book is intended to provide the reader with a guide through the broad and complex materials with which it deals. The essays by Allan Martin and Keith Sinclair are companion pieces designed to survey the historical literature of Australia and New Zealand, as well as to illuminate the sense of evolving identities in the Southwest Pacific. Mary Boyd builds a bridge across the Tasman by tracing the history of Australian–New Zealand relations. The next two companion essays are concerned with foreign policy: the one on New Zealand by F. L. W. Wood and Roderic Alley emphasizing relations with Britain and the one on Australia by Norman Harper having an American thrust. Geoffrey Sawer's essay on constitutional problems provides a key to understanding the Australian political system, namely, its essential conservatism. Joseph Jones explores the literary aspects of the area, including the island literature. The emphasis of his essay is not so much on literary criticism as on the evolution of a literary consciousness which is at once part of evolving national identities and part of a growing international use of English as a world language. The shift from a political emphasis to cultural and ethnic aspects of identity continues with the two companion pieces by W. E. H. Stanner on the Australian Aborigines and by M. P. K. Sorrenson on the New Zealand Maoris, which interpret the place and development of the indigenous inhabitants in the societies of Australia and New Zealand. Deryck Scarr's essay traces the emergence of the island groups from colonial status to independence. In Grattan's concluding essay there is an original interpretation of events in the Southwest Pacific that includes, among other things, the argument that the most significant changes in the region can be ascribed to the break-up of the British Empire. J. D. B. Miller's introductory essay affords an overview of the volume and provides suggestions on the direction of future research and trends of historical understanding.

One or two technical questions deserve explanation because they have led to small aberrations or inconsistencies of usage. We have capitalized such words as Aboriginal, Aborigines, and Pakeha in accord with established usage in Australia and New Zealand. The two countries differ, however, in their spelling of the word "labor." The party in Australia is Labor but that in New Zealand is Labour, and we have tried to conform to local usage in each case. Where the meaning is unspecific or inclusive, we have used the American spelling, which is the same as the Australian.

The book has been long in the making, and we wish to thank the authors and our colleagues for bearing with us. For assistance and contributions at various stages, we also wish to thank Ahmed Ali, Paul and Helen Bourke, A. J. Brown, Keith Campbell, C. M. H. Clark, H. C. Coombs, Sir John Crawford, L. F. Crisp, Peter Edwards,

Sir Keith Hancock, A. D. Hope, K. S. Inglis, Elwyn Lynn, Ian Nish, and C. G. F. Simkin. Our warm thanks go also to Virginia Sevier, who helped in the preparation of the manuscript as well as in the extensive correspondence involved in its development. And we are especially grateful for the unflagging support of our colleague Warren Roberts, former director of the Humanities Research Center at the University of Texas.

William S. Livingston
Wm. Roger Louis

Australia, New Zealand, and the Pacific Islands
since the First World War

J. D. B. MILLER

Introduction

"It was the good fortune of the Australasians," wrote Henry Demarest Lloyd in 1900, "and of us who can see that they are experimenting for the rest of the world, that they could make the history we sigh for, without making the revolutions for fear of which we can do nothing but sigh."[1] His glowing approval was not fully shared by Sidney Webb, who wrote about the same time to his friend Graham Wallas that in Australia the people were "an exceptionally Individualist graft from our Individualist epoch (1840–1870); and they are all of them gambling profit-makers, keen on realising the Individualist ideals of the lower Middle Class of 1840–70 . . . I don't find that the Australian Democracy was or is based on any abstract ideas."[2] Between these two views lies the argument about interpretation of the Australia and New Zealand of the period before the First World War; the echoes of that argument will be found in some of the papers in this book.

It is now clear, however, that the Australia and New Zealand of those days are far distant, whatever affinity may be found with them. The effects of the intervening period have been to make both countries more sophisticated, more complex socially and politically, more closely connected with the major powers of the northern hemisphere though in different ways, and more self-conscious about their national identities and their likely futures. The papers gathered here are concerned with significant changes in the Southwest Pacific since the First World War. In this introductory essay, I wish to emphasize some of the major points made in the papers that follow and to suggest where further research is needed.

As Allan Martin and Keith Sinclair show, there is much more curiosity about the Australian and New Zealand past than there was fifty years ago and much more professional skill employed in its investigation. In each country a rough-and-ready earlier model of its history, sufficient for the education of the young in the 1930s and 1940s, is being taken apart and examined in detail, while new models are crowding in as more historians graduate and more positions become available in tertiary education. The three themes which Martin ascribes to W. K. Hancock—mastering the continent, framing a polity, and forging an identity—are still being pursued, but there is considerable variation upon them. While it is clear that much more research is needed, there is some likelihood that younger historians, reacting against the broad sweep of their predecessors, and anxious to submit all generalizations to close inspection, will finish by knowing more and more about less and less. Miniature painting has its fascination for painter and onlooker alike, but its limitations are soon obvious. The new themes now emerging—the role of women, the relations between immigrants and indigenes, the development of the cities and the significance of cultural and religious movements—provide some guarantee that the broad sweep will still be attempted.

Nonetheless, as Martin points out, some historians suggest that "economic history is the major part of all Australian history," and no doubt the same can be argued of New Zealand. These are countries settled by immigrants who had to make a living; that is the salient fact about them. Having made for themselves livings as good as any in the world, they must continue to find ways of doing so, in the midst of changing markets and confusing economic growth. Willy-nilly, these high-standard countries are linked to other high-standard countries. They are accordingly involved in the trade policies, currency movements, investment programs, and fiscal changes of distant lands. The sense of utter dependence on the British market, which was so strong a feature of Australian and New Zealand life between the world wars, has now utterly disappeared; few are sorry to see it go. It has been replaced, however, by a more general form of economic dependence, expressed in the fear of what may happen if the Japanese steel industry falls into decline and so wants less iron ore, or the beef markets of the northern hemisphere are suddenly closed because of local producers' pressure, or the international oil companies decide not to explore for possible oil leases, or France succeeds in making the European Economic Community a closed market for temperate foodstuffs.

In both countries the contemporary economy is subject to intensive research, in treasuries and reserve banks no less than in universities. Because livelihoods depend on economic policies, and economic policies come from a combination of group pressures and economists' advice, the whole process is intensely political.

Debates about what should be done to reduce inflation and unemployment, and how to regulate economic growth so as to enhance the quality of life, are as much political as economic. Because of the intense concentration of immigrant societies upon opportunities and economic development and because of the difficulties of mastering a continent and some sparsely settled islands, Australia and New Zealand have traditionally regarded "progress" as strictly physical: so many miles of road, so many dams, so much railway development, so many new factories, so much rural electrification, so great an advance in sewer systems and home-ownership. In this sense Webb's statement in 1898 remains true today; but Lloyd's observation is also correct, because he saw the urge toward social justice that has normally run parallel with, but sometimes counter to, the desire for economic improvement.

Not only in New Zealand but also in Australia, much history has been written in terms of "the Long Pink Cloud" mentioned by Sinclair. Historians and students of politics have often been ruled by what they saw as the essential element in their country's history, the rejection of the old world in favor of a better and more egalitarian one. "Mateship," celebrated by Australian writers and historians, provided the substance of what Martin calls the Bean-Hancock-Fitzpatrick vision of Australia and what an alien may be pardoned for calling the Reeves-Beaglehole-Airey vision of New Zealand. It was a broad and extensive vision (Bean, after all, wrote an admiring book on the long-established fee-paying schools of Australia), but it has proved to be inadequate because it does not accommodate the predominantly petit-bourgeois side of Australians and New Zealanders, those "gambling profit-makers" whom Sidney Webb found hard to praise. In this book the reader will find numerous wistful references to the ideals of social justice and the bold initiatives in foreign policy of such men as Fraser, Evatt, Whitlam, and Kirk and relatively few to the virtues of the Holyoakes and Menzieses. Only in Geoffrey Sawer's relatively technical analysis of Australian federalism is much attention paid to the fundamentally conservative, or nonradical, aspect of Australian national character or to its New Zealand equivalent. There must be an equivalent, if only because Labor governments were almost simultaneously wiped out in both countries late in 1975, for very similar reasons. Radicalism was not enough—even more, radicalism appeared to be actively disliked by a majority of those who, if the older historians' visions were correct, might have been expected to respond to it.

The variants of conservatism which Australia and New Zealand have developed still await full research. Studies of political parties are insufficient (for example, the New Zealand National party has certainly not been adequately dealt with). The roots of conservative feeling require examination, and its growth needs to be seen in terms of current conditions of immigration, employment, and public communication. Scholars need to accept as effectively Australian or New Zealand the sense of identity which conservatives have forged and to reconcile it with its radical opposite.

The problem of economic dependence, which has produced so much of the fire and smoke of traditional politics in both countries, is linked with that of political dependence. In the 1930s it was one of the arguments of local conservatives that, because Australia and New Zealand depended upon Britain for markets as well as naval protection, Australia should support Britain in all aspects of policy. This traditional approach was modified by the Savage government in New Zealand; in Australia it persisted until the Pacific war began. Since then, as Norman Harper demonstrates, a new form of political dependence has been the rule, linked rather less closely than the old with economic dependence but pursued with much the same fervor—dependence on the United States. Again, there is some divergence between the two countries. Sir Keith Holyoake's government, though loyal to the American alliance, was slightly more discriminating in its policies, less wholeheartedly determined to place itself firmly in Washington's good books, than its counterpart in Australia. The almost simultaneous appearance of the Whitlam and Kirk governments in 1972, with their comparative radicalism in foreign policy sharpened by the bitter debates over the Vietnam War, made it look for a time as if this dependence might be permanently modified.

However, the Fraser and Muldoon governments elected in 1975 have returned to something like the position held by their predecessors. Neither agrees with the late Norman Kirk in the view, quoted by F. L. W. Wood and Roderic Alley, that "small countries can be strong. The force of ideas can equate with power." It is association with power, not the force of ideas, that the sense of political dependence strives for. The Long Pink Cloud may characterize much of the thinking of Australian and New Zealand intellectuals about foreign policy, but it is the Long *White* Cloud—seen not as Aotearoa but as the conviction that white people should sustain themselves indefinitely in the South Pacific—which governs the thinking of conservative politicians and many of their parliamentary opponents. In this respect, as in others, the radical image is defective: clearly, most Australians and New Zealanders want the protection embodied in ANZUS and are basically conservative in their outlook. To them, forging an identity does not mean going it alone in an unfriendly world.

That Long White Cloud does not preclude the decent treatment of local indigenes or a helpful approach to former colonies and other islands in the South Pacific. Yet for so long, as W. E. H. Stanner damningly indicates, the Australians ignored and despised the Aborigines. Though the New Zealand record in dealing with the Maoris is immeasurably better, the two countries now find themselves struggling with similar problems—the permeation of colored peoples into their cities and the growing resentment of articulate Aborigines and Maoris against the insults of the poor whites and the patronizing attitudes of the rich. There is no lack of research into these problems. The difficulty lies in effective action.

New Zealand appears to have the better chance of solving the problem because of the recognized position of the Maoris in its political structure and the greater degree of intermarriage between Maori and Pakeha (Maori word for Europeans). In Australia the Aborigines are both too few and too far removed from the established structure of authority to give them the same leverage as the Maoris. M. P. K. Sorrenson's picture of "race relations again coming under strain" is true of New Zealand. The strain is even more apparent in Australia, where the problem is enhanced by the fact that the white people who first come into contact with the Aborigines moving into the inner cities are not the traditional Australians but Turks, Syrians, Lebanese, Italians, and Greeks, none of whom is likely to have that mildly guilty conscience about the past which Australians of British descent sometimes feel.

It is easier to deal with colored people abroad than colored people at home. The Australian and New Zealand record in respect of Papua–New Guinea, the Cook Islands, Western Samoa, Niue, and the Tokelaus will stand comparison with most colonial records. Now that independence has come to these former colonies, the problems for the former administering countries have lessened, although their financial responsibilities have grown. Papua–New Guinea is by far the largest recipient of Australian aid; New Zealand has its special difficulties with the volatile politics of the Cook Islands. Yet these problems are small in both cases, and they must be regarded as a slight price to pay for the sense of national aggrandizement which Australia and New Zealand achieved when they originally took over the island territories. Through the South Pacific Forum and other diplomatic agencies, relationships of dignity can now be established between them and their former colonial possessions, as with other countries, like Fiji and Tonga, with which their past associations have been unofficial but nonetheless significant.

For the island territories themselves, the benevolence of Australia and New Zealand will hardly be enough. They have grave problems of independence, well illustrated in Deryck Scarr's paper. These are partly a matter of economics and partly a matter of identity—though perhaps, as with Australia and New Zealand, economics will prove so pressing that action about identity will have to wait until a dependable standard of living has been established. Should they, in Scarr's words, "remain poor in their own way"? Or should they seize whatever chances of enrichment are provided by foreign investors, knowing that these will change their traditional ways of life, but also knowing that those ways have already been changed forever by modern transport, medicine, education, and administration?

Some of their problems are linguistic, as with all excolonial territories. Unless they accept that they are part of that far-reaching phenomenon which Joseph Jones calls "World English," nobody will understand them, and they will, in some cases, not understand themselves. On the other hand, the English language stands not only for communication but also for elitism, in the sense of the reservation of top jobs for people who have managed to achieve a degree of western culture and who will see that their children achieve it too. This is part of the wider problem of how much western technology and administration to adopt. While one speaks of it as a problem, which implies a solution, the matter is not readily resolved in terms of deliberate action. That "fatal impact" of Europeans upon the Pacific, which produced so many initial tragedies, is now producing dilemmas which may never be resolved. To the extent that they can be alleviated or avoided, Australia and New Zealand have a distinct responsibility to help.

Such help is easier for them to provide in the technological field than the cultural, in spite of the earnest efforts of education officers for decades in places like Papua–New Guinea and Western Samoa. Unlike France and Britain, Australia and New Zealand have had no high culture of their own to hand on to their colonial wards. Only in the last period of colonial control did they establish the Universities of Papua–New Guinea and of the South Pacific; and that was only just in time to provide university degrees to local people who would step into positions of authority with the coming of independence. The high culture purveyed in these universities is necessarily a compound of British, American, and occasional Australian–New Zealand elements—an uneasy mixture which would seem a poor hybrid to the French but which, to Australians or New Zealanders, represents something close to the cultural norm of their own intellectual surroundings. The problems of Pacific island writers, mentioned by Jones, are given a special twist by the fact that the people from whom these writers have learned have themselves been products of derivative cultures. Australia and New Zealand are still forging their own identities, though with more assurance and sophistication than when Hancock was chronicling the Australian efforts of the 1920s. The evolution of these identities, especially in relation to Britain and the United States, is one of the major insights of Hartley Grattan's concluding chapter.

A final theme which emerges from this book, most notably in Mary Boyd's paper but sometimes in others, is that of future relations between Australia and New Zealand as sovereign states. No two peoples are more alike than these two; yet the record of their joint activities, outside those of war, is poor in the extreme. Often, as Boyd says, "the will to consult existed but cooperation proved more difficult." The very likeness between them has been a handicap, to the extent that producers of similar commodities in the two countries have viewed each other as rivals to be kept out of their own territory. Australia is news in New Zealand, but New Zealand is hardly ever news in Australia; there is a regrettable sense of superiority about Australians who are involved in negotiations, public or private, with their counterparts across the Tasman. This is maddening to New Zealanders, as it should be, but their indignation stirs no corresponding concern in Australia. The issue of future relations is regarded with much more seriousness on one side than the other, and it is unhappily the weaker side that takes it more seriously.

The means to further cooperation lie ready at hand—in the New Zealand–Australian Free Trade Agreement, in the periodic consultations between ministers and officials, and in the schemes devised by scholars.[3] What is lacking is the will. The glowing sentiments of Prime Minister Whitlam about resurrecting the sense of companionship which produced the Australia–New Zealand Agreement of 1944 soon looked ironic in the difficult circumstances of unemployment in 1975, when both governments began to think of restricting the free movement of labor from one country to the other. If one of the tasks of earlier Australians and New Zealanders was framing a polity, here is a task for the future: to frame not only a set of institutions that will give them greater opportunities to influence one another but also a set of ideas that will make such institutions both comprehensible and necessary. Perhaps the spur will be found in the need to have common policies in Asia and the Pacific; it would be more appropriately found in a greater awareness of the differences and similarities between the two peoples. Books like this will help in that neglected task. Further research, applied to the similarities and differences and to the issues which at present divide the two countries, is needed from both sides.

Notes

1   Henry Demarest Lloyd, *Newest England: Notes of a Democratic Traveller in New Zealand, with some Australian Comparisons* (New York: Doubleday, Page, 1900), 9.

2   A. G. Austin (ed.), *The Webbs' Australian Diary, 1898* (Melbourne: Pitman, 1965), 115. The Webbs came to Australia by way of New Zealand, where they liked the scenery but Beatrice was repelled by the vulgarity of society.

3   By far the most active of these has been the late Alan Robinson of the School of Political Science and Public Administration at the Victoria University of Wellington. See his *Trans-Tasman Futures* (Wellington: School of Political Science, Victoria University, 1972) and other writings.

ALLAN MARTIN

The Changing Perspective on Australian History

At the end of the 1920s, W. K. Hancock remarked on the pride with which the Australian democracy was inclined to consider itself

> Product of the present only
> Thinking nothing of the past.

Though to a degree inevitable in a "new" society, such an attitude could scarcely recommend itself to a historian. Hancock's reaction to it was mirrored in his *Australia*, a book in which, as half-expatriate, he set out to examine his own country—as he subsequently explained—both sympathetically and critically, both at close view and in the perspective of history. What he saw as the "fecklessness" of the boom years then coming to an end gave a special edge to the inquiry. Hancock sensed with deep unease that a tradition bequeathed to Australians by his parents' generation was in danger of being squandered. A book written by such a man in such a spirit could scarcely be unimportant. In fact, as we can see, it marked as nearly as possible a first watershed in Australian historiography.[1]

Many others had written before this, sometimes with considerable distinction, on aspects of Australia's past and changing present. It would be tedious to list their names, invidious perhaps to try to make a selection among them on grounds of interest or excellence.[2] But, in the nineteenth century, early writers, such as James Macarthur and John Dunmore Lang, and later historians, such as G. W. Rusden and H. G. Turner, had recorded events—particularly political events—in their respective colonies with a sense of structure, a fluency, and an often all-too-evident bias which made their work transcend mere chronicle. In Australia, as in most English-speaking communities during that period, the creative writers caught best the flavor of society, though the natural curiosity of strangers about a land which fascinated—first through its physical peculiarities and then through the unusual societies it came to support—supplemented indigenous writings with a constant stream of visitors' reports, impressions, and criticisms. Writings of this kind reached a proximate apogee in the years just before and just after the turn of the century, when outsiders briefly saw Australia as the world's social laboratory. They celebrated in effect a new kind of democracy which had produced both the first Labor party and an advanced liberalism—two forces which acted jointly to produce social legislation clearly far ahead of its time. Federation of the six colonies, effective in 1901, added the spice of nationalism to the solid fare of democracy, and it was primarily this combination which came thirty years later to be the object of Hancock's quest.

The new nation had by then been through the strange experience of war at a distance—the First World War—which at once "blooded" it and split it more terribly than ever before or since. At the Peace Conference of 1919, Prime Minister William Morris Hughes claimed a hearing on the basis of sixty thousand dead, a tragic sacrifice for a people of barely five million to have made in a war at the other end of the earth. No one could ever know what the loss of so many young men would mean for the quality of life in the society they had left; but the legacy of the other sad happening of those years—the division of the nation over conscription—was clear enough. Pride in the fact that Australia's troops were by late 1916 the only purely volunteer forces in the war was more than merely sentimental: it seemed to many the very symbol of the peculiar quality of Australian democracy. But Hughes, though Labor's leader, thought by then that Australian losses in Europe made conscription necessary, and in two referendums he proposed its introduction. He was defeated on both occasions, in passionate struggles which revealed the real complexity—and fragility—of Australia's democratic consensus and resulted in Hughes's leaving the Labor party with a group of followers, to join their conservative opponents in forming a new Nationalist party. After the war the Nationalists repudiated Hughes's leadership and, under S. M. Bruce, embarked on that hard-headed pursuit of material advancement which came to trouble men like Hancock.

There were some voices to claim that continuities bridged the agony of 1914–1918. One of the most notable was that of C. E. W.

Bean, official war historian, who had lived close to the troops. In a new kind of campaign history, he wrote of the fighting as seen from the trenches as well as from strategists' headquarters.[3] Before the war, Bean had reported vividly on life in the bush, and in the Australian soldier—the Anzac—he saw a new exemplification of a national type which he and many earlier writers thought of as having been molded in the stress of frontier pioneering. Tough and self-reliant, comradely, impatient of pretense, and skeptical of the claims of authority, this legendary Anzac, as Heather Radi succinctly puts it, "bridged the gap between pioneering and the present, by giving to the people of the city the right to the qualities of the outback."[4]

At war's end Bean wrote *In Your Hands, Australians*, a little tract in which he appealed to his compatriots to preserve and develop the Anzac tradition as the one sound basis for future social health and as a trust bequeathed by those who had been sacrificed for the nation. Bean thus summed up and idealized an important strand in the Australian experience, though he no doubt exaggerated the generality of its acceptance. There were many Australians who saw the war in a different light and who, if they thought of future social well-being, looked for its coming through conflict (particularly class conflict) rather than through a consensus based on shared values. Still others—and in overwhelming numbers—thought not at all about such things. As historians have reiterated to the point of tedium, the 1920s and 1930s in Australia were, culturally and morally, "mean" decades.

Professional history, however, came to birth in those years, stimulated partly by teachers in the young history departments of the universities (Ernest Scott in Melbourne and G. Arnold Wood in Sydney were the most notable) and partly by the necessity of providing material about Australia for students eager to study their own society in adult classes organized at that time by the Workers' Education Association. Scott and Wood were fascinated with the story of Europeans' discovery and subsequent exploration of Australia; a pair of younger academics, S. H. Roberts and Myra Willard, wrote respectively on the spread of settlement in the nineteenth century and the origins of the drive to create a "White Australia." Constitutional development had its chroniclers and analysts in Edward Sweetman and A. C. V. Melbourne. R. C. Mills's pioneer work on immigration to Australia during the 1830s had appeared during the war. In 1918 T. A. Coghlan, retired statistician of New South Wales, published his four-volume economic chronicle, *Labor and Industry in Australia, 1788–1901*,[5] a work supplemented by the most notable of the first WEA productions, J. T. Sutcliffe's pioneer study of the trades unions. Writings such as these reflect the natural curiosity of the first professional historians in origins, exploration, economic growth, and the establishment of political institutions. As K. S. Inglis once put it, they were pegging out their territory, laying guidelines for the study of who the white Australians were, how they came, how they made a living, and how they governed themselves.

An epitome of the pioneer historians' work appeared in the early 1930s, a special volume of the *Cambridge History of the British Empire*. Though published in the shadow of the Great Depression, the text of this work belongs to the late 1920s—a chapter discussing "Australia since the War" ends in 1928. The tone of the work is celebratory, its central theme the success with which the "planting of English stock in the South Pacific" had been achieved. Theorists of settlement like Edward Gibbon Wakefield, the editors said, "dreamed great things for Australia and New Zealand, yet none more splendid than have come from the anvil of time." Exploration by sea and land, immigration and the extension of settlement, the wool trade and the gold discoveries, the establishment of responsible government, constitutional development, federation, imperial relations, and the Great War were the staple topics treated. Arranged with an overlapping chronology and accompanied by discussions of politics and economics, the articles gave some sense of a developing society. A massive bibliography, heavily British and destined incidentally to remain for many years the major published list of source material, indicated beyond doubt that Australian history could indeed be a respectable subject for scholarly investigation.

Notwithstanding its theme of progress, the Cambridge volume ended on a sour note. Writing of the Australia of 1928–1929, Fred Alexander deplored politicians' reluctance to shoulder "the obligations of that nationhood upon which war had set its seal," expressed pain that "personal jealousies, party animosities, provincial pettiness all played their part" in retarding progress, and explained the country's social and industrial ills in patrician vein. "The levelling democratic structure of Australian life was unrelieved by the presence of a socially or politically dominant caste, inspired by a tradition of public service, sensitive to outside thought and looking beyond the immediate question of material gain or loss."[6]

As we have seen, Hancock's *Australia*, also written at the end of the 1920s and published in 1930, expressed equal disquiet at the temper of the times. But Hancock's emphasis was radically different. His central concern was for the future of Australia's particular brand of democracy, which he approved and which he associated politically with the Labor party, "the most emphatical product of Australian sentiment." Democracy and Labor, he sensed, must soon confront a severe crisis. Labor won federal office in 1929, to face almost at once economic troubles which, as it turned out, heralded the Great Depression; in Hancock's mind there was a question as to whether the party, "designed to enforce orthodoxy at the expense of leadership," would prove flexible enough to handle economic difficulties imaginatively and forge new goals "which it can pursue with the old zest." It is thus easy to sense behind the writing of *Australia* an urgent wish to provide the democracy with self-knowledge and a desire to articulate the spirit which Labor symbolized and to put it in its proper explanatory historical and physical setting.

Not all Hancock's ideas were new, nor were the historical sections of *Australia* the product of close empirical research. The book's achievement came from Hancock's mastery of existing historical materials, his sensitivity to the tone of Australian society, and his genius for seeing woods as well as trees. Therefore, in his account past shaded effortlessly into present, and many of the ideas that emerged came to be of permanent importance, constituting, indeed, something of a straitjacket from which subsequent historians have had to struggle to escape. Among the more important of these ideas were that in Australia an inhospitable continent allowed only sparse settlement, "a big man's frontier," and the growth of the state as "a vast public utility"; that disappointment of the smallholder bred a collectivist social ethos and a nationalism rooted in rural experience and radical in tone; that Australian politics came to be polarized around two forces—Labor parties of "initiative" and non-Labor parties of "resistance." And behind these observations stood an implicit agenda for Australian historians—their chief tasks being to explore the nineteenth-century themes of development (mastering a continent), democracy (framing a polity), and nationalism (forging an identity).

The 1930s saw the realization of many of Hancock's fears. Assailed by the problems of the economic depression, the Labor party lost unity, office, and its sense of direction. Economic recovery proved slow and painful; unemployment remained a chronic problem; and governments formed by the parties of "resistance" were cold to the idea of social experimentation. Brian Fitzpatrick, the most important historian of that decade to take up Hancock's themes, wrote from an avowedly left-wing point of view, picturing the nation's economic growth as a story chiefly of exploitation by British capitalism. To him the political and industrial struggle of the Australian working class against capitalism had been "beyond its class ends an effort to achieve social justice."[7] Fitzpatrick and the other great historian of those years, Eris O'Brien, set new scholarly standards in their use of source materials and their insistence on relating Australian events to the wider world. Their writings were consequently of lasting significance. O'Brien's *The Foundation of Australia*[8] remains a standard work on the origins of the convict system, and Fitzpatrick's picture of economic development in Australia reigned without serious challenge for twenty years. More important still, Fitzpatrick, especially through his eloquent reiteration of the old tradition which saw Labor as a vital source of creativity in Australian society, was to prove a key influence in inspiring and shaping much of the historical research and writing that followed the Second World War.

An oddity in this context was C. Hartley Grattan's *Introducing Australia*, published in 1942: a book of present description mixed with shrewd historical comment, seeking to capture Australia, so to speak, in the round, for the benefit principally of fellow Americans who—thanks chiefly to the war—were now discovering its existence. Grattan's own discovery had begun in 1927. Travel, talk, and study soon turned that discovery into affection and erudition. Those two qualities, seconded by his synoptic skills and his talent for lively writing, made *Introducing Australia* a book of considerable influence in Australia itself. It was fresh and timely— outside the main currents of local writing because it was broader in scope—and it marked its author as the natural editor for the Australian volume in the United Nations series—an important book which the University of California Press published in 1947.

War and its immediate aftermath meantime confirmed for many Australians themselves what might be loosely called the Bean-Hancock-Fitzpatrick vision. The Anzac tradition acquired new meaning and, after the ruling political parties of the 1930s fell apart, Labor governments from 1941 directed the nation through the most serious crisis of its history and then proceeded with reconstruction plans. Those plans could optimistically be interpreted as picking up reformist threads that had been lost, except in fits and starts, since the early years of the Commonwealth. For some writers the heady excitement of those years survived Labor's fall from office in 1949, paradoxically perhaps, since the triumph then of the parties of "resistance" reflected developing cold war tensions and, when the chips were down, the essential conservatism of the electorate.

But, as the country moved into twenty years of non-Labor rule, the shape of politics as traditionally interpreted became progressively less illuminating as a shorthand guide to what was happening to Australian society. It has truly been observed that "the two decades to 1970 comprised years of such profound change in Australian experience as to allow a confident prediction that future historians will see them as a watershed comparable only perhaps with the gold decade of the 1850s."[9] Elements of the change— a doubling of population since the 1940s, reception of European immigrants in great numbers, unprecedented economic development and affluence, attenuation of British influence, and a new sense of involvement in the mainstream of world affairs—could be perceived readily enough. But their meaning, in terms of culture and the ways in which contemporary Australia differed from the provincial society of prewar years, came quickly to be interpreted variously, spilling untidily out of the old conceptual frameworks.

Most of the existing body of serious historical writing about Australia is the product of those postwar years. Inevitably, it has been affected by changing conceptions of relevance, but this has not been the only or, arguably, the most important source of shifting interpretations. The pioneers of whom we have spoken pointed the way and sometimes illuminated special patches of the field, but historians writing after 1945 found that they were in most areas working from scratch. The progressive accumulation of their findings, and the new questions thus raised, have been a principal source of historical reappraisal in Australia.

The rapid growth of historical research is, of course, itself a reflection of cultural sophistication bred of affluence. Though modest by American standards, the expansion of Australian universities took up much of the slack of the educationally austere years of the 1920s and 1930s. A proliferation of history departments progressively provided historians with incentive, training, and audiences. Staff numbers offer a raw index of change: in 1949 about fifteen full-time professors and lecturers taught history in six Australian universities; by 1973 there were sixteen universities and more than three hundred permanent posts. The multiplication of scholarly journals from one in 1955 to six in 1966 shows more graphically and proximately the growing volume of historical writing.[10] Surveying historical monographs in 1959—most of them originating in universities—J. A. La Nauze likened recent production to an "industrial revolution."[11] Four years later, in another assessment, J. M. Ward described the progress of that revolution by arguing that "the day of the brilliant pioneers, who took quick looks at large subjects and reported their findings in general terms, has given way to the day of the meticulous scholar . . . patiently searching for the truth, accurately determined and precisely stated." Ward was convinced that Australian historiography was at a point of transition in that contemporary writers "know both too much and too little. Knowing what they do, they cannot easily indulge in the bold hypotheses that lent brilliance and distinction to the works of predecessors less encumbered by other men's researches. Knowing more than they do, they might have the materials and the confidence for enlightened judgments of real scope and authority."[12]

In 1963 Hartley Grattan and Manning Clark each published important new histories of Australia. In the previous ten years, no less than four other such works had been produced—three by individual scholars (R. M. Crawford, A. G. L. Shaw, and D. Pike) and one by a group of authors working under Gordon Greenwood's editorship.[13] As one reviewer sardonically remarked at the time, of the writing of general histories there seemed to be no end. No doubt the tight clustering of such works in that period signified an urge for self-understanding in a community aware of the onset of deep change. The problem was—as Ward's remarks implied—that, individual quirks and specialties aside, those historians inevitably drew on a common body of research. Furthermore, none could escape the influence of Hancock; although they commanded infinitely more detail than had been available to him, their material seemed to seep into molds he had fashioned. Of course, some important new bearings were evident. Crawford, for example, wrote at length on Aboriginal culture and set the beginnings of history in Australia well before the coming of white persons. Later, in examining the development of an exploitative European society, he detected the influence of an "aristocratic" element not previously treated by historians. Again, Pike pressed for closer examination of variety in Australian experience, suggesting in particular the importance of smallholders who had in parts of the country developed traditions of independence which cut sharply across the collectivist ideal. And Clark sought in the lives and aspirations of representative figures a way of symbolizing the various strands of faith which he saw as the shaping elements in the Australian story, particularly the encounter in a virgin land of those three great European creeds, Catholicism, Protestantism, and the Enlightenment.

One significance of those general histories is that their preoccupations, as well as their timing, put them astride two reasonably distinct phases of La Nauze's historiographic "revolution." In the first of those, which dated roughly to 1960, the outstanding interpretative works were written by historians pursuing Hancockian themes, particulary radicalism. Fitzpatrick, stressing capitalism's ravages and the creative political role of the working class, had already pioneered that tradition, which by 1960 found its most influential expression in the work of Robin Gollan. Gollan identified consistent radical themes in the history of nineteenth-century Australia and depicted their flowering in the emergence of a powerful nationalistic Labor movement which became the driving force in the critical reformist years between 1890 and 1914.[14] And in 1958 Russel Ward offered a view of the connection between radicalism and nationalism reminiscent of Bean's, arguing persuasively that a mythic Australian self-picture, "discovered" in the 1890s but originating in the experiences of convicts and bushworkers even before 1850, validly reflected a set of democratic attitudes central to the Australian ethos—stoic resourcefulness, distrust of wealth and status, and collectivist egalitarianism encapsulated in the ideal of "mateship."[15]

The demonstrable centrality of the radical theme in Australian history made its early pursuit natural for historians of generous sympathies. They worked from a background of idealism generated by Labor's policies of postwar reconstruction and later of disillusion at the reaction which, in the cold war climate of the 1950s, split the Labor party and ushered in a long period of pragmatic bourgeois politics. The heroic origins of social and political reformism were in that atmosphere a natural focus of study. At the same time, interest in class themes received powerful support from the prevailing orthodoxy which was largely derived from Hancock. To quote S. J. Butlin:

> Australian economic history is the major part of all Australian history; from the beginning economic factors dominated development in a way that should gladden the heart of any Marxist. What is true

of any particular strand of economic growth—land settlement, labour relations and labour organisation, immigration, secondary industry—is also true of each major stage in the development of the community as a whole: each is characterised by economic changes which conditioned political, social and cultural changes.[16]

But, by the early 1960s, other work was coming to fruition, and some new bearings were evident. The establishment in Sydney in 1960 of a *Journal of Religious History* was one straw in the wind ("the religious history of Australia," the editors wrote sadly in the first issue, "is only very imperfectly known"). Two years earlier K. S. Inglis had with force and elegance reminded historians that in Australia the Catholic church had a notable historiographic tradition which deserved reexamination and extension.[17] Such an interest was bound to raise queries about the dictum that "economic history is the major part of all Australian history." In two books of documents[18] published in the late 1950s, Clark had challenged that assumption, and his first volume of *A History of Australia* (1963) developed a tragic vision of early New South Wales in which religious themes were of central importance. Catholic historians working in less apocalyptic vein were soon writing afresh of the church's internal politics and growth and of its encounter with Australian society.[19] The history of Protestantism advanced more slowly, though Michael Roe depicted it as beside, and in some senses as a part of, a quest for "moral enlightenment" that before 1850 appeared in eastern Australia as the dominant urban lower and middle-class ideology—and, incidentally, an important cultural strand to be set beside Russel Ward's bush ethos.[20] The appearance of such writings was seen by some as the beginnings of serious intellectual history in Australia—an attempt, as Paul Bourke put it in 1967, "to use public and private talk heuristically . . . as a way of discovering certain features of the social and individual contexts in which such talk has occurred . . . to establish the predispositions, ideas and concepts of past generations and discover their uses."[21]

That sense of variety which some of the general historians had felt was also being documented through the writing of regional history. At least eight major studies published between 1960 and 1973 offered soundings in depth, principally for the nineteenth century, on an arc stretching round the perimeter of the continent from northern Queensland to Western Australia. Their revelation of extensive differences in community, environment, and experi-

ence cut across many received generalizations. Themes prominent
in eastern history—the conflict between labor and capital or religious disputes over education, for example—were muted or absent in F. K. Crowley's account of Western Australia.[22] J. B. Hirst,
considering the peculiar social and political interrelationship of
Adelaide and the country, depicted South Australia as a virtual
"city state" rather than as a colony whose "ample government"
was generated by problems of distance and sparse settlement.[23]
In western Victoria Margaret Kiddle explained the growth from
modest and chiefly Scottish origins of a pastoral aristocracy which
thwarted radical land legislation and evolved a mode of patriarchal
social relations unusual in Australia.[24] Gordon Buxton showed by
contrast how in the Riverina districts of New South Wales the
"free selection laws," contrary to earlier historians' beliefs, created
rural communities of small and medium farmers and graziers, populist in tone, and centered on service towns where lively social
and political life mediated that rural-urban dichotomy conventionally stressed as a feature of Australian history.[25] The thirst
for property was seen to modify the "big man's frontier" in en-
vironments as different as those which created the small sugar
growers of northern Queensland and the migratory farmers of
South Australia.[26] On a broad scale it was becoming clear that
in Australian history geographic determinism, though given a brilliant new twist by Geoffrey Blainey in *The Tyranny of Distance*,[27]
would not survive unscathed in the face of detailed study in particular settings of the interplay between human and environment,
particularly where scholars were working with dynamic conceptions of ecology and trying to allow for the effects on the land
itself of changing patterns of human knowledge and technology.[28]

Biography, hitherto a weak growth in Australian studies, was
also advancing in the 1960s, the most notable achievement being
the establishment early in the decade of a cooperative scholarly
enterprise, centered on the Australian National University, for
planning and producing an *Australian Dictionary of Biography*.
The first five volumes of this work, published between 1966 and
1974, provided new and colorful evidence of variety, especially
as they included not only the eminent but also less notable individuals chosen "simply as samples of the Australian experience." Organized by time periods, the *Dictionary* offered a series
of cross-sectional pictures of Australian society in evolution and
aroused new curiosity—particularly about the significance of
types of people who previously have not found a place in histori-

ans' conventional pictures. Its potential as a revisionist influence must thus be considerable.

But the great revolution of the 1960s was in economic history itself. "Economists' economic history"—informed by theory, highly technical, and based on massive accumulations of statistics—bore its first fruit in Australia; Fitzpatrick's work was eclipsed, at least in its guise as the ruling empirical account of Australia's economic growth. The centerpiece of the new work was N. G. Butlin's *Investment in Australian Economic Development, 1861–1900*, an exhaustive examination of the processes of capital formation in Australia's most remarkable period of nineteenth-century expansion. Butlin concluded that Australian history fell into four distinct periods—"an inauspicious convict beginning," half a century of "pioneering trials," forty years of "massive effort to control the resources of the Australian continent," a final "three quarters of a century . . . preoccupied with the deliberate fostering and perfection of . . . urbanised society"—and wrote with lyricism of his findings about the third of them:

> In 1860 the Australian colonies made up a loosely connected group of economies. No stable society, no effective social order, no sustained utilisation of available new resources . . . no substantial capital equipment and no national capital accumulation had been achieved. . . . Thirty years later the foundations of an enduring western society had been established and the social and productive assets of a coherent efficient economy and of a wealthy society installed. This transformation was a prodigious effort . . . product of a rate of expansion paralleled only by the United States.[29]

Butlin's exploration of such themes had profound implications for almost every aspect of social and political history in this period and beyond. It dealt with the dynamics of growth; it provided a new context for the stories of pastoral expansion, of the state's emergence as what Hancock had called "a vast public utility," and of the depression of the 1890s. It linked the character of development in the twentieth century to an overproduction of social capital in the nineteenth. Above all, it underlined with startling clarity a fact with which Australian historians had never come to grips, the leading role of urbanization in the economic growth.

In one sense Butlin's work was hardly needed to emphasize the importance of urbanization in Australia. That importance often had been commented on in the nineteenth century and had been highlighted in the famous study of 1899 in which Adna Weber, comparing urban growth internationally, thought it "remarkable" that, after barely one hundred years of settlement by Europeans on a continent which they developed chiefly for rural production, a third of Australia's people should be clustered in the colonial capitals. The twentieth century, as anyone who heeded census findings knew, saw a great acceleration of the trend toward concentration. By 1971 nine major coastal urban areas accounted for almost two-thirds of the entire Australian population of 12.7 million, 44 percent of whom lived in one of the two great conurbations centering on Sydney and Melbourne. And yet, as one writer recently observed, in Australia "historians have asked very few questions about the process and politics of urban growth, [or] the nature and quality of the urban life that most Australians have experienced."[30]

We may set down this neglect partly to the relative youthfulness of Australian historiography, remembering as well that even in Britain and the United States urban history is a recent growth. The bush or rural legend also played its part, given its association with a particular tradition of Australian democracy and its importance to artists and publicists long obsessed with the urge to assert Australia's uniqueness. The development in recent years of a more sophisticated culture and of a sense of close involvement in the problems of a wider world community has helped turn Australian attention more toward the city environment, where in any case the issues of pollution, redevelopment, and planning—though often neglected in the past—seem no longer avoidable. So in the 1960s urban studies became a burgeoning field for town planners, economists, and sociologists, in the process arousing inevitable curiosity about the past. A few pioneer urban historians were already at work and, as others took up the interest, it became clear not only that reappraisals of a variety of received historical interpretations might be in store but also that innovative historiographic techniques, involving cross-disciplinary work, might be developed.[31]

Urbanism is, of course, only one of a number of issues with historical dimensions brought to attention by changing circumstances. Others cluster, for example, around the results and implications of recent immigration. The movement of Europeans (only 45 percent of them British) to Australia between 1947 and 1973 produced a direct net gain to the country of 2 million people who, taken together with their Australian-born children, accounted over the same period for 59 percent of the total population growth of 5.6 million. Immigration on such a scale (Australia's population in 1947 was 7.5 million) and of such diversity has dramatically changed the age and ethnic structure of the population. Fewer than half of today's Australians personally experienced life in the insular and parochial society of the years before 1945. Despite much speculation on the ways in which the immigrant wave has affected Australian styles of life (eating and drinking, sport, musical and literary taste), hard evidence is rare in these matters. But study of the problems faced by minority groups and of the adaptations they have made to the host society is further advanced. This work, together with a growing official tendency to replace the "assimilationist" attitudes evident in the early days of the immigrant program with franker recognition of the fact of ethnicity, underlines the pluralistic character of modern Australian society.[32] Some historians wonder how new this phenomenon really is and what fresh light might be thrown on the Australian experience by the study of minority groups in the past. The work of scholars like Charles Price (on southern Europeans in the early twentieth century and on Asian groups in the nineteenth) seems to make the point.[33] So too does the interest displayed, particularly by religious historians, in the Irish in Australia. Above all, there are the Aborigines, that minority whose condition most disturbs a prosperous society whose complacency is upset by having to recognize in its midst the direst poverty and the opprobrium of being guilty of one of the deadliest sins of modern times— racism.

In *Population and Australia* (1975), the first report of the National Population Inquiry, W. D. Borrie observed:

> On every conceivable comparison, the Aborigines . . . stand in stark contrast to the general Australian society, and also to other "ethnic" groups, whether defined on the basis of race, nationality, birthplace, language or religion. They probably have the highest growth rate, the highest birth rate, the highest death rate, the worst health and housing, and the lowest educational, occupational, economic, social and legal status of any identifiable section of the Australian population. Yet less hard data is [sic] available about the Aboriginal population than about the most recent migrant groups . . . it is a measure of the inequality of the Aborigine's position in Australian society that in a country whose population and social statistics rank among the best in the world, there should exist a group for whom the statistics are as poor as those of most developing countries.[34]

What anthropologist W. E. H. Stanner has called "disremembrance," or the "Great Australian Silence," long muffled the facts of Aboriginal conditions and the place of the Aborigines in Australia's history.[35] An estimated three hundred thousand Aborigines inhabited the continent when soldiers and convicts established the first British settlement in 1788; but demographic collapse over the next hundred years reduced those numbers to the point where it seemed inevitable that the race would disappear. This outcome of white settlement, however sad, seemed unavoidable to most Europeans during the heyday of social Darwinism. There were arguments about the impact of exotic diseases, about ecological change, even about a curious psychological "loss of will to live," which served consciously or unconsciously to mask the brutal reality of the violence to which the indigenes had been subjected.

As mentioned earlier, Crawford's *Australia* (1952) had a lively chapter on the Aborigines, but for the most part the general historians were content to repeat Hancock's brisk dictum that "in truth, a hunting and a pastoral economy cannot coexist within the same bounds" and hence to treat the Aborigines as a kind of melancholy footnote to Australia's history.[36] Stanner's description of this approach is apt enough: "A view from a window which has been carefully placed to exclude a whole quadrant of the landscape." But, in any case, the prophets of doom were wrong. Aboriginal birth and death rates steadied in the 1880s, and the Aboriginal people began to hold their own in the demographic sense. By the 1940s their numbers were rising rapidly, and in 1971 demographers were predicting that the Aboriginal population, then 106,000, would double before the end of the century.

In the 1950s and 1960s a virile movement—strongly influenced by black stirrings overseas and championed by many students and other white Australians—began to assert Aboriginal rights and to protest Aboriginal injustices. It was not fortuitous that anthropologists and prehistorians at work on Aboriginal culture began at this time to receive public recognition, the most notable event being the establishment in 1961 of a government-funded Institute of Aboriginal Studies. In less than a decade, the work which the institute made possible in biology, prehistory, linguistics, and anthropology added incalculably to knowledge of the Aboriginal past and present. While prehistorians pushed back the date of the Aborigines' arrival on the continent—once thought to have preceded the coming of whites by only a few hundred years—to a barely imaginable thirty thousand years ago, students of modern history were seeking in a variety of studies to trace the unhappy history of the Aborigines after their dispossession by Europeans began. The major single project was sponsored by the Social Sciences Research Council and led to the production by 1973 of ten volumes. The project's director, C. D. Rowley, presented a comprehensive picture in the three-volume *Aboriginal Policy and Practice*.[37] Besides opening to a wide public the fruits of accumulating scholarly research, those works could be expected to insure that no future general historian should find it possible to ignore the place of Aboriginal culture and experience in Australian history.

The Aborigines form Australia's only significant—and therefore "troublesome"—"colored" minority. This results from restrictions which the individual colonies imposed on immigration in the nineteenth century and which the new Commonwealth adopted as "settled policy" in 1901 to keep Australia "white." For more than half a century, few seriously questioned the morality of this policy, but there is self-consciousness about it now. The contemporary revulsion against "racism" is one source of unease; Australia's heavy dependence, for trade and security, on friendships in Asia is another. The restrictive immigration legislation still stands, though softened since 1966 by blander administration. Despite the agitation of reformers, Australia is a great distance yet from deciding to free immigration to a point that would allow the development of that multiracial society which some visionaries dream of and some down-to-earth people occasionally think of as inevitable. Meantime, self-questioning has been evident in an urge to reexamine the origins and the working of the restrictive machinery. Though here, as in writings on "racism" and the Aborigines, there appears much breast-beating (usually anachronistic and pious or shallowly sardonic), important new light has been shed on Australian social attitudes, and local scholarship has been given a salutary push in the direction of comparative study.[38]

In the most important of the new works on White Australia, for example, Charles Price noticed that in British Columbia, California, Oregon, and New Zealand the history of restriction has been similar. Scholars "peered and pottered and wondered at local minutiae, sometimes becoming lost in intricate and heated debate about origins or procedures," while failing to notice what was happening elsewhere and how seemingly local oddities might in fact be manifestations of wider trends. "Australian scholars, for instance, might have spent less time arguing whether economic, nationalistic or racial motives were predominant in creating and maintaining the White Australian policy had they concerned themselves not only with Australian egalitarianism and pastoral origins but with why virtually identical policies emerged elsewhere at the same time."[39] The meticulous research and sensible conclusions which Price developed on those premises threw new light on the origins of Australia's restrictive policies. His work was also important in a wider sense because of its methodological implications. For few historians have in the past thought it profitable to compare Australia with other societies that display likenesses in origins and experience, though elsewhere the fruitfulness of that method has long been understood.

Price's work may be expected to support an interest belatedly stirred among some Australian historians by Louis Hartz's provocative *Founding of New Societies* (New York, 1964). Though the substance of Hartz's-treatment of Australia in this work does not always please specialists, the comparative framework within which it is couched has stimulated lively discussion and at least one seminal essay. That is J. W. McCarty's "Australia as a Region of Recent Settlement in the Nineteenth Century," which takes cues from Hartz and from Marc Bloch to suggest pitfalls in a conventional wisdom that emphasized Australia's uniqueness and neglected a range of crucial questions which comparative study might bring to light.[40]

It would be misleading to suggest that those and the many other new departures that one might list in a more extended essay have spelled the death of interest in the old radical tradition. That interest has remained alive and well, having received a particularly important fillip at the beginning of the 1960s through the establishment of an Association for the Study of Labour History, whose journal, *Labour History*, quickly became the main forum for discussion in the field. Monographic literature after 1960 continued to expand the range of scholarly understanding of particular phases of Labor's development, and the Fitzpatrick vision of Labor's heroic role in the Australian "class struggle" remained a lively debating point.[41] Historians of more pragmatic bent were seeking to locate the earlier Labor movement in a broader social and political context which gave weight to other, often neglected, reformist impulses or to investigate the contrast between Labor's ambiguous working-class rhetoric and its actual populist composition and performance.[42] And, from both "conservative" and "new left" standpoints, the suggestion was being made that, in Australia's essentially bourgeois society, Labor might better be understood historically as promoter of consensus than as vehicle of class consciousness. Thus, in his significantly titled *Civilising Capitalism,* Bede Nairn pictured nineteenth-century Labor leaders in New South Wales as a kind of creative minority dedicated to improving a capitalist society whose essential contours they accepted unquestioningly, while Humphrey McQueen has written of Australian workers as fundamentally petit bourgeois in attitude, "fog-bound within capitalism," their false consciousness long articulated by the Labor Party.[43]

In 1974, forty years after the appearance of the Cambridge history and twenty years after Greenwood's *Australia,* a group of professional historians under the editorship of Professor F. K. Crowley produced *A New History of Australia,*[44] a book avowedly designed as "a new overview" of the country's history and, perhaps even more than its two multiauthor predecessors, an epitome of the research of the previous twenty years. Over six hundred pages long and arranged in twelve chapters which lack titles but divide the years from 1788 to 1972 into more or less even chronological slabs, it is a formidable encyclopedic work. Although there are some omissions (the story begins, for example, with the coming of white men and women in 1788, neglecting the ancient Aboriginal occupation of the continent), most of the preoccupations we have been discussing are evident in the text. There is a concern to capture regional diversity, to take proper note of religion, to confront racialism, to recognize the existence of the cities, even at times to break through the politicoeconomic crust and give glimpses of a real society underneath. The density of the treatment, that is to say, has thickened as the writers—particularly those concerned with the nineteenth century—draw on specialist studies their predecessors did not have and strain after methods for depicting society in the round and explaining change in structural terms. No doubt the silent influences here were those historians whose great contribution to the revolution of the last few decades has been to suggest ways of looking holistically at past Australian communities—economies limned in the manner of Noel Butlin, for example, or cultural fabrics recreated in the semianthropological style of some of the regional historians, in particular that of Geoffrey Serle.[45]

The accumulation of data reported in the Crowley volume and the proficient and frequent insight with which it was assembled mirrored the great distance Australian historical scholarship had traveled by 1974. Yet, despite brave words in its preface about "radical rethinking of traditional interpretations," much of the story seemed familiar. The editor's decision to leave the twelve contributors "free to apply their own view of the nature of general history, and to emphasize those aspects of their periods which gave them character or ethos" meant that the book was essentially a collection of essays and not a work with consistent and developing themes. In detail, of course, it reflected within particular periods those shifts in perspective which followed the accumulation of "meticulous scholarship" to which J. M. Ward referred in 1963. Although many old themes persisted, they appeared muted or overlaid or placed in a more reasoned and more detailed human context. But, considered as a whole, *A New History*, fine epitome of Australian scholarship though it is, still left it open for someone to tell us what the shape of Australia's past looks like in long perspective from the vantage point of the last quarter of the twentieth century.

The general historians who wrote after the Second World War laid down a structure of periodization which took economic growth, "democracy," and the development of nationhood as central themes. Politics was a main clue to the working out of these themes, and five dramatic events—the gold rushes, two depressions, and two world wars—were the critical markers for defining the main periods to be treated. That perspective, which tempts historians to deal with the quarter century after 1950 as a kind of postscript to the main story, is becoming more and more unsatisfactory, particularly to those who came to maturity in that period. As memories of depression and war receded, as the study of politics lost much of its traditional content, as problems of social justice assumed new forms, and as concern for the quality of life took precedence in many people's minds over the imperatives of "development," the incentive to break—sometimes radically—with traditional approaches to the past was strong. Thus, for example, some suggested that Australian history might be fruitfully rethought as a whole if the character and evolution of the class structure were chosen as the central issue to be investigated and as a possible clue to a new periodization which might bring to the surface rhythms and explanations of change hitherto lost to view.[46]

Similar effects are hoped for from the growth in Australia of that kind of social history (now well developed in Britain) which is concerned to discover such facts as the patterns of birth, marriage, death, household, and kinship and to investigate the changing nature of culture (in the anthropologists' sense of the word) and of ideas as treated by those whom the French call historians of *mentalités*. That is the kind of history which, as R. J. Tawney would have it, explores the "life of society" rather than a series of events. It is a history to "widen the range of observation" from the experience of a single generation in order to encompass systematically that of its predecessors.[47] It is needed by a community beset by a consciousness of change, even of rootlessness, and looking urgently for new interpreters.

Notes

This essay was written in 1974. Although I have added selected references to materials published after that date, I make no claim to have covered the subsequent literature comprehensively.

1   W. K. Hancock, *Australia* (London: Ernest Benn, 1930; Sydney: Australasian Publishing Co., 1945); idem, *Country and Calling* (London: Faber & Faber, 1954), 121–122.

2   The literature of Australian historiography has been discussed in detail in a number of essays. Three are particularly to be recommended, and the information they contain is broadly assumed in what follows in this essay: J. A. La Nauze, "The Study of Australian History, 1929–59," *Historical Studies*, no. 33 (1959), 1–11; J. M. Ward, "Historiography," in A. L. McLeod (ed.), *The Pattern of Australian Culture* (Melbourne and New York: Oxford University Press and Cornell University Press, 1963); K. A. MacKirdy, "Australia," in R. W. Winks (ed.), *The Historiography of the British Empire-Commonwealth* (Durham, N.C.: Duke University Press, 1966).

3   C. E. W. Bean, *Official History of Australia in the War of 1914–18* (six vols., Sydney: Angus and Robertson, 1938–1942).

4   Heather Radi, "1920–29," in F. K. Crowley (ed.), *A New History of Australia* (Melbourne: William Heinemann, 1974), 395.

5   T. A. Coghlan, *Labor and Industry in Australia, 1788–1901* (4 vols., Oxford: Oxford University Press, 1918).

6   *The Cambridge History of the British Empire*, 7, p. 1, (Cambridge: Cambridge University Press, 1933), 625.

7   B. C. Fitzpatrick, *A Short History of the Australian Labor Movement* (Melbourne: Rawson's Bookshop, 1940). The economic histories are *British Imperialism and Australia, 1783–1833* (London: George Allen and Unwin, 1939) and *The British Empire in Australia, 1834–1939* (Melbourne: Melbourne University Press, 1941).

8   Eris O'Brien, *The Foundation of Australia* (London: Sheed and Ward, 1937).

9   W. J. Hudson, "1951–72," in Crowley (ed.), op. cit., p. 504.

10 The figures are taken from Geoffrey Serle, "The State of the Profession in Australia," *Historical Studies*, no. 61 (1973), 686–702.

11 La Nauze, op. cit., 8.

12 Ward, op. cit., 231, 250.

13 R. M. Crawford, *Australia* (London: Hutchinson, 1952); A. G. L. Shaw, *The Story of Australia* (London: Faber & Faber, 1955); D. Pike, *Australia: The Quiet Continent* (London: Cambridge University Press, 1962); Gordon Greenwood, *Australia: A Social and Political History* (Sydney: Angus and Robertson, 1955); C. Hartley Grattan, *The Southwest Pacific to 1900* and *The Southwest Pacific since 1900*, (two vols., Ann Arbor: University of Michigan Press, 1963); C. M. H. ("Manning") Clark, *A Short History of Australia* (New York: Mentor Books, 1963).

14 R. A. Gollan, *Radical and Working Class Politics: A Study of Eastern Australia, 1850–1910* (Melbourne: Melbourne University Press, 1960).

15 Russel Ward, *The Australian Legend* (Melbourne: Oxford University Press, 1958).

16 S. J. Butlin, *Foundations of the Australian Monetary System* (London: Cambridge University Press, 1953), 1.

17 K. S. Inglis, "Catholic Historiography in Australia," *Historical Studies*, no. 31 (1958), 233–253.

18 C. M. H. Clark, *Select Documents in Australian History* (Sydney: Angus and Robertson, 1955); idem., *Sources of Australian History* (London: Oxford University Press, 1957).

19 See W. Phillips, "Australian Catholic Historiography: Some Recent Issues," *Historical Studies*, no. 56 (1971), 600–611. Important monographs include T. L. Suttor, *Hierarchy and Democracy in Australia, 1788–1870* (Melbourne: Melbourne University Press, 1965); P. O'Farrell, *The Catholic Church in Australia: A Short History, 1788–1967* (Melbourne: Nelson, 1968); J. N. Molony, *The Roman Mould of the Australian Catholic Church* (Melbourne: Melbourne University Press, 1969); J. Waldersee, *Catholic Society in New South Wales, 1788–1860* (Sydney: Sydney University Press, 1974).

20 J. D. Bollan, *Protestantism and Social Reform in New South Wales, 1890–1910* (Melbourne: Melbourne University Press, 1972).

21 Paul F. Bourke, "Some Recent Essays in Australian Intellectual History," *Historical Studies*, no. 49 (1967), 97–105.

22 F. K. Crowley, *Australia's Western Third* (London: Macmillan, 1960).

23 J. B. Hirst, *Adelaide and the Country, 1870–1917* (Melbourne: Melbourne University Press, 1973).

24 Margaret Kiddle, *Men of Yesterday: A Social History of the Western District of Victoria, 1834–1890* (Melbourne: Melbourne University Press, 1961).

25 G. L. Buxton, *The Riverina, 1861–1891: An Australian Regional Study* (Melbourne: Melbourne University Press, 1967).

26 G. C. Bolton, *A Thousand Miles Away: A History of North Queensland to 1920* (Brisbane: Jacaranda Press, 1963); D. W. Meinig, *On the Margins of the Good Earth: The South Australian Wheat Frontier, 1869–1884* (Chicago: Rand McNally, 1962).

27 Geoffrey Blainey, *The Tyranny of Distance* (Melbourne: Sun Books, 1966).

28 See especially Meinig, op. cit.; T. M. Perry, *Australia's First Frontier* (Melbourne: Melbourne University Press, 1963); W. K. Hancock, *Discovering Monaro* (Cambridge: Cambridge University Press, 1972).

29 N. G. Butlin, *Investment in Australian Economic Development, 1861–1900* (Cambridge: Cambridge University Press, 1964), xiii, 3–4.

30 Leone Sandercock, *Cities for Sale* (Melbourne: Melbourne University Press, 1975).

31 See in particular the articles by J. W. McCarty, S. Glynn, and G. Davison in *Urbanisation in Australia*, special issue of *Australian Economic History Review*, X (1970). W. A. Bate, *A History of Brighton* (Melbourne: Melbourne University Press, 1962), is the pioneer work in this field. Hugh Stretton, *Ideas for Australian Cities* (Adelaide: Griffin Press, 1970), is the most stimulating historian's book on current urban problems.

32 The best guide to the relevant literature is C. A. Price's periodically updated *Australian Immigration: A Bibliography and A Digest* (Canberra: Australian National University Press, 1966, 1970, 1975). Part 2 of the 1975 issue is a bibliography of immigrant education in Australia, 1945–1975, and is prefaced with an important essay by Jean I. Martin on the change from assimilationist to pluralist policies.

33 C. A. Price, *Southern Europeans in Australia* (Melbourne: Oxford University Press, 1963); idem, *The Great White Walls Are Built: Restrictive Immigration to North America and Australasia, 1836–88* (Canberra: Australian National University Press, 1974).

34 W. D. Borrie, *Population and Australia: A Demographic Analysis and Projection* (Canberra: Australian Government Publishing Service, 1975), vol. 2, p. 455.

35 W. E. H. Stanner, *After the Dreaming* (Sydney: Australian Broadcasting Commission, 1969), 18 ff. See also his essay elsewhere in this volume.

36 Though it should be noted that in *Discovering Monaro* (1972), Hancock saw the Aborigines in a very different light.

37 C. D. Rowley, *Aboriginal Policy and Practice*; vol. 1, *The Destruction of Aboriginal Society*; vol. 2, *Outcasts in White Australia*; vol. 3, *The Remote Aborigines* (Canberra: Australian National University Press, 1970–1971). On Aboriginal antiquity see D. J. Mulvaney, *The Prehistory of Australia* (London: Thames and Hudson, 1969, revised 1975). Geoffrey Blainey's *Triumph of the Nomads* (Melbourne: Sun Books, 1975) is a popular epitome of the main work in the field.

38 See P. Corris, "Racialism: The Australian Experience," *Historical Studies*, no. 61 (1973), 750–759, for a critical guide to the literature. The administration of the "White Australia" policy is examined in A. T. Yarwood, *Asian Migration to Australia: The Background to Exclusion 1896–1923* (Melbourne: Melbourne University Press, 1964), and A. C. Palfreeman, *The Administration of the White Australian Policy* (Melbourne: Melbourne University Press, 1967).

39 Price, *Great White Walls Are Built*.

40 J. W. McCarty, "Australia as a Region of Recent Settlement in the Nineteenth Century," *Australian Economic History Review*, X (1970), 107–137.

41 Among numerous works note especially Ian Turner, *Industrial Labour and Politics: The Dynamics of the Labour Movement in Eastern Australia, 1900–1921* (Canberra: Australian National University Press, 1965), and D. J. Murphy, *Labour in Politics* (St. Lucia: University of Queensland Press, 1975).

42 The literature here is extensive. But see especially B. E. Mansfield, *Australian Democrat: The Career of Edward William O'Sullivan, 1846–1910* (Sydney: Sydney University Press, 1965); P. Loveday and A. W. Martin, *Parliament Factions and Parties* (Melbourne: Melbourne University Press, 1966); D. W. Rawson, *Labour in Vain: A Survey of the Australian Labor Party* (Melbourne: Longmans, 1966).

43 N. B. Nairn, *Civilising Capitalism* (Canberra: Australian National University Press, 1973); H. McQueen, *A New Britannia* (Ringwood, Victoria: Penguin Books, 1970); J. Playford and D. Kirsner, *Australian Capitalism: Towards a Socialist Critique* (Ringwood, Victoria: Penguin Books, 1972).

44 F. K. Crowley (ed.), *A New History of Australia* (Melbourne: William Heinemann, 1974).

45 Geoffrey Serle, *The Golden Age: A History of the Colony of Victoria, 1883–1889* (Melbourne: Melbourne University Press, 1963); idem, *The Rush to be Rich: A History of the Colony of Victoria, 1883–1889* (Melbourne: Melbourne University Press, 1971).

46 See R. W. Connell, "The Shape of Australian History," *Labour History*, no. 28 (1975). Connell is critical of mainstream empirical historiography and is working with T. H. Irving on a historical analysis of class in Australia. His *Ruling Class, Ruling Culture* (Cambridge: Cambridge University Press, 1977) is a collection of important essays setting out some of his key ideas and, incidentally, suggesting the special usefulness of a "class" approach after the Liberal "coup" in federal politics at the end of 1975. The burgeoning field of women's studies is a special aspect of the new social history. See especially Miriam Dixson, *The Real Matilda* (Ringwood, Victoria: Penguin Books, 1976); Beverley Kingston, *My Wife, My Daughter and Poor Mary Ann* (Melbourne: Nelson, 1975); Anne Summers, *Damned Whores and God's Police* (Ringwood, Victoria: Penguin Books, 1975); A. Curthoys, S. Eade, and P. Spearrett (eds.), *Women at Work* (Canberra: Australian Society for the Study of Labour History, 1975); K. Daniels, M. Murnane, and A. Picot, *Women in Australia: An Annotated Guide to Records* (2 vols., Canberra: A.G.P.S., 1977).

47 See E. J. Hobsbawm, preface to J. F. C. Harrison, *The Early Victorians, 1832–51* (London: Weidenfeld and Nicholson, 1971); F. B. Smith, "Recreating the Life of the Common Man," in D. Duffy, G. Harman, and K. Swan (eds.), *Historians at Work* (Sydney: Hicks Smith, 1973). K. S. Inglis, *The Australian Colonists: An Exploration of Social History, 1788–1870* (Melbourne: Melbourne University Press, 1974), the first of four volumes "exploring" Australian society from its beginnings to the 1970s, is the most important work in this genre.

KEITH SINCLAIR

The Changing Perspective
on New Zealand History

The New Zealand historians of the late nineteenth and early twentieth centuries did not search in Colonial Office records and rarely referred to unpublished sources at all in collecting their data. They had not been trained in the school of von Ranke or, with rare exceptions, in any rigorous intellectual discipline. But it does not seem that many striking features of their subject escaped their attention altogether. Nor is that surprising. Few of them were fools. And the perspectives in which New Zealand history could be viewed, the aspects which could be emphasized, were very restricted. Almost nothing certain about prehistory, before Abel Tasman's discovery of the country in 1642 and between then and Captain James Cook's rediscovery in 1769, was known to Europeans. The effective range of historical vision began in 1769, and after that little was certain before, say, 1800.

It was impossible to ignore the dominant role of the Maoris up to the mid-nineteenth century. The first history, A. S. Thomson's *The Story of New Zealand* (1859), like the books of G. W. Rusden and William Pember Reeves at the end of the century, placed the Maoris in or near the focus of attention. General histories before 1900 also stressed the Anglo-Maori wars of the 1840s and 1860s as principal historical features.

Other happenings that seemed without reflection to assume the status of historical events were the Treaty of Waitangi with the Maoris, the British annexation of the country, and the arrival of the first New Zealand Company settlers, all in 1840. Usually not much was said of the earlier, putatively raffish and unprepossessing if not positively criminal, European settlers on the principle of "the less said the better." The foundations of other organized settlements, such as Otago in 1848 and Canterbury in 1850, were also landmarks, as were the gold rushes of the 1860s and Julius

Vogel's overseas borrowing and economic development program of the 1870s, both of which brought in large numbers of immigrants.

One striking political phenomenon was the evolution of the constitution and of the practice of responsible government. The new status was symbolized by the assumption in 1907 of the title "Dominion of New Zealand," though that title did not denote the wholly independent condition known later as dominion status. At that time the name seemed to many people grandiloquent. No one appears to have thought it might imply British dominion over, and hence continuing possession of, the former colony.

The other political feature given most emphasis in the late nineteenth and earlier twentieth centuries was the Liberal government of 1891–1911. William Pember Reeves was a prominent and the most radical member of that ministry and later the country's best-known historian. When he wrote his short history, *The Long White Cloud,* in 1898 he had already, like most of the leading writers, artists, and intellectuals for another forty years, become an expatriate, living in Great Britain. In his books he stressed state control—radical governmentalism—as the predominant feature of New Zealand politics. So did the French political scientist, André Siegfried, in *La Démocratie en Nouvelle-Zélande* (1904). In 1909 Guy H. Scholefield's pioneering attempt to write an "industrial, economic, and political" history, *New Zealand in Evolution*, likewise stressed New Zealand socialism. There was in fact little "socialism" in a Marxist sense. But there was a tradition of public ownership of railways and other utilities and much government initiative in economic and social affairs, which commonly passed for socialism in those days.

To historians, to politicians, and to the public, reasonably enough, indeed inescapably, their history was that of a British colony. It was traditional to stress that the pioneers were not refugees or convicts but "selected stock"—selected by the supposedly efficient filtering screens of Edward Gibbon Wakefield's theories of colonization and the companies they inspired. New Zealand, it had been proclaimed since 1840, was, and would be, "the Britain of the South." It was the *Britishness* of the colony which most impressed its white population and the many visitors who wrote travel books about it.

That new Britain had its own imperial "civilizing" mission in the Pacific, and it was by virtue of that mission that the Pacific Ocean entered the New Zealand Europeans' consciousness. An eminent line of missionaries, governors, and politicians, like their

Australian counterparts and rivals, had wished that the Australasian colonies should administer an array of Pacific islands, including at least part of New Guinea. Those ambitions received emphasis in an early history of the Pacific, *The Pacific: Its Past and Future* (1919), by Scholefield. But it was the recent and continuing connection with Great Britain—not New Zealand's ancient past, when for a thousand years or more it had been the largest of the Polynesian island groups—on which the white New Zealanders focused their attention.[1]

Not much change in these emphases is to be detected in the decade after the First World War, or even in the 1930s. W. P. Morrell, stressing the inspiring influence of the Gallipoli campaign and the heroic—near mythical—deeds of the Anzacs (members of the Australian and New Zealand Army Corps), wrote in *New Zealand* (1935)[2] of his country's history as the growth of a nation. But little overt nationalism is to be detected in books written at that time. A school book, widely used in the 1930s, was called *Our Nation's Story*. It did, indeed, refer to the need to develop a national spirit. But it was subtitled *A Course of British History*. It contained long sections on the British and other empires and concluded with a list of the English sovereigns since 1066.[3]

Nor is this surprising. Even in the 1920s, most of the adult males of mature years, who presumably ran the country, were immigrants, though a majority of the white population had been New Zealand–born as long ago as the 1880s.[4] Almost all the members of the first Labour cabinet, elected to power in 1935, were immigrants, mostly from Australia.

Colonial history, British history, were still what mattered. That was true for historians and, in a more general sense, for politicians, newspaper editors, and the public. Speeches and editorials were littered with pious references to Home, Mother Country, and the Empire.

Writers who were self-consciously New Zealanders, like the historian J. C. Beaglehole or the poet Allen Curnow, wondered what it meant to be a New Zealander. The latter wrote:

> Not I, some child, born in a marvellous year,
> Will learn the trick of standing upright here.

The lack of change in historical and hence sociological perspective (or mythology) may be illustrated by two quotations. In 1902 two writers, R. F. Irvine and O. T. J. Alpers, dogmatically asserted that the "stock from which the New Zealanders are sprung" was "not only British but the best British."[5] In 1930 the economic historian J. B. Condliffe (later an expatriate in the United States) wrote that this "stock" had been "rigidly selected . . . physically, mentally, and morally."[6]

To historians writing in the late 1930s there had been change, but *plus ça change, plus c'est la même chose*. To Beaglehole, in his essay *New Zealand: A Short History* (1936),[7] and to W. B. Sutch, in his *The Quest for Security in New Zealand* (1942),[8] the long depression of the 1880s and the radical Liberal legislation of the 1890s seemed as important as they had seemed to Reeves. Those notable events had been followed by the First World War, conservative inaction in the 1920s, and then another traumatic economic depression in the early 1930s, which led to further radical and welfare legislation. Thus twice, in the late nineteenth and early twentieth centuries, economic history (boom, slump, boom, slump) was paralleled by and produced its political history (conservative, radical, conservative, radical). Both Beaglehole's and Sutch's books were largely, as the latter said in his preface, studies of poverty, unemployment, and their legislative products.

There were signs of new outlooks, for instance, in the series of books edited by E. H. McCormick and published in 1940 by the Labour government to celebrate the country's centenary of being British. McCormick's own contribution, *Art and Letters in New Zealand*, examined with sensitive scrupulosity a feature of history previously scarcely mentioned. F. L. W. Wood's *New Zealand in the World* was the first history of foreign relations and the beginnings of foreign policy. But it is difficult to feel that new approaches had made much of a dent in the received historical traditions originally summed up so neatly and memorably by Reeves.

There is little doubt that the perspectives in which their country's past is viewed by New Zealanders have changed much more since the Second World War than they did in the previous half century. For this conclusion several reasons will be suggested. Some of the main changes in outlook occurred no doubt in response to developments in the outside world. As the world changes, so does New Zealand, and its history appears different as perspectives change. But some of the new points of view have also arisen internally. Great social or political problems of the past have receded, faded, been dropped or solved. One example is the temperance and prohibition movements, which were as strong in the colony as the drink generously imbibed by its population. The pubs closed at 6 P.M., by popular will, from during the First World War until 1967. Now they close at 10 P.M.; licensed restaurants are permitted and numerous. The public seems, if anything, more sober. Consequently, the quasi-religious, moralistic band of anti-alcohol reformers appears as a passing phase of New Zealand's puritanism and not as a trend. Marijuana, moreover, in the opinions of many of the not-so-young, makes alcohol seem almost harmless. Such social changes must affect as yet unwritten general histories, not by causing historical strands to be excised altogether—censored (as it were) from the historical consciousness—but because some past events will be seen as completed and "in perspective."

Politics has changed, and past political issues already appear in new lights. For instance, one of the major political issues from the 1880s to the 1920s concerned land taxation and land tenure: land nationalization, freehold versus leasehold, and the taxation of the unearned increment on land. Those were once hot political issues, gone cool since the 1920s. Historians will continue to discuss them as they seek to know the scarcely penetrable minds of the dead, but to the public the issues recede into a dark background.

The former vice-chancellor of the University of Canterbury, the historian N. C. Phillips, once playfully referred to New Zealand's history as "the Long Pink Cloud." Certainly, most of its most prominent historians from Reeves to Beaglehole, Sutch, and W. T. G. Airey have sounded politically left of center. For some reason that might be debated, much the same could be said of Australian historians, many of whom, at least until recently, were conspicuously "lefties."

In New Zealand some of the more prominent features of the historical landscape have appeared in a lurid light to observers at all points of the political compass. The great strikes of 1890 and 1913 and the wharf conflict of 1951 can scarcely be ignored. Indeed, the present writer would give greater prominence now to the 1913 strike of the "Red Feds" (disciples of the American IWW) than would have seemed reasonable a few years ago. The physical confrontation of urban striking unionists with the government and its mounted (farmer) special police, W. F. Massey's "Cossacks" or "Uhlans," was the most dramatic example of class, or ideological, conflict that this country has experienced. The 1951 strike, as that of 1890, also aroused violent class and sectional emotions. The depressions of 1879 to 1895 and of about 1928 to 1935 also retain their historical importance, not merely because they changed social attitudes but because they gave birth, as we have seen, to brief periods of radical politics, in 1891–1898 (Liberal) and 1936–1938 (Labour).

These periods of radicalism were of major importance because they greatly sharpened the welfare and statist features of our historical profile. They were periods of volcanic eruption, mountain forming. But sober and later reflection showed that they were indeed brief phases. Of the long years of Liberal and Labour government, few were devoted to such radical legislation. The Liberals under Richard J. ("King Dick") Seddon after 1893 and J. G. Ward after 1906 can scarcely be regarded as left-wing. They became substantially a farmers' and lower-middle-class respectable or establishment party after Reeves left, despite notable achievements like old-age pensions in 1898. Labour introduced the most comprehensive system in the world of social security (pensions, "free" medicine and medical care, etc.) in 1938. But, then, Prime Minister Peter Fraser created an efficient wartime administration. Despite major legislative innovations, such as universal and generous child allowances in 1946, his became a right-wing government. Indeed, he was a cold war warrior in the late 1940s, introducing compulsory military training, after a referendum in which the government threw all its weight into achieving a "yes" vote.

During the Second World War, it was possible for people to overlook, not to see, this change, but in 1949 a National party government, led by Sidney Holland, was elected to power. Under him and then Keith Holyoake, Jack Marshall, and R. D. Muldoon, it retained power to the late 1970s, with only brief and tenuous interruptions under Walter Nash, who had a parliamentary majority of two (minus the Speaker) from 1957 to 1960, and again under Norman Kirk and Wallace ("Bill") Rowling from 1972 to 1975. Twenty years of non-Labour power—often relatively right-wing— have altered the way things look. Twenty years of almost uninterrupted and increasing prosperity have made people less radical, have made the radical episodes of the past seem briefer, and have made both the poverty of depression and the old class feelings seem remote.

New Zealand history now seems more capitalist and more conservative than it did to Reeves, Beaglehole, or Sutch. The economic depressions have for many years ceased to be experiences central to the public vision of the past. One would hesitate, however, to say that this change is permanent. It is true that, while deflation used to be the economic devil of the poor and the unemployed, inflation came to replace it as the nightmare of a wealthy, property-owning democracy. But inflation now stimulates renewed fears of a depression.

Perhaps the clearest way of expressing how time alters appearances is simply to say that New Zealanders enjoyed one of the highest standards of living in the world from 1865 to 1879, from 1895 to 1921, less surely from 1922 to 1928, and from 1935 to 1973. Although their standing in the world statistics of GNP per person has slipped from about fourth to about twentieth, as that of Japan and western European countries has risen, it is still very high.

A modern history of New Zealand would be about a capitalist society, but one that on two occasions was somewhat ahead of other capitalist societies in modifying the effects of competition by state action to redistribute income and protect the helpless. In this altered view, some past achievements seem less notable. For instance, the tradition of state control and intervention in the economy goes back to Vogel and even earlier governments and still continues. But what was fascinating to late-nineteenth-century English, American, or French radicals is now a commonplace in the world. Similarly, the welfare state has been sustained and extended. The poor are still with us, mostly old-age pensioners, superannuitants, and some Polynesians, but they are not as hungry as the unemployed were during two major depressions. What has changed is that welfare systems are now as widespread as the labor legislation which made Reeves an innovator in the 1890s.

Whether the points of view outlined in these paragraphs will persist depends upon world economic trends and also upon domestic political developments.

Some of New Zealand's historical experiences, however, are of increasing importance in the modern world, relevant to modern problems, and still living in the thoughts of many New Zealanders. Race relations, which loomed large in the historical memories of 1859 or of 1898, still seem quite as important as they did then, perhaps more so.

In some respects this renewed emphasis undoubtedly reflects the growing importance of race relations—and racism—in international politics, and in the domestic politics of many countries, in Africa, in the U.S., Australia, Malaysia, and even in Great Britain. But this is not the whole truth. Except for a brief period in the late nineteenth century, racial questions have always been predominant concerns in New Zealand to Maoris and Pakehas (whites) alike.

The Maoris since 1840 have formed an important proportion of the population—not quite half in 1858, and nearly 10 percent in 1970. With large, well-organized tribal political units, they could have prevented at will the initial settlement or destroyed the early townships, whatever backlash from the British army and navy that might have produced. In published histories, as we have seen, their importance has always been recognized. In the histories of the U.S., Canada, or Australia (but not South Africa), the pre-European populations have received less attention. Yet, strangely, though the Maoris themselves have loomed large in European thinking, the Maori (or Anglo-Maori) wars have never captured the popular imagination. When the author was young, New Zealand boys played cowboys and Indians, with six-shooters and bows and arrows. No one then or since relived the defense of Rewi Maniapoto at Orakau in 1864: *"Ka whawhai tonu ake! ake! ake!"* ("We shall fight on forever!") he cried—and escaped when their ammunition had run out.

In *European Vision and the South Pacific* (1960), the Australian scholar, Bernard Smith, wrote of European conceptions of "soft" and "hard" primitives. In the early nineteenth century and later, the Maoris were regarded as intelligent, tough, warlike—and these adjectives were warranted. After European settlement began, curiously ambivalent attitudes developed toward them. Sometimes, especially during the wars of the 1860s, they were referred to as "niggers." But at the same time attitudes of regard and respect were also expressed. Visitors often noted that the Maoris were regarded by settlers as superior to other "savages," and especially to the Australian Aborigines. Humanitarian and missionary opinion joined with this popular notion and proclaimed that the Maoris were eminently civilizable. To "elevate" them, this patronizing but benevolent opinion held, meant that they should be induced to abandon their own culture and become brown Europeans.

Most of the early books describing the Maoris express markedly favorable sentiments toward them. After the wars, as the Maori population declined, a certain sentimentality crept in too toward a supposedly dying race. Although it is easy to cite striking exceptions, at no stage did the English-language literature, except for some newspapers and pamphlets, generally express anti-Maori prejudice. Although white people bought and confiscated Maori lands, from the Treaty of Waitangi onward, there were always many Europeans who hoped for a happy solution to the problems of racial and cultural conflict.[9]

In the late nineteenth and early twentieth centuries the Maoris produced new leaders—prophets like T. W. Ratana,[10] politicians (in the New Zealand Parliament), lawyers and doctors, like Apirana Ngata and Peter Buck—to direct a new effort to come to terms with European society.

Although in many ways modern Maoris suffer disadvantages—in education, housing, and income—their situation is favorable in comparison with that of North American Indians or Australian Aborigines. There is no room, however, for smugness. Young Maoris now often assert their Maoritanga, their Maoriness, their cultural identity, in aggressive voices echoing those of American blacks or of Africans. The term "brown power" is sometimes heard but is not yet always taken seriously.

Another factor has made race relations a cause of active concern. Nearly thirty thousand Polynesian immigrants—from Samoa, Niue, the Cook Islands, and elsewhere—have come to New Zealand. The adaptation to European and urban life has not always been easy. For this reason, too, interracial questions are likely to maintain their place near the center of future histories, as of past ones, of New Zealand.

There are other ways in which world changes have combined with local evolution to produce reassessments of New Zealand's past and of new social attitudes. Confident, even brash assertions of national identity, rare in the 1930s, became more common after the Second World War. Perhaps it is true, as Karl Stead wrote in an essay on New Zealand literature, that such affirmations, at least in poetry, were in some ways less convincing than "the apparent gestures of defeat" of older poets like Allen Curnow.[11] They had the merit, however, of being new.

The growth of a postcolonial sense of nationalism was due in part to the fact that, for most New Zealanders, Great Britain, no longer talked of with nostalgia by parents and grandparents, became increasingly remote, not central to their sense of identity. But that was paralleled by the decline of Britain as a world power, especially as a Pacific power, and the decline of the once British Commonwealth as a useful international organization. Thus events necessitated what sentiment demanded—the search for a meaningful and regional sense of identity to replace "the Empire" and the consciousness of being British as the focus of self-regard.

Changes in the Pacific basin also profoundly altered the world in which New Zealanders had to exist. Once, white New Zealanders felt themselves members of a remote and isolated community cast up on antipodean islands by an imperialist wave. That imperialism was their link with the great European world where things happened. Now that wave has receded, but they no longer feel cut off. Air travel has been important but, more important, all the great world powers now border on the Pacific. Some of the secondary powers, like France, retain a Pacific presence. (In that particular case, one strikingly unpacific, as the French persist in making tests at Mururoa of "safe" nuclear devices. Those tests would be inexpedient at home, whether under- or overground.) Moreover, some of the major world crises since 1941 have occurred in Asia and Southeast Asia and have involved New Zealand. All of those changes have forced New Zealanders toward new attitudes, new policies, and a new independence of outlook.

All histories of New Zealand have stressed the British imperial connection. Historically that was and is just. But the conception of patriotism and citizenship "almost wholly in imperial terms" encouraged an "imperviousness to happenings in the outside world," except in Great Britain.[12] It was possible for Reeves to write a history which scarcely mentioned any foreigners except explorers and the few early French settlers. That would scarcely be feasible now. Britain seems diminished and has joined the European Economic Community. Australia and New Zealand joined defensive alliances with the U.S.—the ANZUS treaty of 1951 and the SEATO treaty of 1954—in response to the real or supposed threats from a possibly remilitarized Japan or from communist China. Pearl Harbor and the Korean and Vietnam wars meant that New Zealanders have looked somewhat less toward Britain and more toward Asia, the U.S., and the Pacific.

Symptomatic of this changing attitude is the rise of the study of Asian, Pacific, and American history in the schools and universities and the publication of numerous pamphlets and a few books on foreign policy, such as M. P. Lissington's surveys of New Zealand's relations with the U.S. and Japan.[13] Foreign policy, particularly in regard to Vietnam, became an election issue for the first time in 1966. Australia and New Zealand signed a free (or freer) trade agreement (NAFTA) in 1965. Both government and business are increasingly active in the Pacific and Southeast Asia. Future historians are likely to give more emphasis to the origins of the external policies of this small, independent state, such as its numerous activities in the League of Nations, the United Nations, and the complex world of international diplomacy.

Parallel to and part of this more cosmopolitan attitude toward the country's past and future is a growing interest in its ancient history. After about 1915—when S. Percy Smith promulgated the theory that the Maoris came in a fleet of canoes[14]—it became usual to believe that the Polynesians arrived in New Zealand about 1350. Little could be said of the supposed earlier inhabitants. As far as is known, New Zealand was one of the last groups of Pacific islands to be occupied by humans. But archeology has shown that by the eleventh century the country was settled from the north to its southern tip, a thousand miles in length. The original settlement must have been over a thousand years ago.

That date in prehistory reinforces the new emphasis on Pacific history rather than merely on a western European one and provides ancient links with the western Polynesians, the Malay-speaking people, and probably with southern China, through a long history of maritime migration. Austro-Polynesian-speaking peoples had spread over a greater part of the earth than any others before the migrations of English-speakers to America, South Africa, and Australasia.

Some of the new attitudes which have been outlined have already affected the writing of New Zealand history. Other, even more recent points of view may lead to equally great reassessments, though which of today's interests will persist and lead to historical investigations is as yet speculative. A student once asked the writer why the Labour government of 1935–1949 did not introduce "equal pay" for women doing the same work as men. Good question? It had been discussed, of course, long before and had been part of the policy of the Political Labour League in 1905. But at the end of the depression of the 1930s, to give pay to unemployed men seemed an all-absorbing problem. The next Labour government, 1957–1960, did introduce equal pay for white women public servants, while in 1972 a National government extended the principle to the whole working population. One may imagine that future historical attitudes will stress the subjection of women, even in one of the first places to introduce votes for women (in 1893).[15]

If present, usually youthful, talk of zero population growth persists, it too will lead to historical reevaluations. Almost always it has been assumed by politicians, historians, and the public that a reasonably high population increase was desirable and a sign of achievement. Similarly the modern stress on protecting the environment from pollution and desecration may lead people to regard with a jaundiced eye the brutal assaults on the landscape by settlers, businesses, local and central governments, railway, electricity, and other departments. But that would not really be novel. In 1898 Reeves published his poem, "The Passing of the Forest," which lamented that the price of progress was "beauty passed away." It was learned and recited by the next generation of schoolchildren.

As popular interests and attitudes change, history is often rewritten as part of the reconsideration of past experience. But a great deal of the change in historical outlook is due simply to the acquisition of new knowledge, even though the inquiries that led to it may have been inspired by changing social attitudes. There can be little doubt that an important reason for advances in knowledge and understanding has been the rapid growth of universities, as society has become more complex and sophisticated. Change in historical, anthropological, and other branches of knowledge thus results from orthodox research, from the desire to satisfy curiosity, gain esteem, or earn a Ph.D.

Our increasing insight into prehistory largely derives from the application of modern archeological techniques in the Pacific. Much has been discovered about the Polynesian settlement of New Zealand. Moreover, it is seen in a new perspective because archeologists have shown that people have inhabited the Pacific for thousands of years. Southeast Asia and Australia now seem not prehistorical backwaters but early centers of human settlement and even of civilization. Archeology used to be Europe-centered too.

Revisionism in historical research has also been fruitful. Much of it has been in the history of the Maoris and race relations. These subjects are far from exhausted: no significant book has appeared based on a thorough knowledge of the written Maori language sources. But some progress has been made. Andrew Sharp's *Ancient Voyagers in the Pacific* (1956) produced a lively debate on Polynesian migrations. H. M. Wright's *New Zealand, 1769–1840* (1959) and Judith Binney's *The Legacy of Guilt: A Life of Thomas Kendall* (1968) have led to a continuing debate on the effects of European contact on Maori society, and particularly on the response of the Maoris to Christianity, which has greatly deepened our understanding of pre-1840 history. We also know infinitely more than before the Second World War about government Maori policy, the Maori king movement, and the Anglo-Maori wars of the 1860s, as about later Maori political and religious movements. Perhaps this has not produced a radically new way of looking at the past, but increasing understanding may not be without its returns to society at large.

Many other historical topics have similarly been subjects of detailed investigation—for instance, the politics of the period 1870 to 1900, which saw the establishment of the tradition of statism and of radical and democratic legislation. Very much more is known about Vogel, Seddon, and Reeves and their works. It is doubtful whether that has led to a substantial reassessment. Governors have fared less well. The "Good Governor Grey" (Sir George Grey) of the school books has become, if not bad, at least shifty.

New social interests that have caused novel inquiries have included university history: the records of four universities have been published out of a possible six—plus one agricultural college. Some work has been done on urban and business history. Provincial histories, which reflect states of mind in the original settlements and provincial governments, have not attracted much attention recently. The provinces seem less important. Their powers were not great, and they did not always correspond with economic regions. Provincial rivalries survive in sport but (except in rugby football) are scarcely as savage as they were a century ago. Local histories, based on real regional differences, are flourishing.

Not all efforts at revision have succeeded. Attempts to suggest that the Treaty of Waitangi did not derive mainly from a humanitarian concern for Maori welfare have been unconvincing to historians and public. Indeed February 6, when the first group of chiefs signed the treaty in 1840, has been appointed a national holiday. And this seems justified. It still appears accurate to say, with C. Hartley Grattan, that the treaty was "a statement of intent," of an intention to establish a "biracial society in New Zealand with equality of rights for both races." [16]

It would not be difficult (though it might be tedious) to go on with a list of historical reassessments. [17] It is equally easy to say where historians (and political scientists) have failed to make the assessments which might have changed public attitudes. There are two recent biographies of Labour leaders, Keith Sinclair's *Walter Nash* and Erik Olssen's *John A. Lee*, [18] but no history of any government since 1935 has been published by any of the legion of academics. Perhaps it is too recent to permit many significant works to have appeared. But the gap is important. Since we have no detailed investigation of the non-Labour (and sometimes unconservative) National governments since 1949, it is difficult for historians to see the past, except dimly, in the light which the present and recent past might shed on it. For this reason and many others, New Zealand's history will continue to be seen in ever changing perspectives.[19]

Notes

1 For earlier views on New Zealand history the reader should refer to Arthur S. Thomson, *The Story of New Zealand* (originally published 1859; reissued 1970 by Praeger, New York, with an introduction by C. Hartley Grattan), and William Pember Reeves, *The Long White Cloud* (London: Horace Marshall & Son, 1898). For the sense of position in the Pacific see Angus Ross, *New Zealand Aspirations in the Pacific in the Nineteenth Century* (Oxford: Oxford University Press, 1964), and Peter Munz, *The Feel of Truth* (Wellington: A. H. and A. W. Reed for the Victoria University of Wellington, 1969).

2 William Parker Morrell, *New Zealand* (London: Ernest Benn, 1935).

3 Anonymous, *Our Nation's Story: A Course of British History* (Christchurch: Whitcombe and Tombs, n.d. [ca. 1930]).

4 F. Rogers, "The Single-Tax Movement in New Zealand" (M.A. thesis, University of Auckland, 1949), 135–136.

5 R. F. Irvine and O. T. J. Alpers, *The Progress of New Zealand in the Century* (London: W. & R. Chambers, 1902), 421.

6 J. B. Condliffe, *New Zealand in the Making* (London: Allen & Unwin, 1930), 373.

7 John C. Beaglehole, *New Zealand: A Short History* (London: Allen & Unwin, 1936). The most recent short histories are William H. Oliver, *The Story of New Zealand* (London: Faber & Faber, 1960), and Keith Sinclair, *A History of New Zealand* (Harmondsworth: Penguin Books, 1959).

8 William B. Sutch, *The Quest for Security in New Zealand* (2d ed., Wellington: Oxford University Press, 1966). Sutch's book is a radical account of some aspects of economic, social, and political history, not reliable in detail but written with the "inside knowledge" of a senior civil servant.

9 On the early period see Ian Wards, *The Shadow of the Land: A Study of British Policy and Racial Conflict in New Zealand, 1832–1852* (Wellington: Historical Publications Branch, Department of Internal Affairs, 1968), and John A. Williams, *Politics of the New Zealand Maori: Protest and Cooperation, 1891–1909* (Seattle: University of Washington Press, 1969). For further references on the role and position of the Maoris, see the essay by M. P. K. Sorrenson in this volume.

10 See J. McLeod Henderson, *Ratana: The Man, the Church, the Political Movement* (2d ed., Wellington: A. H. and A. W. Reed and the Polynesian Society, 1972).

11 Keith Sinclair (ed.), *Distance Looks Our Way* (Auckland: Hamilton, 1961), 90.

12 Condliffe, op. cit., 470–471.

13 M. P. Lissington, *New Zealand and the United States, 1840–1940* and *New Zealand and Japan, 1900–1941* (both Wellington: Government Printer, 1972).

14 D. R. Simmons, "A New Zealand Myth: Kupe, Toi and the 'Fleet,'" *New Zealand Journal of History*, 3, no. 1 (April 1969).

15 On votes for women, see Patricia Grimshaw, *Women's Suffrage in New Zealand* (Auckland: Auckland University Press and Oxford University Press, 1972).

16 C. Hartley Grattan, *The Southwest Pacific to 1900* (Ann Arbor: University of Michigan Press, 1963), 375.

17 Other recent studies exemplifying a new departure or new interests include Robert McD. Chapman, William K. Jackson, and Austin V. Mitchell, *New Zealand Politics in Action: The 1960 General Election* (London: Oxford University Press, 1962); Gary K. Hawke, *Between Government and Banks: A History of the Reserve Bank of New Zealand* (Wellington: Government Printer, 1973); Robin Kay (ed.), *The Australian–New Zealand Agreement, 1944* (Wellington: Historical Publications Branch, Department of Internal Affairs, 1972); William H. Oliver and Jane M. Thomson, *Challenge and Response: A Study of the Development of the Gisborne East Coast Region* (Gisborne: East Coast Development Research Association, 1971); Herbert O. Roth, *Trade Unions in New Zealand Past and Present* (Wellington: Reed Education, 1973); and Russell C. J. Stone, *Makers of Fortune: A Colonial Business Community and Its Fall* (Auckland: Auckland University Press and Oxford University Press, 1973).

18 Keith Sinclair, *Walter Nash* (Auckland: Auckland University Press and Oxford University Press, 1976), and Erik Olssen, *John A. Lee* (Dunedin: University of Otago Press, 1977).

19 For further references on New Zealand history see the detailed bibliographical essay by Keith Sinclair, "New Zealand," in Robin W. Winks (ed.), *The Historiography of the British Empire Commonwealth* (Durham, N.C.: Duke University Press, 1966), 174–196.

MARY BOYD

Australian–New Zealand Relations

Australia and New Zealand in 1919 were autonomous communities within the British Commonwealth and separate members of the League of Nations—bent on going their own separate ways in the modern world. Federation and the First World War had destroyed the old sense of being colonials belonging to one or another of the seven colonies of Australasia. On April 25, 1915, when the men of the Australia–New Zealand Army Corps landed at Gallipoli, the consciousness of a separate and distinct Australian and New Zealand nationhood had been born. Participation by W. M. Hughes and W. F. Massey in the Imperial War Cabinet and at the Paris Peace Conference had fostered dominion status as well as imperial partnership.

The new Anzac relationship, which gradually replaced the old intercolonial relations, was essentially a family relationship rather than an international relationship—one that could generally be taken for granted and did not need to be formalized. It was deeply rooted in the past. Four of the six Australian colonies and five of the six provinces of New Zealand were founded from Great Britain; the others were extensions of the colony of New South Wales. Successive waves of British immigrants filtered through the Australian colonies to New Zealand, although the backwash was considerable. The number of Australian-born in New Zealand reached a peak of 50,693 in 1911 and then slowly declined; the same was true in Australia, where the New Zealand–born reached a peak of 31,868 in that same year and also declined. But these expatriates were only the tip of the iceberg of trans-Tasman migration. The flow was regulated principally by local economic conditions. The two countries became a common labor market for all who could afford a steerage ticket.

A common British heritage was reinforced by the common experience of beginning life all over again on the frontier (the "crucible of democracy") and by sharing in the evolution of "colonial style" nationalism. The Australians and New Zealanders who emerged were not rugged individualists like Americans. Rather they looked to their mates and to the state for help and sustenance. Yet the myths evolved that they were typical frontiersmen—strong, courageous, independent, enterprising, hospitable, casual and down-to-earth, ingenious improvisers at need. Their utopia was rural, agrarian, democratic, egalitarian, and respectable.

At Gallipoli, the frontier ethos transformed military defeat into glorious victory. Whether they wore slouch hats or "lemon-squeezers," the "diggers" were intensely loyal to their "cobbers" or mates in khaki. Thereafter Anzac Day, April 25, became a national day of mourning throughout the length and breadth of both countries, which helped very much to keep this spirit alive.

Shared myths and many points of contact in separate but parallel histories are valuable clues as to how Australians and New Zealanders came to regard each other—not as one and the same people—but as brothers, neighbors, and close friends, who had a lot in common but felt in their bones that they were different. The differences became more apparent as the colonials shed their British heritage and came to terms with their own local environment. The Australia to which they adapted was an island continent lying partly in the tropics, a harsh, sun-baked land of dusty gums and golden wattles, kangaroos and koalas. New Zealand was three remote, wind-swept islands more temperate in climate, with mountains, lakes, and forests (the habitat of native birds) running down to plains and sea. Australia's distinctive qualities were "strangeness and a brooding sense of the vast and half-known"; New Zealand's were "variety and romance."[1]

Australia by 1919 had five million people concentrated in an arc of seaboard cities located around vast sheep runs and wheat lands which were devastated by periodic droughts and edged into a great empty desert—"a nation for a continent and a continent for a nation." A small sprinkling of tribal Aborigines lived on the outer fringes of the European settlements and on large reserves in the tropical north. Over half New Zealand's population of about one million was also urban. It was concentrated in four main centers and scattered in country towns. Less than 5 percent were Maori, and most of them dwelt in rural North Island villages.

The Tasman Sea was not only a bridge but a barrier. As Sir John Hall, premier of New Zealand from 1879 to 1882, had tersely remarked: "Twelve hundred obstacles to Federation will always be found between Australia and New Zealand."[2] New Zealand with its biracial heritage, better race relations, and long-established rights of local self-government remained aloof. Its leaders had no desire to step down from their exalted positions as representatives of a dominion in London or Geneva and go to Canberra. Its national self-interests were better served by imperial partnership than by Australasian federation. Indeed its fear of being absorbed by Australia naturally pushed it into the arms of England. To the former it displayed "a distrustful independence,"[3] but for the latter it reserved all its loyalty and devotion.

Differences in size, resources, and national character made relations unequal and abrasive though still within the family circle. Australians were regarded by New Zealanders as more aggressive, go-ahead, and extrovert than themselves. New Zealanders seemed quieter, more restrained, and a little old-fashioned to Australians. While New Zealand could not be the tail that wagged the dog, Australia could not afford to ignore or ride roughshod over its smaller, weaker brother and neighbor.

Between the Wars

The forces of Australian and New Zealand nationalism that appeared triumphant in 1919 abated during the 1920s and early 1930s. Both countries still looked to Britain for men, money, markets, and military protection. Thus they remained anxious to preserve the wartime imperial partnership. Despite increasing contacts across the Tasman in business and the professions and in sports and recreations, political relations barely existed. If their leaders informed and consulted each other, it was invariably through the Dominions Office in London and at imperial conferences.

Economically they advanced along similar paths of development. Wool and refrigeration had made them distant farms of Britain, and there was little they could exchange with each other without upsetting some domestic interest. After federation, Australia placed stiff tariffs on New Zealand primary produce and treated New Zealand as "an Asiatic country" with regard to preferences. Erstwhile trading partners were now unevenly matched competitors in overseas markets. Trade relations became more retaliatory than reciprocal. Though each granted the other British preferential rates, in 1922 those preferences made little difference. To protect plants from disease and local interests from competition, each imposed embargoes on the other's vegetables and fruits. In a period of falling prices and rising unemployment, said Professor Keith Sinclair, they were "shoving one another into depression."[4] While New Zealand remained a primary-producing, low-tariff country, Australian secondary industries, developed since federation behind a high tariff wall, gained an increasing share of the New Zealand market. By 1930 the balance of trade was two to one in Australia's favor.

As the depression deepened, trade relations deteriorated. Australian devaluation in 1931 reduced the limited amount of protection that existed for New Zealand industries and encouraged New Zealand to import small orders from Australia instead of bulk orders from Britain. Threatened with the loss of its citrus market by continued embargoes, the federal government initiated negotiations that led to the 1933 trade agreement. The tariff concessions it offered New Zealand were in practice insignificant, as were negotiations to lift embargoes and regulate the Tasman trade in fruits and vegetables in the interests of plant protection. New Zealand in 1935 introduced more tariff protection for local industries and higher preferences for Britain. These were followed in 1936 by the Labour government's policies of economic insulation and trade diversification, with first preference for Britain and second preference for commonwealth countries on the basis of reciprocity. Thereafter trade relations became more cordial—some concessions being made on both sides, although the introduction of severe import licensing in New Zealand to conserve overseas funds was a new irritant. By 1939 the balance of trade was three to one in Australia's favor. Moreover, as wartime supplies from Britain fell away, New Zealand needed more and more from Australia.

In the 1920s and early 1930s, the attitudes and interests of the two governments in defense and foreign policy were basically the same. Both believed that the most likely threat to their future security was Japan. Yet they appreciated that Japan had played the game during the First World War, convoying their troops and offsetting Britain's naval weakness. Consequently, they wanted the Anglo-Japanese alliance renewed. The only conceivable alternative, said Hughes, was an American assurance of safety. They had perforce to be content with the Washington treaties and the 5:5:3 naval ratio among Britain, the United States, and Japan in place of the old two-power standard.

As strategy and finance dictated that Britain's main fleet would be concentrated in European waters, the two dominions accepted a proposal to help build a base at Singapore which, in the event of a major emergency in the Far East, would hold out until reinforcements arrived and which would also make possible the operation of capital ships in the area. They were prepared to bear their fair share of the cost as insurance for the future. New Zealand contributed promptly and substantially to the base and reestablished and maintained its own division of the Royal Navy. Australia was slower off the mark and, when the future of the base was in doubt, decided to devote all its contribution to building up its own navy. This virtually ruled out a joint naval agreement.

Neither country had sufficient power to pursue an independent foreign policy. Provided they were informed and consulted by Britain, they were generally content to align themselves with it. But when their vital interests diverged from Britain's, primarily over Pacific security, they protested vigorously and acted together. Old fears of foreign intruders in the South Pacific and of Chinese immigration were transmuted into new anxieties about Japan's long-range ambitions and "the Yellow Peril." New Zealand defended the policy of building the Singapore base when the British Labour government proposed first to abandon it and then to slow down its construction. Australia actively sought to foster good relations and expand trade with Japan. When Japan invaded Manchuria in 1931, the response was slow and smothered in both countries partly because they were preoccupied with the problems of the depression. New Zealand's anxiety was more muted than Australia's for it had no bridge of islands linking it to Asia and no vast, empty spaces to fill.

After 1935 the two governments took different stands on foreign policy. New Zealand's Labour government supported a strong League of Nations and Covenant, and universal collective security, and publicly opposed British appeasement policies. The Australian government, on the other hand, supported the British, though not simply because it was politically more conservative. Australia's main line of communications to Europe was through Suez and the Mediterranean, and the Far East was its Near North. Yet, when war became imminent, both countries stood together with Britain. The more independent-minded Labour government in New Zealand declared war on its own account. The Australian government adhered to the view that, when Britain was at war, Australia was automatically at war too.

The War Years

The Second World War brought the imperial phase of Australian–New Zealand relations to an end. Common danger rapidly transcended political differences and forced the two governments to work more closely together. Complete military interchange of information between governments instead of individual services was suggested by New Zealand's prime minister, M. J. Savage, in 1938. However, Australia's prime minister, J. A. Lyons, preferred that the information exchanged should be at the discretion of the governments concerned.[5] The first real attempt to insure concerted action in defense was the Pacific Defence Conference, held in Wellington in April 1939 on Savage's insistent invitation and attended by British, Australian, and New Zealand delegations. Its main purpose was to discuss the lack of defense preparations in the South Pacific, a matter of particular concern to New Zealand, which at that stage was pushing for closer political liaison with Australia and a more independent line in Pacific policy.[6] But coordination in defense policies was still lacking when war broke out. The New Zealand government's decision to send a special force overseas to the traditional Middle East theater precipitated a similar decision by the Australian government, which regretted that prior consultation had not been possible.[7]

The Pacific war encouraged better collaboration. After he had been informed of the possible withdrawal of the 9th Australian division, Peter Fraser took great care to consult John Curtin over the return of the New Zealand division from the Middle East in the face of the Japanese threat. Fraser's final decision to leave the division in the Middle East infuriated Curtin, whose shores were more threatened and who was strongly of the opinion that all New Zealand troops should be available for the Pacific. While Fraser was concerned that their different decisions would jeopardize their good relations, he insisted that the circumstances of the two countries were different, granted their strategical interdependence.[8]

The most compelling reason for wartime collaboration was Britain's warning in June 1940 that it would not be able to send reinforcements to the Far East in what was then seen as the unlikely event of Japan's taking the opportunity to alter the status quo, and that the British would have to rely on the United States to safeguard their interests there.[9] The same month a New Zealand delegation went to Australia to speed up defense supply arrangements, and it was agreed that New Zealand would be "regarded as one of the Australian States" in these matters.[10]

The Japanese attack on Pearl Harbor and advance south into New Guinea made the security of "the British antipodes" essential to the U.S., and they became its forward bases. But the South Pacific was their region, and naturally they felt that they must have "an eye, an ear, and a voice" wherever decisions affecting them were being made. Diplomatic representation in Washington and a Pacific War Council provided information but not participation in top-level decision making. When Australia was included in the Southwest Pacific area under General Douglas MacArthur and New Zealand in the South Pacific under Admiral Chester W. Nimitz, both protested that they were inevitably one strategic whole in which the substantial military and economic cooperation that had already been achieved should not be jeopardized,[11] but all in vain.

To add to the stresses and strains of the wartime alliance, there were growing anxieties about American postwar intentions in the Pacific and fears of being excluded from the peace settlement. High commissioners were exchanged in 1943, and the Australian minister of external affairs, H. V. Evatt, invited a New Zealand minister to Canberra for preliminary talks on a proposed conference of countries with Pacific interests. The Cairo Declaration of December 1, 1943, which they first heard about in the newspapers, confirmed their fears that the great powers would, without consultation, decide issues which vitally concerned them. When Fraser arrived in Canberra for further talks in January, he found that Evatt wanted "a solemn Treaty or Pact." He doubted the constitutional propriety of this but agreed with about 75 percent of what Evatt proposed. The outcome was the Australian–New Zealand Agreement of January 21, 1944, also known as the Canberra Pact.[12]

In it the two countries demanded to be consulted and represented at the highest level in planning an armistice and a general international organization. They agreed to work together in the South Pacific and to call a regional conference as soon as possible. They insisted that no change in control or sovereignty in the area should be made without their consent. They proposed a regional zone of defense centered on themselves and the arc of islands stretching from New Guinea to the Cook group. Also proposed was a regional organization for the economic, social, and political advancement of Pacific peoples, with permanent secretariats to be created within their Departments of External Affairs to carry out the agreement. Not only was this a reassertion of their traditional aspirations to a Monroe Doctrine for the South Pacific, it was also an attempt to apply the principles of the Atlantic Charter and the doctrine of trusteeship to all the Pacific island territories under colonial rule. New Zealand, however, rejected a further proposal that they should offer to take over the Western Pacific High Commission territories, for it wanted Britain to remain in the region. Allegations that the agreement was an attempt to keep the U.S. out of the region had caused concern in Washington and London, but such allegations were dismissed by its authors as unwarranted and misleading. Indeed, Fraser went to great lengths to deny them and to stress the importance of good relations with the U.S. The chargé d'affaires of the U.S. legation in Wellington quite rightly commented that Australia apparently was "the aggressive partner but smaller and more distant New Zealand does not want to be forgotten either."[13]

In the event, they failed to secure the right to participate directly in wartime policy making concerning the Pacific. Moreover, three years elapsed before they were able to arrange a regional conference in Canberra to establish the South Pacific Commission. Its advisory powers on social and economic matters were less than they had wanted, but regional collaboration to accelerate political development was unacceptable to the other four metropolitan governments represented—Britain, France, the Netherlands, and the U.S.

A major achievement of the Canberra Pact was the working partnership of Evatt and Fraser at San Francisco. The amendments they suggested to the Dumbarton Oaks proposals for a future international organization were based on conclusions reached at a ministerial meeting in Wellington in November 1944. Although they failed in their attack on the principle of unanimity of permanent members in the Security Council (the veto), they succeeded in getting the substance of what they wanted on trusteeship and economic and social policy. Canberra Pact objectives were incorporated into the United Nations Charter.

Secretariats provided for in the pact were established in both Departments of External Affairs, but they had difficulty in finding anything to do. An ever increasing volume and variety of work on Australian–New Zealand affairs was handled by the departments and the offices of the high commissioners and trade commissioners. Telephone and air services facilitated it. Flying boats in 1940, replaced by land-based planes in 1954, reduced the Tasman crossing from four days to seven hours and later to three or four hours. The elaborate machinery for consultation proposed in the Canberra Pact was not needed. The two countries were so close together that they preferred to conduct much of their business on an informal, ad hoc basis. No two other countries exchanged information so freely or had such free access at all levels to each other—a result of the Canberra Pact, which was increasingly valuable as each expanded its diplomatic representation overseas after the war.[14]

The Postwar Period

The close collaboration of the war years became a permanent feature of the external relations of both countries in the postwar period. Changes of government made little difference in day-to-day relations, though they did introduce new considerations and new interpretations of policy matters into the discussions. Moreover, the frequency and intimacy of consultation at the top political level changed.

After 1945 growing international tensions and endeavors to involve the U.S. in postwar commonwealth defense in the Pacific initiated a new phase in Australian–New Zealand relations. Both countries feared renewed Japanese aggression and wanted a hard peace treaty. Both were becoming increasingly concerned about the threat of communism at home and abroad, and the formation of NATO encouraged the idea of a Pacific pact. The U.S., however, became willing to negotiate only when the Korean War made a soft, early Japanese peace treaty desirable. In Canberra, the new Australian minister of external affairs, Percy Spender, seized the initiative to get the U.S. and New Zealand to agree to tripartite regional security arrangements, partly as a quid pro quo for a soft peace. The outcome was the ANZUS treaty of 1951. Thereafter, regular meetings of the ANZUS council gave Australia and New Zealand machinery for top-level consultation with the U.S. Mutual commitments in ANZUS were broadened by SEATO (Southeast Asia Treaty Organization), AMDA (Anglo-Malayan Defense Agreement), and ANZUK (Five-Power Defense Arrangements in Malaysia and Singapore). Both countries contributed forces for the occupation of Japan, the Korean War, the Malayan emergency, the Vietnam War, and the defense of Malaysia and Singapore—the fulfillment of British Commonwealth, United Nations, and regional obligations.[15]

Governments of the late 1960s also tended to regard such military commitments as "insurance" for future great-power protection. The exigencies of cold war politics had substituted "forward defense" in Southeast Asia for a South Pacific zone of defense within the framework of an international security system.

From 1950 onward, T. B. Millar said, Australian–New Zealand cooperation in defense "developed from a by-product of crisis to a day-to-day activity." [16] This was formalized in part by the 1969 memorandum of understanding concerning cooperation in defense supply[17] and in part by the establishment in 1972 of a Consultative Committee on Defence Cooperation for periodic discussions at the senior level.

Despite the meshing of Australian and New Zealand forces a joint defense union was unlikely. In 1972 Australia spent ten times more on defense than New Zealand, though its population was roughly four times larger and its gross national product five times. Furthermore, Australia could become a nuclear power. It was also conscious of the presence of New Guinea, Indonesia, and other Asian countries to its north and west in a way that New Zealand was not.

After the war trans-Tasman trade increased considerably. Because Australia was rapidly developing its mineral resources and industries at a time when New Zealand, with less varied natural resources, continued to rely principally on primary production, the balance became nearly four to one in Australia's favor. Moreover, New Zealand's margins of preference were steadily eroded. A fall in export prices, which had particularly adverse effects on New Zealand, prompted ministerial trade talks in 1958. Changing patterns in world trade, Britain's bid to enter the EEC, and the restructuring of the economies on both sides of the Tasman encouraged more regular consultation on trade matters. In 1960 it was decided to establish an Australian–New Zealand Consultative Committee on Trade consisting of senior officials, and to hold ministerial meetings at least annually. New Zealand, with its rapidly expanding forest industry, wanted a free-trade area in forest products; Australia wanted a broader balance of advantage. The outcome was the New Zealand–Australia Free Trade Agreement (NAFTA) on August 31, 1965, negotiated by John McEwen and J. R. Marshall.[18] Their basic philosophy was that prosperity and expansion in one country were in the best interests of the other. Free-trade provisions were applied to selected goods set out in schedule A of NAFTA. Most of those included initially were already free of duty, and the intention was to add to them gradually. To facilitate that process a transitional stage was provided in article 3:7 of NAFTA, whereby duties on agreed goods or classes of goods could be remitted or reduced in whole or part. Provision was also made for a phasing-out process on dutiable goods, for safeguards to sensitive industries in both countries, and for import licensing for balance-of-payment reasons. All together 60 percent of the existing Tasman trade was covered in the original free-trade arrangements, 86 percent of New Zealand's exports and 53 percent of Australia's.

The will to consult existed but cooperation proved more difficult. Vehement opposition to free trade came from protected sectional interests, such as Australian dairy producers and New Zealand manufacturers. Some Labour critics in New Zealand argued that NAFTA would jeopardize manufacturing in depth, full employment, and social welfare and make New Zealand an economic colony of Australia.

From 1965 to 1972 the Tasman trade increased by 78 percent and more than doubled in value, most of the increase being in manufactures, notably New Zealand forest products and Australian motor vehicles. The expansion of New Zealand's industrial exports was assisted by devaluation in 1967, and at least some of its industries were proving they could hold their own. Australia by 1973 supplied over 20 percent of New Zealand's imports; indeed, New Zealand was its largest market for manufactures, whereas less than 3 percent of its imports came from New Zealand. The trade imbalance declined to two to one in Australia's favor in 1969, then rose again to almost three and one-half to one in 1972. The proportion of duty-free trade included in schedule A did not increase significantly, for there was a marked resistance on the part of industry to move from limited free trade facilitated by article 3:7 arrangements to unrestricted free trade. Despite NAFTA the pattern of trade remained substantially unchanged. Nonetheless, at the industry level cooperation gathered force. Joint Consultative Committees composed of officials and industry representatives of both countries were established for forest products in 1968 and for dairy products in 1972. From 1967 annual meetings were held between officials and the manufacturers' organizations of both countries. The growth of cooperation, rationalization, and interdependence in industry facilitated by article 3:7 was one of the increasing advantages of NAFTA.

New opportunities for cooperation and consultation in the late 1960s were created by the decolonization of Oceania. Newly independent or self-governing island states looked to both countries for increased trade and aid and for relief from population pressures. New Zealand initially and Australia somewhat later became increasingly aware of their interests in the region and of their obligations to help their poorer neighbors.

In the South Pacific Commission, they warmly supported changes which transferred responsibility for determining the work program and annual expenditure from the six metropolitan commissioners to the island delegates in the South Pacific Conference.[19] When France and the U.S. insisted that the conference should not discuss politics, New Zealand took the initiative in August 1971 in establishing the South Pacific Forum, an informal meeting of prime ministers of independent and self-governing island states with Australian and New Zealand representatives. The SPF set up the South Pacific Bureau of Economic Co-operation in Suva to change the pattern of trade in the region "whereby the territories previously dependent had supplied raw materials to metropolitan countries but were unable to manufacture many of the goods they required."[20] A free-trade area in the South Pacific wider than NAFTA became a possibility. Australia and New Zealand were becoming the hub of a new network of family relationships between commonwealth members and their associates in the region. Furthermore, consultation and cooperation were developing among the island states, as well as between the island states and themselves.

The election of Labor governments on both sides of the Tasman toward the end of 1972 produced new initiatives and new perceptions in Australian–New Zealand relations. Although fundamental interests and policies remained unaltered, changes in 1973 seemed "real and deep." Developments taking place in great-power relations and international relations generally provided a favorable climate. With the emergence of the new multipolar world, both countries could adopt a more independent stance on foreign policy and become more self-reliant.

One of the first things Norman Kirk did after he became prime minister of New Zealand was to telephone the new Australian prime minister, Gough Whitlam, suggesting that they might meet in Wellington on the anniversary of the Canberra Pact. "The first thing we want to talk about," he said, "is how to revitalize and further strengthen the day-to-day partnership between our two countries."[21] At lengthy and intimate discussions on January 20–23 they reaffirmed the principles of the Canberra Pact and "indicated their intention to work for the closest possible consultation and collaboration on all matters—political, economic, defence, social and cultural—which affected their joint interests, particularly in the South Pacific region." They also agreed to complete the abolition of passport and visa requirements for travel and immigration between them for citizens of both countries and for commonwealth citizens with resident status. The practical effect of this was to extend to New Zealand's Polynesians and Asians the freedom of movement already enjoyed by others, a demonstration of the sincerity of both leaders in stating "their belief in the equality of every citizen in a multi-racial society and the right of all to the enjoyment of equal opportunities."[22]

Compared with the Canberra Pact the joint communiqué of January 1973 was more sober and realistic. Contemporary needs were assessed and new forms of social cooperation were indicated. Australia was quietly and effectively reminded that it could not ignore New Zealand politically.

In 1973 consultation and cooperation advanced at a rate unmatched in the past. Both governments took proceedings in the International Court to examine the legality of French nuclear testing in the South Pacific, and the Australian government and the Royal Australian Navy supported the presence of the two New Zealand frigates in the nuclear-test zone during the testing period. Both governments launched a proposal to finance the South Pacific Commission partly on a voluntary basis by each contributing $NZ 250,000 toward the 1974 work program. New initiatives on tariff restructuring took place under NAFTA after Britain entered the EEC and ended the contractual obligations to extend to Britain tariff preferences which each also extended to the other. Australia's 25 percent tariff reduction dramatically telescoped the duty-reduction provisions of NAFTA. New Zealand, though not consulted beforehand, was treated generously. Manufacturers agreed to set up joint industry panels to increase overall sales in both countries. A measure of agreement was reached to cooperate in trans-Tasman shipping services. More ministers than ever before met for both formal and informal discussions. A solid working relation between Australia and New Zealand was being established at all levels.

Bridgebuilding across the Tasman has been a long, slow process which, until the Pacific war, proceeded in fits and starts. After diplomatic representation was exchanged in 1943 the trading of information and consultation became routine. More daily cooperation developed in defense after ANZUS and in trade with NAFTA, though still largely in watertight compartments. It must be said, however, that political initiatives at the top level have been more evident in periods when Labor governments with basically compatible policies have held office on both sides of the Tasman.

Collaboration has been not only between governments but between persons, and it has inevitably reflected their different styles and characters; Evatt, the brilliant lawyer, and Fraser, the astute wartime statesman; Whitlam, the colorful, academic leader, and Kirk, the self-educated, able politician. All of them have been idealists and men of vision. All have believed that their countries had a leading role to play in world affairs, particularly in their own region. Yet there have been marked differences between them which have reflected differences between their two countries—not only in size, resources, power, and capability but also in national character. Fraser and Kirk took their stand on moral principles and were concerned about human rights, the rule of law, and the role of small nations in international affairs. Evatt and Whitlam submerged similar ideals and aspirations beneath realpolitik. Australia has generally been more confident, more forceful, and more ambitious. New Zealand has been a restraining influence. Yet on occasions New Zealand's quiet diplomacy has been more effective than Australia's "crashes through."[23]

Australian–New Zealand relations generally have been closer in periods when each country has been following a more independent foreign policy rather than a policy determined by the views and interests of its most influential ally: at one time Britain, more recently the United States. Sovereign independence and a strong sense of nationhood, as well as kinship between the two countries, have been the essence of a full and equal trans-Tasman partnership.[24]

Notes

1   W. P. Reeves, *State Experiments in Australia & New Zealand* (London: G. Richards, 1902), I, 22.

2   Ibid., 179.

3   André Siegfried, *Democracy in New Zealand* (London: G. Bell & Sons, 1914), 358.

4   Keith Sinclair, "Fruit Fly, Fireblight and Powdery Scab: Australia–New Zealand Trade Relations, 1919–39," *The Journal of Imperial and Commonwealth History*, I, 1 (1972), 34.

5   For the relevant documents see Robin Kay (ed.), *The Australian–New Zealand Agreement, 1944* (Wellington: Historical Publications Branch, Department of Internal Affairs, 1972), 1–4.

6   F. L. W. Wood, *The New Zealand People at War: Political and External Affairs* (Wellington: War History Branch, Department of Internal Affairs, 1958), 80.

7   Kay, op. cit., 5–7.

8   Ibid., 7–16, 25–38.

9   *Documents Relating to New Zealand's Participation in the Second World War, 1939–45*, III (Wellington: War History Branch, Department of Internal Affairs, 1963), 206n. (hereafter cited as *Documents*, III).

10 J. V. T. Baker, *The New Zealand People at War: War Economy* (Wellington: Historical Publications Branch, Department of Internal Affairs, 1965), 120.

11 *Documents*, III, 190 passim. See also Kay, op. cit., 17–20.

12 Kay, op. cit., 140–148.

13 Ibid., 164n.

14 *New Zealand Foreign Policy Statements and Documents, 1943–1957* (Wellington: Ministry of Foreign Affairs, 1972), 17.

15 On these mutual and shared commitments, see the essay on "New Zealand Foreign Policy" by F. L. W. Wood and Roderic Alley elsewhere in this volume.

16 T. B. Millar, *Australian–New Zealand Defence Co-operation* (Canberra: Australian National University Press, 1968), 2.

17 Ken Keith (ed.), *Defence Perspectives* (Wellington: Price Milburn for the New Zealand Institute of International Affairs, 1972), 110–111.

18 New Zealand Treaty Series 1966, no. 1.

19 T. R. Smith, *South Pacific Commission: An Analysis after Twenty-Five Years* (Wellington: Price Milburn for the New Zealand Institute of International Affairs, 1972), 72–75.

20 Ken Piddington, *The South Pacific Bureau: A New Venture in Economic Co-operation* (Wellington: New Zealand Institute for International Affairs, 1973), 10.

21 *New Zealand Foreign Affairs Review*, 22, 12 (December 1972), 13–14.

22 Ibid., 23, 1 (January 1973), 4–5.

23 The phrase is Whitlam's.

24 Since this essay was written, Australia–New Zealand relations have been thoroughly and capably researched by Alan and Robin Burnett. See their *The Australian and New Zealand Nexus* (Canberra: Australian Institute of International Affairs, New Zealand Institute of International Affairs, 1978).

F. L. W. WOOD and RODERIC ALLEY

New Zealand Foreign Policy

New Zealand in 1919 felt no need for a deeply considered foreign policy. That was a matter for the empire, of which it was a junior though active and respected partner. New Zealand tradition was, indeed, one of emphatic—even strident—speech when its interests were threatened; but by preference as well as necessity the government's views were expressed in confidential discussion, not in public confrontations. This was a matter of realism as well as good manners. Its leaders, though fresh from participation in the Imperial War Cabinet and in the peacemaking at Versailles, understood clearly enough—perhaps even exaggerated—New Zealand's insignificance in world politics. But New Zealand, unlike some of its fellow dominions, was well content with its situation. In the euphoria of victory, the British Empire-Commonwealth was a congenial as well as a triumphant power group, and New Zealand had an overriding confidence both in the good will and (by and large) in the wisdom of those who made decisions in London. In September 1925, Prime Minister J. G. Coates accurately described the procedure: when negotiations were in hand, New Zealand expressed its views but was content to leave final decisions to British statesmen, who knew all the facts and (presumably) had an empirewide perspective. Less cautious New Zealanders clothed the situation with emotional language which gave grounds to frequent statements that New Zealand was the most loyal, conservative, sentimentally British of all the commonwealth communities. W. F. Massey, prime minister until early 1925, uplifted by wartime experiences, clung with a plain man's obstinacy to the faith that in peace also the empire could act as one. In addition, New Zealand's most distinguished lawyers insisted in public that, as far as this dominion was concerned, the imperial structure remained legally intact.

In their wishful thinking, and in their expressed loyalty to and trust in British leadership, the politicians accurately represented the views of the vast majority of New Zealanders. What they did not make clear, however, was the underlying reservation. The tradition of plain speech in defense of New Zealand's interests was never lost; it was merely quiescent. New Zealand has never lacked national viewpoints or national policies—though they commonly have had more to do with butter and loan moneys than with guns—but in the 1920s New Zealand judged that its major interests were better served by the existing system than by the kind of modifications sought, for example, by the Canadians. New Zealand's foreign policy was being carried out, cheaply and effectively, by Britain.[1]

Nevertheless, the cosiness of that situation barely concealed the omens of change. On significant matters of detail—immigration, for example—the most conservative of New Zealanders insisted on exercising that autonomy which in constitutional principle they rejected. In 1928 a trade treaty with Japan was negotiated directly, not through British diplomatic machinery. Much more seriously, there were signs that, in the future as in the past, differences might arise about one of the main concerns of foreign policy—defense. Time and again in years past, New Zealand had thought that the British government had quite insufficiently appreciated the dangers of the Pacific situation. It was on that subject that the New Zealand government had (in May 1915) sent to London its most sharply worded warning: "bitter resentment" would arise if New Zealand opinion were to be ignored. No doubt the vast majority of New Zealanders retained their faith in the Royal Navy and agreed with Prime Minister Massey that that navy, traditionally omnipotent and omnipresent, was the best guarantee of their safety. Nevertheless, the feeling grew that in the Pacific situation Japan was uncomfortably strong and that the navy was both uncomfortably distant and loaded with priorities higher than the defense of the South Pacific. The situation naturally looked different when seen from London. British strategists produced soothing arguments, and the Singapore base was designed to enable the navy, after an inevitable delay, to operate effectively. But in New Zealand there was an undercurrent of opinion that was likely to stimulate interest in foreign affairs and to develop a local perspective in the study of defense problems.

Other factors also stimulated independent thought. One was the evolution of nationalism, a sense of identity which valued the New Zealand way of life and claimed for New Zealand the dignity of an adult, independent community. Perceptible in the days when

New Zealand stood aside from Australian federation, it gathered strength between the wars in literature, art, and music—and ultimately in politics. Its influence is hard to assess, but it can, perhaps, be associated with a line of thought that was made definite and significant because it was adopted by a major political party. In the early 1920s, the leaders of the Labour party had criticized the Treaty of Versailles as vengeful and the League of Nations as an organization of victorious imperialist powers, but they became convinced that the League represented the hope of the future— the hope that in international affairs the rule of law might one day displace that of the jungle. The League's achievements had admittedly fallen far short of the hopes of its founders. Nevertheless, it provided a world forum in which New Zealand like other small powers could participate as of right, and its weaknesses were due to the disloyalty of leading members, who sought short-term advantages rather than the establishment of correct principle. It followed that the Covenant should be strengthened and honestly implemented, and the League become a democratic, welfare-oriented, law-enforcing, morality-guided international force. For those New Zealanders who could conceive such an ideal, however remote from present possibilities, there was a guideline for policy: New Zealand should put its small weight behind the work of international institutions and should be prepared to make its fair contribution—including sacrifice if necessary—to make collective security work. Critics—who were many—said that such thoughts involved disloyalty to the empire and lack of faith in the navy; supporters held that there was no conflict of loyalties, for the British Commonwealth was (or should be) animated by precisely the same political morality as the Covenant. For them collective security was a reinforcement, not a substitute, for the protection given by partnership in the empire.

By the mid-1930s, then, New Zealand's deep attachment to Great Britain, still overwhelmingly important, was to some extent qualified. Many, perhaps most, New Zealanders remained obstinately colonist-minded, "good imperialists," but on an increasing number of practical issues they were (however unconsciously) coming to behave a little like citizens of a small nation economically and culturally tied to Europe, but isolated and Pacific-based. A situation was accordingly developing in which it was no longer axiomatic that New Zealand's interests, as it saw them, would be best served by decisions taken at imperial headquarters in London. A case in point arose soon after the Labour party won an overwhelming victory (on domestic issues, of course) in 1935, and New Zealand's new government pressed its views on collective security. After all, collective security was a notion particularly attractive to small powers who needed external guarantees but perhaps less so to a European-based major power with worldwide responsibilities. Accordingly, in 1936 the New Zealand government took a stand quite contrary to British policy on a major issue—the reform and strengthening of the League. This was shortly followed by advocacy of collective security's corollary, opposition to "appeasement." During the next few years, New Zealand proclaimed in an international forum, not just in private intercommonwealth discussion, that it had a foreign policy of its own.

That flash of independence caused some stir, though it was truly a development, not a departure, from New Zealand's historic tradition—which was to speak up if one had something significant to say. But, by the time Labour took office in 1935, the scent of war was in the air; in the next few years the menace grew, both in Europe and in the Pacific. Labour's leaders (M. J. Savage, Peter Fraser, and Walter Nash) and that remarkable civil servant, Carl Berendsen, were admittedly idealists in their pro-League policy and in their view that New Zealand should form its own judgments and not be any powerful friend's yes man. But they were also knowledgeable realists, and on the world scene some disagreeable facts stood out. If war came, it could be lost as of old in Europe. From New Zealand's viewpoint, it could perhaps also be lost in the Pacific. The possibility that the Japanese might become active enemies, the hope that Americans would prove active friends, the fear that the Singapore base might not effectively protect the South Pacific—those things had a higher importance to responsible New Zealanders than to imperial statesmen living in London under Hitler's shadow. No one, of course, doubted its involvement if Britain were at war. But it could no longer be thought that New Zealand was a member of an inevitably victorious power-group with the sole function of paying its way if need arose. Nor could it be presumed that policy directed from London would always be wise. Indeed, there was a strong opinion in many countries that current crises were largely due to avoidable mistakes by the great powers, including Britain. In those circumstances an idealist-realist government saw the opportunity, even the obligation, to formulate and express its views not only in confidential commonwealth discussions but occasionally on a world forum, and increasingly through the normal diplomatic machine.

New Zealand was at first ill equipped for the diplomatic game. In Wellington there was no organization to support a handful of keenly interested politicians and officials. Overseas there was but one post, that in London, where the high commissioner was traditionally concerned with immigration, trade, and finance rather than diplomacy. The enormously voluminous information that came to New Zealand had been skillfully collected by the Foreign Office, but to serve specifically British purposes. It often arrived too late to permit serious study before policy decisions were made: "consultation," the lifeblood of the commonwealth, often seemed to amount merely to generous information about what the British were doing. All those problems were of old standing, and they could be tackled only gradually. A properly organized and ably led Department of External Affairs (later the Ministry of Foreign Affairs) was set up in 1943. Diplomatic posts were established, beginning with Washington (1941), Ottawa (1942), Canberra (1943), and Moscow (1944). Fraser as prime minister and minister of external affairs traveled frequently and established effective personal relations. Consultation with Australia in particular grew close,[2] and the two dominions acted vigorously together on specific issues—notably in criticism of the policy to fight a holding war in the Pacific until Hitler had been beaten—and on the more general principle that small powers should participate in policy making as well as in fighting and should not have decisions affecting their vital interests made cavalierly by great powers without consultation. This principle was forcefully expressed—to the annoyance of the Americans—in the Canberra Pact of 1944. New Zealand and Australia had in fact a wide range of common though not identical interests. As to tactics, however, Fraser—true to New Zealand tradition—was more dignified, indeed more realistic, in dealing with powerful allies than was Australia's flamboyant Evatt; and New Zealand attitudes remained distinctive.

New Zealand's wartime policy predictably began with support of Britain's war effort—and later that of America in the Pacific—to the very limit of human and material resources. Equally predictably, New Zealand insisted that decisions concerning its armed forces should remain in principle under its own control: the story of the Expeditionary Force which contained a very substantial portion of its young manpower, was a case study of the problems involved in combining military efficiency with cooperative independence. And, in the wider field of world politics, the keynote was the same. New Zealand contributed its critical appraisal of policy while putting its whole strength loyally behind a united effort. On the main issues, its government formed careful judgments and supported them by determined advocacy—sometimes, though fortunately rarely, alone. There was a New Zealand policy in prewar days on the Spanish civil war and on Japan's attack on China, and during the "phony war" on relations with Russia and on the need to define war and peace aims in terms that would command support from thoughtful democrats. New Zealand was uneasy about western conservatives' views about Russia, and Fraser welcomed and supported Winston Churchill's prompt decision to regard the U.S.S.R. as an ally from the moment of the German attack. But Fraser was equally firm later on, in the days of Russian victories, that correct principles of foreign policy should be applied to dealings with friend and foe alike. Indeed, there is a consistent line of policy in New Zealand's actions from prewar crises through war to the peacemaking, sustained in the disappointing atmosphere of the cold war, and handed as a legacy to the age of the great inflations and monetary upheavals, Vietnam, the rise of communist China, and the detente between East and West Europe. Its definition lies in New Zealand's rebellious memo on reform of the League in 1936, in its vigorous support (in principle anyway) of the International Labor Organization, and in Savage's stance at the 1937 Imperial Conference. The establishment of the rule of law was of course the first essential, together with machinery for peaceful change. But, added Savage, international like domestic tensions commonly had economic roots, which to his simple and benevolent mind meant that economic hardships as well as political injustice must be remedied. And, in a selfish and shortsighted world, moral principle was seen as the best guideline—"that which is morally wrong can never be politically right."

To hard-boiled politicians such views smacked of unworldly idealism, and critics said that moralistic attitudes were all very well for a small power without responsibilities and safely isolated in the South Pacific. Nevertheless, in prewar Westminster and Geneva and in wartime London and Washington, New Zealand could and did speak its mind; and advocacy of principle had a slightly different aspect after the failure of the Hoare-Laval plan and of Neville Chamberlain's claim for peace in our time after Munich. Moreover, New Zealand continued to stand up for its principles to a creditable extent when its government (if not its people) saw plainly that risks were involved. In the prolonged crisis preceding Japan's entry into the war, it was increasingly evident that American pressure might help precipitate a southward thrust, which for reasons inherent in domestic American politics might (initially at any rate) have to be met without direct American help. In those circumstances New Zealand's adherence to principle led it—even on occasion against Australian policies—to oppose trends toward "appeasement" for Japan, an opposition that was consistent with its earlier policy, even though on Pacific as on European issues it was increasingly and sensibly salted with realism.

Thus under the pressure of impending crises in its Near North, New Zealand increasingly forged its own position on foreign affairs, paying due deference to British leads and keeping a careful eye on the evolution of U.S. policy. The independence of that position emerged from the growing realization that its views of the world could well be different from any assessment likely to be reached (without strenuous prompting) in London or Washington. In the conduct of the Pacific war this stance led to some active attempts to influence the decisions of New Zealand's great overseas friends, for example, in the pressure for more equipment and for the right of New Zealanders to participate in frontline fighting. New Zealand, together with Australia, pressed hard for the creation of machinery by which they could have some continuous share in the formulation of grand strategy. A Pacific War Council was in fact set up in Washington, in which small-power representatives met with the president.

It may well be doubted, however, whether New Zealand, or any other small power, had much influence over grand strategy (which gave priority to the European war) or over military decisions reached in Washington. American servicemen were firmly in charge and, after all, overwhelming agreement on the need to fight efficiently—which in the Pacific meant, in practice, to support the Americans and let them run the war—swamped lesser issues. It was a different matter, however, when it came to thinking about peacemaking and the strategy of the postwar world.

When the San Francisco conference met in April 1945 to build the United Nations Organization, the fundamental problem was inevitably that of the maintenance of peace. New Zealand had a policy, consistently advocated since 1936 and passionately believed in by its leaders. In its view, defeated enemies should be treated firmly but fairly, so that the seeds of wars of revenge should not be sown as at Versailles. New Zealand believed in welfare politics, not only as an attempt to relieve current distress through UNRRA but as a long-term utilitarian and humanitarian strategy.

Above all, it believed that the specter of war could in the end be exorcised only through a worldwide collective security system in which peace and the rule of law would be guaranteed by a strong world organization against any challenge, however powerful. That was a small-power concept which would be workable only on two conditions. First, the great powers must abdicate their hegemony, and all nations, great as well as small, must agree to accept internationally derived decisions even when their "vital interests" as defined by themselves were involved. Second, the great powers must manage in peacetime to work together, to trust each other, and to make sacrifices for the common good to a greater extent than they had achieved in war. In April 1945 the prospects that those conditions could be fulfilled were slim. No great power (and perhaps few small ones) was likely to submit its "vital interests" to international adjudication, and great-power cooperation was already breaking down. Indeed, in May 1945 New Zealand was an unwilling participant in a fortunately brief confrontation between East and West when its troops met those of Marshal Tito in Trieste.

In all these circumstances the small-power campaign, in which New Zealand was very active, could have only a modest success. The powers of the UN Assembly were enlarged, the status of the Economic and Social Council was upgraded, and the system of international trusteeship was created under the guidance of New Zealand's Fraser—achievements which significantly influenced the work of the United Nations in years to come. But on major issues the great powers stood firm and there was no abdication. The constitutional expression of that firmness was their insistence on the power of veto on the Security Council. The small powers were accordingly faced with a stark alternative: a UN with a great-power veto, or no UN at all.

Confronted thus, New Zealand's decision was a foregone conclusion: it must accept the UN Charter and strive to remedy its defects. At the Paris peace conference of 1946 New Zealand continued the fight for small-power status, for the use wherever possible of UN machinery, and for fair treatment of wartime enemies. It proved a conscientious and reasonably independent-minded member of the United Nations. When the Security Council became paralyzed by the veto (or more accurately by great-power disagreements), it supported moves to circumvent the stoppage by the use of the small-power domination in the UN Assembly. It participated in United Nations peace-keeping activities and would have liked to do more. Nevertheless, the small-power vision of a universal, firmly enforced system of collective security quickly faded before the realities of the Berlin blockade, the Czech coup d'etat, conflict in Palestine, and the Korean War.

The failure of the Security Council was a grave disappointment, but that was not the only reason that for New Zealand the first years of peace lacked the euphoria which had followed victory in the First World War. That failure, on the contrary, challenged New Zealand to evolve its own foreign policies. It was no longer possible merely to work through London, exploiting the traditional partnership arrangements. New Zealand was now inextricably involved with two great overseas friends. Economically, culturally, sentimentally, the country was still tied to Britain. Geographically and strategically it was a Pacific country, under the shadow of the U.S. Accordingly, it was essential for its peace of mind, possibly for its safety, that the policies of the two powers should broadly coincide, and thus a prime object of its own foreign policy must be to promote harmony between them. Further, however much New Zealand might wish to construct its defense and foreign policies within the framework of the historic commonwealth, the lessons of wartime could not be long forgotten. In the Pacific, British power was weak, and in Southeast Asia, though still formidable, it was waning. Accordingly in matters of defense, unless New Zealand were to rely for protection on its isolation and insignificance, it was intimately concerned with American policy, which would determine whether help would be forthcoming and which would profoundly influence the conditions that might threaten New Zealand's territorial security.

The immediate problem, of course, was that of a peace settlement with Japan. New Zealand's claim for an effective share in policy making was no doubt conceded in principle—it was represented on the Far Eastern Commission at Washington and at occupation headquarters in Japan—but in practice the Americans went their own way in the first few years of peace. And their policy veered sharply in a way alarming to New Zealand. At first all agreed that peace terms should be such as to make impossible a resurgence of Japanese militarism. However, in the developing cold war situation, American attention became increasingly switched to the dangers of international communism, and Japan came to be seen as a possible ally or at least as a country whose resources should be denied to the new enemy. Such thinking indicated a "soft" peace for Japan, especially as Americans felt optimistic about General Douglas MacArthur's progress in educating the Japanese in democracy. New Zealand, however, and still less Australia, could not so easily forget the threat under which they had lain. The new phase of U.S. policy, together with memories of anxious days in 1941, accordingly stimulated the search for a definite assurance that in a new crisis American friendliness would be expressed in immediate practical help. Since it was no longer possible to hope that such a guarantee would be provided through a worldwide security system, the only practical alternative seemed to be some local or regional scheme—such as that crystallized in NATO in 1949 to organize the defense of western Europe. To apply a comparable scheme to the Pacific involved a significant change of stance not only for the U.S. but also for New Zealand. Acceptance of a regional treaty, however consistent with the UN Charter, meant some deviation from New Zealand's long-sustained insistence on the principle of universalism; and in any case its preference was at first for an American commitment in the form of a presidential declaration. However, matters were precipitated by the outbreak of war in Korea in 1950. New Zealand responded quickly to the UN call, which meant aiding American forces in the good company of many other countries, including members of the commonwealth. The Korean War, following hard on the victory of Chairman Mao Tse-tung in mainland China, sharpened America's fear of communism and its wish to conclude peace with Japan on generous terms. In 1951 the ANZUS treaty of mutual guarantee between the U.S., Australia, and New Zealand was signed almost simultaneously with the Japanese peace treaty. Increasingly good relations soon developed between New Zealand and Japan.

The conclusion of ANZUS signalized New Zealand's independence in foreign policy, as well as its Pacific consciousness.[3] Against any conceivable form of attack on its territory, the U.S. and, on a smaller scale, Australia are the only powers that could give effective assistance; therefore, with those countries New Zealand needs a special relationship.[4] It is not just a matter of a single treaty, a piece of paper. Such a document is a result, not a source, of cooperation and common interests, but it can be a focus and provide the occasion for systematic high-level consultations. ANZUS operated in that way, and in the late 1970s it remained the foundation of New Zealand's defenses.

For New Zealand, ANZUS had a weakness in that Britain was not a party. Britain's involvement in the Manila treaty of 1954 was a powerful reason why New Zealand should accept this new extension (under American impulse) of Pacific regional security, involving as it did some commitments on mainland Asia. New Zealand already had, of course, some forces in Southeast Asia under the so-called ANZAM arrangement whereby British, Australian, and New Zealand servicemen had worked closely together since 1949 to plan the defense of Malaya and the Southwest Pacific. Small New Zealand forces helped deal with such problems as the Malayan "emergency" and the Indonesian "confrontation." New Zealand's traditional commitment to send a substantial force to the Mediterranean area (where there were still some New Zealand forces) in the event of war seemed increasingly outmoded; after the usual consultations in London, that commitment was transferred to Southeast Asia in 1955. New Zealand forces joined the Commonwealth Strategic Reserve in Malaya and, at the wish of the Malaysian and Singapore governments, remained there after independence. In 1969 New Zealand made clear its willingness to keep them there despite the British Labour government's decision to withdraw its forces from east of Suez.

Both as a member of the commonwealth and as an American ally, New Zealand was thus deeply involved in regional security arrangements for the Pacific and Southeast Asia—arrangements which had as a major objective, especially in American eyes, resistance to possible "communist aggression." New Zealand shared to some extent its partners' fears of communist expansion in Asia—that was a major reason for the introduction of conscription in 1949—but like them it was also conscious of the challenge of Asian poverty. New Zealand saw in attempts to relieve that poverty a means of meeting the communist threat. Hence its continuing support for the Colombo Plan, the commonwealth-originated strategy for helping developing Asian countries. New Zealand considered that Colombo Plan costs were a contribution to regional security, as well as the discharge of an affluent country's moral obligation.

New Zealand actively cooperated, then, with Britain and the U.S. in building that regional security on terms which it insisted were consistent with the UN Charter and which seemed the best available substitute for a universal system. Neither the commonwealth nor the American connection, however, could restore (even if it had wanted it) the comfortable feeling of the 1920s that both her safety and the skillful conduct of foreign policy were taken care of by junior partnership in a congenial, world-dominant empire. For one thing, British and American policies sometimes diverged. In 1950 New Zealand, like the United States, hesitated to recognize "Red" China. Subsequently, it became increasingly conscious that mainland China must one day be represented in the United Nations and its regime recognized but suggested uncomfortably that China must work its way back to acceptability, and in the end did not act until 1972, after America had moved decisively toward detente. In the Suez crisis of 1956, New Zealand stood with Britain, perhaps a little hesitantly, against American criticism, but as the tragedy of Vietnam developed it followed the lead of America, not of Britain, who stood aside. As the U.S. became more and more deeply involved in the Vietnam morass, many New Zealanders judged—without too much concern for the details of the case—that, treaty obligations apart, a prudent junior partner should rally round; perhaps suspicion of communism was also involved. The New Zealand government accordingly sent a small volunteer force to help the Americans, an action which led to vigorous controversy until the last servicemen were withdrawn at the end of 1972. Public interest in New Zealand's own foreign policy, aroused as never before, did not die down.

There was in fact a growing realization in New Zealand that it had national interests which neither of its great friends could be expected to serve on its behalf. The fierce debate about Vietnam was one of the developments emphasizing this fact and underlining New Zealand's involvement in the increasingly complicated problems of the Pacific area. Simultaneously, a drastic change affecting the European half of New Zealand's dual personality taught the same lesson. Britain's long trek into the European Economic Community threatened, and in the end virtually destroyed, a long-established basic factor in New Zealand's prosperity—privileged access to British markets, based of course on mutual self-interest. This development had psychological as well as profound economic implications, especially when changes in British immigration laws imposed restrictions on New Zealanders' hitherto automatic rights of entry; inevitably there was a sense of rebuff, strong as the old ties undoubtedly remained. In dealing with this new situation, the first task was one of intense diplomatic activity, calling for economic as well as political skills—to make known New Zealand's case, to secure the best possible terms for trade with the enlarged EEC, and to explore other markets in Europe. In this exercise New Zealand had British support; but the expert knowledge and thrust had to be its own. The second task—long foreseen but now urgent— was to modify New Zealand's economy and trading patterns in order to make the best of changing circumstances. This involved increased efforts to diversify its efficient but overspecialized and therefore vulnerable economy, especially by the development of manufactures. It also involved market diversification for agricultural products. The prosperity and friendliness of Japan in the postwar world seemed to open a door, while opportunities lurked not only in the tricky markets of the U.S. but in Latin America, in parts of mainland Asia, and in Australia. It became an obvious task of New Zealand foreign policy to help seek them out and to try to promote the peaceful and prosperous conditions in which trade could develop. Progress was made. In 1950 Britain took 66 percent of New Zealand's exports while its three chief markets in the Asian-Pacific area (the U.S., Japan, and Australia) took a total of 13 percent. In 1971 the figures were 34 percent and 35 percent respectively; and, if mainland Asia and the Pacific islands were included, the Asian-Pacific proportion rose to 41 percent. However, the world evidently did not feel that it owed New Zealand a living. Its standards of living could be maintained only by a successful fight for trade, not only on the familiar battlefields of Europe but in untried and challenging areas nearer at hand.

One of these areas, though of relatively small economic potential, has played a notable part in the development of New Zealand's sense of nationhood, namely, the Pacific islands. Some nineteenth century statesmen had the vision of a British island-empire based on their country or, alternatively, of a New Zealand–led federation reaching out into the Pacific. Such ambitions bore little fruit: principally the Cook Islands, the Tokelaus, Niue, and the trouble-laden conquest from the Germans in 1914 of long-coveted Western Samoa. Well-meaning but misguided rule of Western Samoa under a League of Nations mandate led to conflict, to a repudiation of New Zealand's paternalism, and to disillusionment. However, in the late 1930s the Labour government did something to regain the islanders' confidence, and in the postwar world New Zealand applied to its island territories the principles of international trusteeship which Fraser had preached at San Francisco in 1945. Indeed, New Zealand took the lead, to the embarrassment of other colonial powers, in the decolonization of Oceania. Western Samoa became independent on January 1, 1962. Somewhat contrary to decolonizing orthodoxies, its constitution retained significant elements of traditional politicosocial structure. And, by Samoan wish, the Treaty of Friendship of August 1962 provides that New Zealand may, on request, act for the government of Western Samoa in the conduct of foreign affairs. Departures from rigid orthodoxy were repeated in 1965 when the Cook Islands became internally self-governing and freely associated with New Zealand on the basis of a continuous right of self-determination. Economic aid continued to these territories as a matter of course; nor was it confined to them. An influential body of opinion held that in the islands, and among Pacific islanders settled in New Zealand, it had a unique duty and opportunity to render effective aid and to do so with improved generosity and skill. Support for the South Pacific Commission was of course one of the channels for such aid. That commission—an international regional organization to promote the welfare of Pacific islanders—was established in 1947 as the fruit of New Zealand and Australian initiatives. New Zealand both pulled its weight in its work and took a lead in transforming it from something looking like a club of benevolent colonial powers to an organization more representative of the island peoples whom it was created to serve.[5] Outside its machinery, these peoples, together with New Zealand and Australia, have since 1971 each sent a chief minister to the periodical informal but fruitful meetings of the South Pacific Forum, consisting of the independent and self-governing countries of the area.

New Zealand, it could be said, was precipitated into full nationhood by four almost simultaneous events: Britain's final entry into the EEC, the enunciation of the Nixon Doctrine, the perception that New Zealand need fear no threat from Asia in the foreseeable future, and the election (in November 1972) of New Zealand's third Labour government under Norman Kirk (who was tragically to die after twenty months in office). Britain turned to continental Europe with a new intimacy; Nixon announced a partial American withdrawal from overseas commitments; and Kirk picked up the challenge. In essence, however, Kirk in his clearheaded way was carrying to their conclusion (and expertly defining) established principles of New Zealand policy. Like his predecessors he had to hold the delicate balance between idealism and realism, between a small power's independent judgment and the necessity to work with great powers and through international institutions, and between New Zealand's Asian-Pacific and its North Atlantic involvements. His first comprehensive statement on foreign policy had some highlights: a firm stand against apartheid sport; a stepping up of international aid, particularly for the South Pacific area; emphasis on moral principle; diplomatic recognition of China; the reopening of the Moscow embassy; and leadership in world protest against nuclear testing. Openness about the government's foreign policy attitudes was promised; military and security considerations were given less emphasis; vigor and initiative were conveyed as the dominant tones. Its main significance, however, was that it spelled out the extent to which—partly by force of circumstances and partly by deliberate choice—New Zealand had undertaken a "self-reliant foreign policy" and proposed to see issues through its own eyes, not through those of any powerful "protector."[6]

The new approach was encouraged by a variety of forces. Within New Zealand itself, there was a vague if real public uneasiness about foreign policy actions of the recent past, particularly over Vietnam. The country seemed ready for a lead that would redefine its international role in ways promising greater independence and self-respect. As Prime Minister Kirk himself was later to state, a certain hyperbole notwithstanding: "My Government came to office . . . with a mandate for change: change in the pace of development, change in a greater regard for the well-being of the ordinary man. And change above all in the approach of New Zealanders to the world around us."[7] In fact, sections of public opinion had already been moving ahead of the politicians in a number of foreign policy areas prior to Labour's arrival in office. There were already vocal groups urging a substantial increase in official aid, a withdrawal of troops from Vietnam, a more positive attack on French nuclear testing in the Pacific, a rupture of sporting ties with South Africa, and a strengthening of links with the South Pacific.

Externally, conditions were also propitious for new initiatives. The increasingly multipolar relations among the major powers was interpreted by advisers and officials in New Zealand as necessitating a more broadly based range of diplomatic contacts with key capitals. A central thrust of the Nixon Doctrine in Asia—much greater self-reliance and sufficiency—pointed up a need for identification and cooperation with, if not direct membership in, regional political arrangements, such as the Association of South-East Asian Nations. With British entry into Europe, New Zealand's long-standing traditional tie with the United Kingdom was now irretrievably altered toward a more conventional, much less intimately bilateral relationship. To these considerations should be added the growing awareness in New Zealand of interdependence as an international dimension affecting economics, race relations, social justice, and environmental questions within and between countries.

It was Norman Kirk's capacity to capture the mood of these altering conditions and voice them locally that helped impart a sense of direction to New Zealand's foreign relations. That ability to expound foreign policy objectives in clearly understood terms was a considerable strength, and his views, therefore, deserve scrutiny. Here he compares quite favorably with Labour predecessors in developing an approach to international affairs derived from conscious attempts to wed acquired understanding to personal beliefs and convictions. And, as with such forerunners as Fraser and Nash, his resulting philosophy featured internationalist, pragmatic, humanitarian, and activist principles.

For Kirk, however, there was an acute awareness that disparity and inequality constituted central, ubiquitous international problems that were found within as well as between nations. Whether bred of ethnic, geographical, economic, or social considerations, such disparities constituted a human dilemma, a moral affront, and a threat to international stability.

Yet such problems were soluble. But for such an achievement it was necessary, in Kirk's view, to have these issues forced to higher levels of consideration upon the international agenda. Any implementation of policies designed to ameliorate disparity required stable patterns of cooperation between governments. And for this to solidify, genuine attitudes of partnership and realistic expectations of mutually advantageous rewards were needed. Within the Asian, and Pacific regions, for example, Kirk saw these habits best furthered by building an interlocking network of political ties—agreements on trade, aid, and technical assistance and more formalized multilateral structures for the purpose of consultation to solve joint problems. While New Zealand might not be a direct participant (as in the ASEAN, for example), it was clearly in its interest to nudge others toward strengthened confidence in the values of such regional cooperation.

These ideas also underlined Kirk's readiness to view foreign policy as an activity where planning rather than just reaction and response to initiatives of others, was possible and desirable. The capacity to plan is perhaps one of the advantages enjoyed by a state as small and isolated as New Zealand, though this is not a readily identifiable attribute of its past international conduct. It was Kirk's belief, however, that international conditions were increasingly auspicious for small-state initiatives. "Small countries," he said, "can be strong. The force of ideas can equate with power."[8]

Failure to act could also involve costs. With New Zealand's neighborhood in mind, Kirk claimed that, if the small countries of the area did not move reasonably soon to develop some regional political fabric of their own devising, then they could not complain about having to live by decisions made by others.

On some occasions, Kirk spoke of small states as an international collectivity—even a trade union—while elsewhere he underlined the importance of the rule of law to them. Parallel to this were apprehensions about super-power detente and major-power relations which were regarded as potentially fragile and dangerous, thinking reflected in the attacks made upon nuclear testing and related calls for a nuclear-free zone in the South Pacific.

Finally, Kirk was anxious to project what he regarded as certain domestic values into New Zealand's foreign policy. These included, in his view, humanitarianism, decency, compassion, and especially racial tolerance. Thus: "The standards that we have forged in New Zealand to create the basis of a humane society should be the standards that underlie every foreign policy action."[9] The same linkage was applied by the late prime minister when announcing his domestically controversial decision in 1973 to have the New Zealand Rugby Union "postpone" its invitation for a South African team's visit to New Zealand. Such a tour "would exacerbate differences of attitude on racial matters within New Zealand and create strains within our society. It would damage New Zealand's broader international relations by reducing its standing and credibility as a decent humane country with a successful multiracial society."[10]

Yet, if these were some of the more important assumptions and operational concepts underlying the new Labour government's approach, how nearly did they relate to its subsequent foreign policy actions? As one might expect, actual performance and outcome have borne mixed results.

Toward the South Pacific, New Zealand has substantially increased its volume of aid, conscientiously promoted regional cooperation, and furthered diplomatic initiatives aimed at the complete cessation of nuclear testing. A full diplomatic mission was established in Papua–New Guinea. The South Pacific Bureau of Economic Cooperation, established in 1973 as a servicing and coordinating agency for South Pacific Forum members (Fiji, Tonga, Western Samoa, the Cook Islands, Papua–New Guinea, Australia, and New Zealand), has been actively supported by Wellington. Those South Pacific states involved in the European Economic Community's Atlantic-Caribbean-Pacific 1974 trade and aid agreements probably benefited by the bureau's existence. At a public

level there is now a greater awareness of New Zealand's changing role within the South Pacific. Nevertheless, much practical
policy cooperation has to be accomplished before the New Zealand government can derive any clear satisfaction about trends
in South Pacific regional cooperation. Problem areas needing greatest attention are shipping, air transport, immigration, and trade
complementarity.

A second major point of New Zealand's neighborhood circum-
ference is Australia. Here the record is far more mixed, especially
when initial objectives are contemplated. Following their elections
in 1972, Gough Whitlam and Kirk met for talks in Wellington.
Although the importance of revitalizing and strengthening trans-
Tasman intergovernmental consultation was confirmed, various
problems remained. Little was involved that might be termed
"high politics"; instead it was issues such as maritime policy,
movement of people, and particularly the workings of the so-called
Free Trade Agreement that displayed misunderstanding and faulty
communications across the Tasman. New Zealand proposals for
a nuclear-free zone in the South Pacific received but lukewarm
support from Australia, whose understandable preoccupations
with Papua–New Guinea's birthpangs of nationhood possibly ob-
scured its view of wider Pacific needs and trends. Moreover the
volatile, not to say turbulent, political situation within Australia
itself was hardly conducive to such a perspective.

In January 1973, when the first Whitlam-Kirk exchange occurred, the two leaders offered to join in "appropriate efforts" to
bring Asian and Pacific states together in "a new collective endeav-
or." They nevertheless expressed "understanding and support" for
the desire of the ASEAN countries to limit outside interference
in the affairs of Southeast Asia and sympathy for their efforts to
make the area a zone of peace, freedom, and neutrality.[11]

Less ostentatious than a similar Australian initiative, the New
Zealand government in 1973 sounded various Asian capitals with
a proposal to establish some form of consultative structure. Their
replies tended to emphasize delay rather than refusal, which was
an understandable response given the then fluid and uncertain outcome awaiting Indochina. At a later stage, Kirk spoke of a more
limited grouping that would possibly include Indonesia, Papua–
New Guinea, Australia, and New Zealand. Such a group "would
not only discuss development problems relating to New Guinea—
in itself a major issue for the area—but it would also act as something of a link between the South Pacific and Asia."[12] Though

such plans remain in abeyance, New Zealand has not relaxed its efforts to encourage such regional cooperation as already exists in Southeast Asia.

At less specifically regional policy levels, recent New Zealand foreign policy has sustained a more independent line. This has been seen in its handling of international economic and resource questions. Unlike some of its Organization for Economic Cooperation and Development partners, for example, New Zealand supported the new conception of the international economic order endorsed by the United Nations Special General Assembly of 1974. Following the 1973 Yom Kippur war (especially after the massive increase in oil prices that followed in its wake), the New Zealand government prudently and almost imperceptibly moved from what had been a basically pro-Israeli to a more neutral, outlook toward the Middle East. Trade, and particularly the sale of technology (for example, in agriculture and geothermal energy) has also been significant as a component in newly established relations New Zealand has cultivated with Iran, Eastern Europe, China, and Pacific-seaboard Latin America. Better trade and aid terms for lesser developed countries have also been strongly supported by New Zealand through the United Nations, the commonwealth, and the Colombo Plan. Playing a part in this approach has been a continuing quest for more diversified yet stable outlets for primary products, an increased sense of moral obligation to assist poorer nations, and an anxiety not to be too readily identified as a rich, white, affluent country.

While increasing independence was the major theme of the 1972–1975 Labour government's foreign policy, that theme received varying emphasis according to the issues involved and the man at the top. At public, declaratory, and even symbolic levels of enunciation, Kirk voiced that particular appeal to greater effect than his successor, Wallace Rowling, ever did. Indeed, after he assumed the leadership in 1974, Rowling was heavily preoccupied with domestic economic, not to mention electoral, considerations while his handling of foreign relations was diligent and prudent if not inspired. Within a small state such as New Zealand, the personal traits, attitudes, and skills of any given prime minister are of considerable importance in the handling of foreign relations since they help define the salience of foreign policy questions before the public at large. That the late Norman Kirk could present those questions with such vigor was one of his important skills, and the principles he thus supported, one of his important legacies. The policy initiatives he bequeathed to his successors in office afford some useful guidelines for at least the foreseeable future. After Kirk's death in August 1974, New Zealand foreign policy entered a quieter phase under Rowling, but one is entitled to doubt whether that quiet will continue to characterize the administration of Robert Muldoon, who became prime minister in December 1975 after Labour's defeat by the National party. Muldoon is as vigorous as Rowling was restrained, and it would be surprising if that vigor did not carry him into new initiatives in foreign policy as well as in domestic politics.

Although foreign policy is not in any sense a major public issue in New Zealand (in the late 1970s it is still only rarely debated in Parliament), a shift toward a more discerning, self-realized position in the South Pacific and in the wider world has become increasingly evident in recent years, and that new position is likely to be maintained for some time to come.

Notes

1 For historical background on this point see F. L. W. Wood, *New Zealand in the World* (Wellington: Department of Internal Affairs, 1940).

2 On this theme see the essay by Mary Boyd, "Australian–New Zealand Relations," elsewhere in this volume.

3 On the development of ANZUS as it affected New Zealand, see Bruce Brown's essay, "Political and Strategic Relations: A View from Wellington," in Bruce Brown (ed.), *Asia and the Pacific in the 1970s* (Canberra: Australian National University Press, 1971), 119–136.

4 See the essay by Boyd in this volume.

5 T. R. Smith, *The South Pacific Commission* (Wellington: New Zealand Institute of International Affairs, 1972).

6 Ministry of Foreign Affairs, *Annual Report* (Wellington, 1973), 3–17.

7 *New Zealand Foreign Affairs Review*, 24, no. 1 (1974), 12.

8 Address to the New Zealand Institute of International Affairs, *New Zealand Foreign Affairs Review*, 23, no. 8 (August 1973), 7.

9 Ibid., 4.

10 Ibid., no. 4 (April 1973), 27.

11 Ibid., no. 1 (January 1973), 8.

12 Norman Kirk, "New Directions in New Zealand's Foreign Policy," *Journal of International Studies*, 3, no. 2 (Autumn 1974), 94.

NORMAN HARPER

Australian Foreign Policy

T. B. Millar has pointed out that "there were 113 years from the First Fleet to federation of the Australian colonies, and nearly 40 more years before an Australian government took independent action in foreign affairs."[1] Foreign affairs are related essentially to defense and security. While distance may have exerted some tyranny over Australian economic development, it did have some advantages. Sydney, the terminal port of an imperial shipping line, was twelve thousand miles from Europe and remote from threats of military attack. Asia was closer, but Japan alone in the twentieth century possessed a powerful fleet. Like the Monroe Doctrine in the nineteenth century, Australian security rested on the broad back of the British navy.

1919–1941

Australian nationalism contributed to federation in 1901 and to the demand for a separate Australian navy, finally to be integrated into the Royal Navy. Nationalism was immensely strengthened by the landings at Gallipoli in 1915, which resulted in the development of the Anzac legend, and also by participation in the military campaigns in France and Palestine. The new self-confidence, largely bred on the battlefields, brought membership of the Imperial War Cabinet, separate representation at the Peace Conference in 1919, and foundation membership of the League of Nations. Dominion status was a heady concept leading to a demand for a greater measure of autonomy in foreign relations, but Australia remained reluctant to assume the financial responsibilities for defense and diplomatic representation.

The Paris Peace Conference produced the first serious initiative in Australian foreign policy and a head-on collision between President Woodrow Wilson and William Morris Hughes, the fiery Welsh-born prime minister of Australia. The points of controversy were the future of German colonies south of the equator and the principle of racial equality. The battle over a mandate system for German colonies led to the famous confrontation between the two men, who did not understand one another and whose policies were diametrically opposed. "Mr. Hughes, am I to understand that if the whole world asks Australia to agree to a mandate in respect of those islands, Australia is prepared still to defy the appeal of the whole civilized world?" "That's about the size of it, President Wilson," replied Hughes as he moved his ear trumpet close to the president. He subsequently reminded Wilson that he "represented sixty thousand dead."[2] Hughes helped mobilize West Coast opinion in the United States against President Wilson on the question of racial equality put forward by Japan as an amendment to the Covenant of the League of Nations. He regarded it as a threat to Australia's restrictive immigration policy. Wilson declared the Japanese amendment lost because the vote was not unanimous.

Friction between Australia and the U.S. over the Versailles settlement persisted over the future of the Anglo-Japanese alliance and the problem of stability in East Asia. It was aggravated by Australia's attempt to secure separate representation at the Washington Conference in 1921–1922. Washington did not understand the new Australian nationalism, and London regarded it as adolescent and simplistic in the area of foreign policy. The end result was the inclusion of Sir George Pearce, the Australian defense minister, in the British delegation. In Australia it was thought that the network of treaties signed at Washington would stabilize the situation in the Far East; in fact it established Japanese naval preponderance in the western Pacific.[3]

Australia's independent initiative in foreign policy in 1919–1920 was short-lived, and for almost two decades it lapsed into semi-isolation. The Washington Conference in 1922 and criticisms of British policy at Chanak were in a sense a swan song as "men, markets, and money" became the central issues of Australian politics. Strategically the Singapore base, regarded essentially as a British project in a commonwealth context, became the key point of Australian defense policy.

Such interest as Australia had in foreign policy was centered on the Commonwealth of Nations and a barren attempt to obtain a common imperial foreign policy. The battle for dominion autonomy was won by the Balfour Declaration (1926). The Statute of Westminster (1931) put into concrete legislative form the finely spun phrases of the Balfour Declaration. Australia (and New Zealand) was largely content with status rather than function and was less active than Canada and South Africa in taking initiatives in foreign policy. In 1924 Australia had appointed R. G. Casey as its liaison officer in London, reporting direct to the prime minister. Foreign affairs were handled by the Prime Minister's Department until 1935, when a separate Department of Foreign Affairs was established. Australian information about international affairs was thus largely derivative. It was not until 1942 that Australia ratified the Statute of Westminster: autonomy meant a willingness to have affairs rather than relations. That inability to formulate a foreign policy led in the long, rather than the short, term to what J. R. Poynter has called "yo-yo variations" in policy at a variety of levels—political, military, and economic.[4]

The real question was, who held the strings? Lacking independent sources of information and diplomatic posts abroad, Australia depended on consultation with London. There was a flow of dispatches from London to Canberra, but it was difficult to determine whether there was real consultation before decisions were taken by Whitehall. In 1938 Casey expressed the view that consultation was the important thing so that a commonwealth foreign policy might be framed that would "attain the common aims of all members and at the same time serve Australian national and regional interests. . . . British foreign policy may accordingly be regarded in a very real sense as Australian foreign policy." London obviously held the yo-yo string.[5] During the Munich crisis, Australian Prime Minister J. A. Lyons seemed content to be supplied with information rather than being formally requested for "the expression of an opinion by Australia or for any acceptance by Australia of the responsibility which would flow from active participation in the shaping of policy."[6]

It was an increasing restiveness with, and concern about, Australian security and British policy that led Lyons to take the initiative in proposing the establishment of a regional security system through the conclusion of a Pacific pact. Japanese expansion in China (1931–1937) breached the Washington treaty system of 1921–1922 and threw a long shadow south of the equator. The Lyons proposals for a Pacific pact which might replace the Washington agreements met with a lukewarm reception in the United States and all the other centers of power. This lonely Australian initiative failed; Australia continued to rely on Britain as the protecting angel and to speak with a muted voice. That voice was so muted that the U.S., as late as the 1940s, saw the dominions as the "nondescript appendages" they had seemed in the 1920s. On the other hand, despite the close economic ties spelled out in the Ottawa preference system, strain developed between Canberra and London over defense priorities. Britain's interests were primarily European, while Australia became increasingly concerned with the changing balance of power in East Asia, where Japan's expansionist policies posed new threats to regional security. The result was "a radical solution to [Australia's] dilemmas in the form of a separate Australian diplomacy."[7] Casey became the first Australian ambassador to Washington in May 1940, and J. G. Latham took up his post in Tokyo later that year.

The essential change in Australian foreign policy at the end of the interwar period was the growing reorientation of Australian foreign policy toward the Pacific and especially the establishing of closer relations with the U.S. This essay is mainly concerned with that reorientation. The pioneer flight of Kingsford Smith's *Southern Cross* from San Francisco to Brisbane in 1928 foreshadowed a closer physical relation between the two countries, but the ocean shrank slowly until new developments in aircraft took place.

Australian relations with the U.S. after the Ottawa Conference in 1932 were primarily economic. The chronic imbalance in trade between the two countries was approximately four to one in America's favor. The crunch came when Australia adopted the "trade diversion policy" in 1936, a disastrous experiment designed to rectify that imbalance with the U.S. and Japan. Pearce, Australia's minister for external affairs, told the American consul general in Sydney, Jay Pierrepont Moffat, that "the feeling of comradeship and confidence [between Australia and the United States] had now almost entirely disappeared."[8] Raymond Esthus, in his *From Enmity to Alliance*, has exaggerated the extent of friction. There was perhaps irritation and frustration, perhaps yo-yo variations in relations, but not enmity. There was some resentment of general American attitudes on economic matters after the "trade diversion policy" ended in 1937, and wool, meat, and zinc continued to bedevil economic relations in the post–Pearl Harbor era.

The exchange of ministers in 1940 contributed to the removal of misunderstanding between Washington and Canberra. Casey quickly established rapport with Cordell Hull. The main thrust of Australian policy at that stage was to secure American cooperation in the use of the Singapore base. The State Department resisted all pressure to send American ships to visit Singapore as an indication to Japan of American concern with the security of Southeast Asia, but some warships did visit Sydney and Auckland in April 1941, perhaps as a hint of American interests in the region.

As Hartley Grattan has pointed out, Australia was a country of low visibility in Washington until the full impact of Japan's warmaking capacity was felt; then it appeared above the horizon as an indispensable but menaced base. Pearl Harbor was the catalyst. On December 27, 1941, the Australian prime minister made his dramatic appeal for American assistance. "Without any inhibitions of any kind, I make it quite clear that Australia looks to America, free of any pangs as to our traditional links of kinship with the United Kingdom." John Curtin's appeal did not involve a breach of relations with the United Kingdom but, rather, a reorientation of defense and foreign policies hypnotized by the belief in the impregnability of the Singapore base. His appeal met with an immediate response, primarily for American strategic reasons.[9] Brig. Gen. Dwight Eisenhower had already advised Lt. Gen. George C. Marshall (December 14) that "Australia was the base nearest the Philippines that we could hope to establish and maintain and the necessary line of air communications would therefore follow along the islands intervening between that continent and the Philippines. If we were to use Australia as a base it was mandatory that we procure a line of communication leading to it. This meant that we must instantly move to save Hawaii, Fiji, New Zealand and New Caledonia, and we had to make certain of the safety of Australia herself." Marshall replied laconically, "I agree with you. . . . Do your best to save them." Australia was strategically indispensable for the conduct of the Pacific war and the defeat of Japan.[10] President Franklin D. Roosevelt had already decided (October 28) that the defense of Australia was vital to that of the U.S.

Curtin's appeal to the U.S. meant, not the cutting of the umbilical cord with Great Britain, but an independent assessment of Australian strategic and foreign policy when the international scene had changed dramatically since the heyday of British imperialism. Australia realized that matriarchy was inadequate. Where did power lie? Which was the "powerful and willing friend" upon which a small independent state could rely for support to preserve its independence?

1941–1972

The fall of Singapore on February 15, 1942, and the collapse of British naval power in Southeast Asia meant the crumbling of the old bases of Australian security. Curtin's disagreement with Winston Churchill over the return of Australian troops from the Middle East, the traditional zone for Australian contributions to imperial defense, was accompanied by the establishment of a close working relationship with General Douglas MacArthur. Australian troops fought in New Guinea alongside American forces, and the American fleet played a vital role in halting the Japanese advance toward New Guinea and Australia. The battle of Coral Sea, fought May 4–8, 1942, checked a dangerous Japanese threat to Australian territory. It was "the first major fleet-air battle in history": the opposing ships neither sighted one another nor exchanged shots. The engagement was fought by carrier- and land-based aircraft.

As Australia became the springboard for a joint offensive against Japanese armies in Southeast and East Asia, it experienced for the first time a mass contact with Americans. Almost a million American servicemen used Australia as a Southwest Pacific base in the war against Japan or visited Australia for recuperation. The typical American image of Australia "as a large blank continent with a zoological sense of humor" was modified by the large influx of Americans.[11] Despite minor clashes between troops with different outlooks and rates of pay, which led inevitably to fierce competition for feminine favors, a wider understanding developed between the two countries. Mutual respect replaced suspicion, and many Australians began to look eastward across the Pacific as well as westward to Europe and Britain.[12]

Increasing Australian awareness of California and of the East Coast of the United States was accompanied by a rethinking of Australian priorities in foreign policy and defense. The independence which had led to clashes with Churchill was matched by a growing Australian insistence on consultation by the U.S. on policy issues, strategic and political, in the Pacific war. Although H. V. Evatt in his first speech on foreign policy (November 27, 1941) had stated that the "recent change of Government in this country does not imply any vital change in Australia's foreign policy," he was primarily responsible for the reorientation of Australian wartime and postwar foreign policies. His firm insistence that Australia was an independent middle power rather than a

British imperial satellite led the American government to agree that Australia should sign the instrument of surrender with Japan and become the commonwealth member of the Allied Council in Japan.

The Evatt period in Australian postwar foreign policy (1945—1949) was marked by an essentially nationalistic approach to problems and by a sensitivity to a recognition of Australian rights. In a sense there was a return, sometimes abrasive, to the anti-British nationalism of the 1890s. Dr. Evatt glimpsed the need to find, as Sir Robert Menzies later said, a new "powerful and willing friend" to protect Australia against external threats. He knew that the 1939 power structure in the Pacific had disappeared, that western colonial empires had collapsed, and that new nation states were emerging in Asia. He challenged the great powers at San Francisco in 1945 on a number of issues[13] and while recognizing the increasingly important role of the U.S. in the postwar Pacific, he disagreed with American policy in occupied Japan. He disliked the new American policy of using Japan as a bastion against the spread of communist influence in East Asia. His emphasis on the important role of the United Nations in international relations, leading to his election as president of the General Assembly in 1948, placed him far ahead of the rank-and-file members of the Australian Labor party (ALP) and of the Australian government. Washington regarded him as "an active source of both irritation and uncertainty."[14] The wartime honeymoon was over. The differences over the role of Japan in East Asia were strengthened by Australia's fears that a new American-backed Japan might become a new threat to stability in Southeast Asia and to Australia's security. On September 21, 1949, the People's Republic of China was proclaimed, and in December the Australian Labor party was defeated in the federal election. Menzies became the new prime minister and the Liberal-Country party coalition remained in power, despite cabinet changes, for a generation. On December 2, 1972, a Labor government was elected and Australian foreign policy in general, and Australian-American relations in particular, had to be reexamined.

To Australia, the central problem was one of security—how to prevent any threat of the post–Pearl harbor kind from developing. The Japanese bombing at Darwin on February 19, 1942, had brought home to Australia the inability of Great Britain to provide a defense shield. Despite the deep Menzies attachment to Great Britain and the commonwealth, it was evident that Australia needed a new "powerful and willing friend" to shield it from an attack. The potential threats were envisaged as coming from a resurgent, re-armed Japan or an expansionist China pursuing either ideological or traditional imperialistic objectives. Security became linked with the problem of the kind of peace treaty to be concluded with Japan and with the question of the recognition of the People's Republic of China. The Korean War gave added point to Australian fears of the People's Republic. Its swift decision to supply troops to the United Nations force in Korea, commanded by General MacArthur, was not unrelated to the hope of establishing a firm working arrangement with the U.S. in other areas in Asia. With the British commitment in Asia extending only to Singapore, with Hong Kong an exposed and undefendable outpost, and with American defense responsibilities ending at the Manila base, the main objective of Australian defense and foreign policy in this region centered round the closing of the gap between Manila and Singapore. That involved securing a firm American commitment to Southeast Asia. Evatt had tried to secure such a commitment by offering the U.S. a base on Manus Island.

The immediate problem in 1950 was the conclusion of a peace treaty with Japan. When John Foster Dulles visited Canberra on February 15, 1951, Percy Spender told him that the Australian government "was not prepared to accept a Japanese peace treaty unless: 1. reasonable limitations were written into the treaty against Japanese re-armament; 2. a satisfactory security arrange-ment in the Pacific was able to be agreed to. This arrangement should take the form of the tripartite pact between the three coun-tries that I had been contending for."[15] Spender's primary concern was a security treaty, and he insisted on concentrating discussion of that before dealing with the Japanese peace treaty. The substan-tial terms of the treaty were agreed upon at that time in Can-berra, although it was not formally signed until September 1, a few hours after the text of the proposed Japanese peace treaty had been published.[16]

The ANZUS treaty became the central pillar of Australian se-curity. "Each party recognizes that an armed attack in the Pacific area on any of the parties would be dangerous to its own peace and safety and declares that it would act to meet the common danger in accordance with its constitutional processes." Article V provided that "an armed attack on any of the parties is deemed to include an armed attack on the metropolitan territory of any of the parties, or on the island territories under its jurisdiction in the Pacific."[17]

The treaty was "an historical milestone" in Australian-American relations. It gave a firm basis to the vague relationship that had been inherited from the Second World War. It involved common assumptions about the chief threat to Pacific security and a reassessment of the relations between Australia and the United Kingdom. In a sense, it was a logical development from Curtin's appeal in 1941. Spender told the Commonwealth Club in San Francisco on March 15, 1950, that the main Australian objective was "to build up with the United States somewhat the same relationship as exists with the British Commonwealth."[18] Despite Churchill's considerable objections, a British request to send observers to the first meeting of ANZUS ministers to discuss defense problems was rejected.[19]

The second important link in the American alliance was the Southeast Asia Treaty Organization (SEATO), set up by the Manila treaty on September 8, 1954. The collapse of French power in Indochina produced both the Geneva settlement and the loosely drawn SEATO treaty, designed to stabilize the region and to commit western as well as Asian powers to the checking of aggression. The obligations assumed by the eight signatories were similar to those binding the three ANZUS partners, "to meet the common danger in accordance with its constitutional processes" and immediate consultation "in order to agree on the measures which should be taken for the common defence" of any state whose territory or political independence was threatened. There was no automatic commitment to action under either treaty. Although Australia deliberately declined to sign the American understanding attached to the Manila treaty, that "action would apply only to Communist aggression," it accepted the American view that the chief danger to stability in Southeast Asia came from Chinese expansion, ideological or imperialistic. Casey felt that the treaty gave Australia two strings to its bow and flatly rejected a suggestion from Dulles that the ANZUS treaty should go out of existence.

Attempts were made to clarify some of the loose phrases[20] in the two treaties. ANZUS council meetings in Canberra in 1962 and Wellington in 1963 made it clear that the treaty umbrella also covered the Territory of Papua–New Guinea: ". . . a threat to any of the partners in the area, metropolitan and island territories alike, is equally a threat to the others." The ANZUS treaty declared in simple and direct terms that in matters of defense Australia, New Zealand, and the U.S. stand as one. Australian attempts to include Borneo and Malaysia in the treaty area when confrontation developed between Indonesia and Malaysia received little support from the State Department.[21]

SEATO action was at first handicapped by the convention that unanimity was necessary before any military initiatives could be taken. On March 6, 1962, the Rusk-Khoman agreement provided for unilateral aid by the United States to Thailand under the SEATO treaty when communist pressures built up along its borders. Australia and New Zealand, as well as Great Britain, followed the American lead and sent small forces to Thailand to bolster its defenses. This greater flexibility in interpreting obligations paved the way for Australian and New Zealand assistance to the U.S. in Vietnam. The specific inclusion of Papua–New Guinea in the ANZUS treaty area was an American *quid* for the Australian *quo* in Thailand and Vietnam. The decision to send thirty military instructors to Vietnam was announced on May 24, fifteen days after the ANZUS council meeting in Canberra.

The third link in the American alliance was the agreement for the use of Australian bases for communications purposes. Two days after the Canberra meeting of the ANZUS council, Australian Prime Minister Menzies announced the establishment of a naval communications center at North West Cape in Western Australia. A formal agreement, leasing a twenty-eight-acre site to the U.S. for at least twenty-five years, was not concluded for another year. The base was equipped with low-frequency radio to enable it to communicate with Polaris nuclear submarines in the Indian Ocean. The base was to be under sole American control but was to be used only for defense communication unless the Australian government expressly gave consent for its use for other purposes. The Australian minister for external affairs, Sir Garfield Barwick, justified the agreement on the ground that it would increase "the individual and collective capacity" of the ANZUS partners to "resist armed attack." A deeply divided Labor opposition finally accepted the bill to establish the base as "a grim and awful necessity." A special conference of the ALP federal executive voted nineteen to seventeen to support the bill. The debate made it clear that, should a change of government take place, an attempt would be made to renegotiate the agreement.[22]

Subsequent agreements led to several other American installations: a Joint Defense Space Research Facility at Pine Gap near

Alice Springs and a Joint Defense Space Communications Center at Nurrungar to analyze and test data provided by American satellites. Other installations were equipped to monitor nuclear tests in the atmosphere, on the surface, and underground. None of them forms part of a weapons system, and Australia has access to the data provided by the installations.

The close political and defense relations built up between the two countries by these three major treaty arrangements involved constant consultation on broad issues of foreign policy and defense procurement. The agreement about the F-111 plane is perhaps the best illustration of that consultation.

The Australian commitment to American policies in Southeast Asia reached its peak as the war in Vietnam escalated after the Gulf of Tonkin incident in August 1964. The number of Australian advisers was increased to one hundred early in 1965. On April 29, Prime Minister Menzies announced the government's decision to send an infantry battalion of eight hundred men to Vietnam.[23] The Australian force was increased by his successor, Harold Holt, to four thousand five hundred. After his sweeping victory in November 1966, largely on the issue of Vietnam, further increases took place. Partly as a result of a visit to Australia by Clark Clifford and General Maxwell Taylor on October 17, 1967, Holt told Parliament that the Australian task force in Vietnam would be increased to eight thousand by the dispatch of a third battalion and the necessary support troops. He firmly resisted suggestions by Clifford for a further increase in Australian forces.[24]

The Australian decision to commit combat troops to Vietnam, to go "all the way with LBJ," was justified by the government in terms of its SEATO obligations in the same way that President John F. Kennedy had responded to a request for aid in 1961. At the same time, Australia had in mind the long-term problem that dominated its views about security: the danger that could face Australia if a political vacuum developed in Southeast Asia. The government was aware that it could not from its own resources defend the country against external attack. It was necessary for Australia to find another "powerful and willing friend," and the U.S. was the dominant power in the Pacific. As the United States became increasingly drawn into the Vietnamese quagmire, the Australian government looked at its obligations under the American alliance. The escalation of its forces in Vietnam from thirty military advisers to eight thousand combat troops was a calculated insurance policy to keep the ANZUS treaty alive.

The American alliance has never been a "debatable" alliance in the full sense of the term. There had been criticisms of particular American policies before Vietnam, but all major political parties accepted U.S. policies in principle. The Vietnam War, however, provided the catalyst for a reexamination of Australian foreign policies and the assumptions underlying them. As Whitlam said on March 10, 1966, "the Australian people are more divided on the issue of this war than on any in which they had ever been engaged." Increasingly, criticism of the Vietnam War in the trade unions, in academic and church circles, and in the streets centered round a belief that the war was "an unnecessary and an unwinnable one." The chorus of public disappointment matched criticism in the U.S. There was increasing support for the view that "we are fighting to protect an error in American foreign policy."[25]

Criticism centered in part on the nature of the American alliance and the relation between senior and junior partners in an alliance. Could a junior partner really influence important political or military decisions? Had the Vietnam War made Australia and New Zealand appear before the rest of the world "as satellites of the United States" and as sealed into "the alliance straitjacket into which they had deliberately fitted themselves?"[26] The government repeatedly claimed independence of action and vigorously denied the satellite suggestion. Evatt's policy during the occupation of Japan and Menzies's support for the United Kingdom over Suez in 1956 are two notable illustrations of independence of action in the early postwar years.[27] Australian ministers have always argued that the ANZUS treaty gave Australia a privileged access to the U.S. and that Canberra acted as a bridge between Washington, London, and various Asian capitals. There is much evidence to support this view and the assumption that "when you cannot live without your friends you do not argue with them or disagree with them in public."[28] Although there were many opportunities for privileged access, it is less certain that they were used by Washington. When the crunch comes, the junior partner's criticism may be brushed aside. Prime Minister John Gorton admitted the harsh realities of any alliance when he said that "if there were great changes in United States' involvement in Vietnam, Australia would be forced to accept them."[29]

Closer military ties between Australia and America were accompanied by rapidly expanding economic relations. Australian exports rose from 8.3 percent (Canada and the U.S.) in 1937–1938 to 11.9 percent in 1966–1967 and 14.2 percent in 1968–1969. Imports were almost halved between 1937–1938 and 1950–1955 but rose to an average of about 25 percent in 1970–1971. Meat became by far the largest export (45 percent in 1970–1971) despite friction over quality and quotas. The American duty on wool imports remained a handy perennial in negotiations between the two countries. Trade with Japan expanded much more rapidly than with the U.S., and Japan replaced the United Kingdom as Australia's best trading partner.[30] Overseas investment in Australia rose sharply during the 1960s, increasing more than threefold. The American share in investment increased slightly over the British, especially between 1965–1966 and 1970–1971. The economic ligaments between the two bodies politic had become very strong indeed, especially with the growth of American ownership of some sectors of Australian industry.[31]

Cultural relations between Australia and the United States expanded considerably between 1950, when the Fulbright and Smith–Mundt programs were introduced, and 1971, when the Australian-American Education Foundation replaced the earlier programs with substantially greater Australian financial support. The traditional intellectual pulls toward Oxford, Cambridge, and London became less strong; and Australian academics, graduates, students, and technical experts were increasingly attracted to American universities. Interest in Australian history, politics, and literature, however, remained confined to a handful of American universities.[32]

The flow of people and ideas across the Pacific was accelerated when Pan American began its first commercial service from San Francisco to Sydney in 1945—seventeen years after the pioneer flight of the *Southern Cross*. British Commonwealth Pacific Airlines (BCPA) followed a year later, and the first Qantas plane crossed the Pacific in 1954. The publication of regional editions of *Time*, *Newsweek*, and part of the weekly edition of the New York *Times* expanded Australian knowledge of the United States. Wire services were expanded and Australian journalists were stationed in the U.S. Yet the flow of information and the expansion of knowledge was largely a one-way process despite sentimental memories and tourist visits.

The American alliance developed out of the wartime alliance, and it took shape during the postwar period in the atmosphere of the cold war. World politics became bipolar and, with the establishment of the People's Republic of China, the central problem of foreign policy tended to become the containment of the spread of communism. That appeared to be the main threat to the stability of Southeast Asia and to the security of Australia: an expansive communist China had replaced a revived militant Japan as the potential danger. The deduction was clear: a powerful American presence was essential between Singapore and Tokyo now that the British presence in the region was much less visible.

1972–1975

On December 2, 1972, the Australian Labor party won the federal election and was returned to power for the first time in twenty three years. Three days later, Prime Minister Gough Whitlam indicated that the "change of government provides a new opportunity for us to reassess the whole range of Australian foreign policies and attitudes. . . . Our thinking is towards a more independent Australian stance."[33] He realized, however, that the election would not "change the essential foundations of [Australia's] foreign policy"; there must be "continuity within change," he said, at a time when the setting of foreign policy had changed dramatically since 1949 and especially since 1968.

The apparently monolithic communist world had disintegrated with the confrontation between Moscow and Peking and with discontent in eastern Europe. Japan had emerged as a major world economic power with a considerable military potential. Britain had entered the European Economic Community, and its presence in Asia became a token one as it decided to withdraw its military forces from Singapore. The nuclear balance had changed as France and China acquired a nuclear capacity while refusing to join the club. The rapid expansion of the Soviet navy and the entry of a Soviet fleet to the Indian Ocean foreshadowed a significant shift in the naval balance of power. The international balance of power had become at least quadrilateral rather than bipolar.

Washington had begun its own reassessment in the late 1960s as it realized the strength of internal opposition to its policy in Vietnam and recognized that it was overcommitted there. That reassessment led to a searching review of foreign policy priorities and a limitation on the range of American commitments. It was begun under President Lyndon B. Johnson and was largely completed by President Richard M. Nixon and Secretary Henry Kissinger. The new policy was sketched out at Guam on July 25, 1969, and then filled out in a series of major statements to Congress between February 18, 1970, and May 5, 1973.

It involved both a contraction of American commitments and a continued willingness to participate in the defense and development of allies and friends. The problem was one of dimensions and priorities: "America cannot—and will not—conceive *all* the plans, design *all* the programs, execute *all* the decisions and undertake *all* the defense of the free nations of the world. We will help where it makes a real difference and is considered in our interests." [34]

The new priorities meant a reversal of the Asian emphasis of Dulles in favor of Europe and a gradual detente with the Soviet Union, disengagement from Southeast Asia but not a retreat into isolationism. There were to be no more Koreas or Vietnams, but American treaty obligations were to be honored. The new priorities saw American interests in the Northwest Pacific outranking those in Southeast Asia and the Southwest Pacific. Tokyo and Peking became central and Australia peripheral to those interests. The Nixon visit to Peking reflected that new orientation. In a sense, the wheel had come full circle after a generation.

Australian rethinking of its foreign policy lagged behind the American. Before the election of 1972, Gorton had accepted the American decision to wind down the war in Vietnam and then withdraw. Prime Minister William McMahon began a revision of Australia's China policy which moved belatedly toward a "Two China" policy in 1971. With the withdrawal of most British forces from Singapore and the formulation of the Nixon Doctrine, both "powerful and willing friends" were leaving the area regarded as crucial to Australian defense. This raised the question of the new implications of what Bruce Grant has called "loyalty to the protector." Was a "protector" now necessary or possible in a world in which a new four-power balance would develop east of Suez? [35]

The major reassessment of Australian foreign policy in general, and of the American alliance in particular, was made by Whitlam after the Labor party assumed office. Labor had been the party which, under Curtin, had forged the alliance or, in the words of A. A. Calwell, had "first forged the links which bind our nations"; it was also a nationalistic party which, under Evatt, had been very critical of great-power domination of wartime and postwar policies.

Whitlam saw Australia as a middle power whose interests were primarily regional rather than global despite a determination to diversify and widen the range of diplomatic contacts and to revise Australian policies in the United Nations. His five-point program involved national security, a secure and friendly Japan, independence for Papua–New Guinea, close relations with Indonesia, the removal of the taint of racism, and the promotion of "the peace and prosperity of our neighborhood."[36] With those objectives went a deep awareness of the importance of Australia's mineral resources and their effect on the policy options for Australia: strategic, political, and military.

Immediately after he became prime minister, Whitlam said that his new government would adopt "a more constructive, flexible and progressive approach to a number of issues . . . towards a more independent Australian stance in foreign affairs and towards an Australia which will be less militarily oriented and not open to suggestions of racism."[37] But the only major new initiative was one that had been commenced by the previous government— namely, the recognition of Peking. The recognition of communist regimes in East Germany, North Vietnam, North Korea, and Poland was largely cosmetic, a gesture toward flexibility and the left-wing elements in the Australian Labor party.

In his first important speech on foreign policy, Whitlam said that the Labor government's "mandate and duty" to maintain the American alliance was equally clear. "This," he said, "we will do."[38] The American decision to withdraw from Indochina removed the only serious difference between the two governments. But, at the same time, it was clear that Whitlam saw the alliance in a different perspective as he set out to end what he regarded as an imbalance in Australia's foreign relations. The swift recognition of the People's Republic of China and the withdrawal of the Australian ambassador to Taiwan were part of the effort to correct that imbalance. In a sense Australia was adopting a policy parallel to Washington's, but it was a policy based on quite different premises.

The significant thing was his decision to convert the American "alliance" into the American "connection." Inheriting the Evatt mantle and representing the "new nationalism," he rejected the idea that Australia would automatically endorse American policies, and he repudiated emphatically the satellite syndrome, what Senator Fulbright referred to as almost "a semi-colonial relationship." After Whitlam's visit to Washington on July 29–30, 1973, he reported that "the American administration now fully accepts that Australia is not a small and relatively insignificant country as it was once called there, but a middle power of growing influence in the South-East Asian and South Pacific regions." As the U.S. ambassador, Marshall Green, said: "It was a time to recognize that Australia has parallel interests with the United States but not necessarily identical ones . . . we were not locked in step and . . . were not trying to stand over you."[39]

As a pragmatic nationalist, Whitlam reexamined the main instruments of the American connection: ANZUS, SEATO, and the bases agreements. The ANZUS treaty still remains the centerpiece of the connection. At the same time it was not to be "the only significant factor in our relations with the United States" any more than "our relations with the United States are the only significant factor in Australia's foreign relations."[40] SEATO, the main legal basis for Australian intervention in Vietnam, was now much less useful and has now been largely dismantled as a military organization.

The status of American bases in Australia had always been criticized by the ALP while in opposition. The two central points of criticism were that the agreement involved a surrender of Australian sovereignty over part of its territory and that Australia had no control over messages received by the North West Cape base. The Australian fear was that the station might be used to send signals that could trigger a nuclear war in which the base itself and Australia could be targets. That fear was strengthened during the Middle East crisis of October 6, 1973, when a global alert was issued by Washington. Australia was not officially informed about the alert, which did apply to the North West Cape installation.[41] Whitlam resisted left-wing pressures within the ALP to scrap the bases; they contribute, he said, "to the maintenance of global peace and security" and "specifically to the improvement and development of Australia's defense system." The 1963 agreement was renegotiated on January 9–10, 1974, so that the base would now be operated jointly, with Australian participation in its management, operation, and technical control. Australia established its own communications center, but the U.S. communications building remained wholly under American control.[42]

Southeast Asia was the area where new evaluations were made. The end of the Vietnam War in March 1973, and the subsequent fall of Cambodia altered the whole strategic pattern. American troops were phased out of Thailand by July 1976. As Kissinger pointed out in a comment on the Nixon Doctrine, "We have commitments only in those areas where our interests are involved. . . . Where the difficulties arise are in the grey areas where historical evolution may take care of the requirement."[43] The areas that are grey for the United States but vital for Australia are Malaysia, Singapore, Indonesia, and Papua–New Guinea. Here Australia for-

mulated its own policies based on close relations with Indonesia
and the abandonment of forward bases. American attitudes and
policies will be only one part of the jigsaw puzzle. Where differences arise, discussion will take place privately rather than in ban-
ner headlines or television announcements.[44]

The reorientation of Australian foreign policy in the grey areas
of Southeast Asia involved the reduction of Australian military
forces in Malaysia and Singapore under the Five-Power Defense
Agreement and the winding down of military cooperation with
SEATO. At the same time Whitlam tried to establish closer relations with the ASEAN nations—including closer economic ties
and interest in proposals for a "zone of peace" in either or both
of the Indian and Pacific oceans. But the establishment of closer
ties with ASEAN was slowed by the recognition of Peking. Not
even Australia's upgrading of relations with Japan (as in the negotiations for expanding trade between Australia and Japan) did
much to allay the suspicions of Australia's new Asian policy
among the ASEAN countries.

On the other hand, the public revision of Australia's racial policies improved its image in Asia, the United States, and the Pacific
islands as well as in Africa. In the UN General Assembly, Australia
supported tough resolutions on Rhodesia, the Portuguese colonies,
and apartheid; it also ratified the International Convention on the
Elimination of All Forms of Racial Discrimination in 1965. Its
immigration policy was revised administratively to remove much
of the "stigma of racialism," and the revision of its policy toward
Aborigines to provide for greater economic, educational, and social justice helped break the old image of a "White Australia."[45]

Australian-American relations at the official level have usually
been interpreted in political and military terms. Economic and
cultural matters have been kept in more or less watertight compartments. The development of Australian mineral resources means
that Australia has become a resources-rich power, but one determined to become "neither a quarry nor a sheikdom."[46] Control
of those resources and of the capital necessary for that development has increased the area of potential conflict between Canberra
and Washington. With the growth of multinational corporations,
many of them American-based, the nationalistic Australian government became very sensitive to capital inflow and takeover bids.
It now asked in a new context the old socialist question, "Who
owns Australia?" Was Australia in danger of becoming a sphere
of American economic influence? What the Australian govern-

ment was doing was to treat the American connection, and especially the ANZUS relationship, as part of the total Australian scene—political and military, economic and cultural. Mainly what the Whitlam government did was to accelerate changes that were already under consideration. Despite its concern with new Australian initiatives, few of its designs got much farther than the blueprint stage.

The reorientation of Australian foreign policy—that is, the attempt to formulate an independent foreign policy—has meant the reexamination of its relations with both London and Washington. This reexamination has been carried out with a realization of the changed position of Japan vis-à-vis Australia: Japan has replaced Great Britain as Australia's major trading partner and has also become a crucial element in the new balance of power in the Pacific. One component of this reorientation has been a stress on regional cooperation, epitomized in the growing importance of ASEAN. Another component, which must be regarded as a shift in emphasis, though perhaps not a major shift, is Australia's increasing interest in the Pacific islands. Its early interest in those islands had been essentially strategic, overlaid to some extent by a desire to import cheap kanaka labor. The annexation of southeastern New Guinea by Great Britain was a result of pressure from the Australian colonies. The Versailles clash between Hughes and Wilson concerning a mandate over German New Guinea reflected this sensitivity about control of an island very close to the Australian continent. Australian administration of its colony of Papua and of the mandated territory of New Guinea was combined in 1948. Independence has always been the terminal point for mandated territories. In September 1975, Papua–New Guinea achieved independence.

The Pacific islands proper, as one might call them, were merely of peripheral interest to Australia until the Second World War. War meant that the islands became important links in the supply route from California and Panama to Australia. The Curtin government, partly Fabian socialist in outlook, supported postwar decolonization. In 1944 Evatt invited the prime minister of New Zealand to a conference in Canberra, where he produced for the surprised New Zealanders the draft of the ANZAC agreement. It contained, among other provisions, one for the setting up of a commission to promote the welfare and advancement of native peoples in the Pacific. The effective outcome was the South Pacific Commission, which came into being in 1948. Australia,

France, the Netherlands, New Zealand, the United Kingdom, and the United States were the original members, all of them controlling island colonies in the Pacific.

The initiative in organizing the South Pacific Commission was Australian, and Australia provided the largest contribution to its budget. But interest in it waned after the change of government in 1949. ". . . it lacked not sympathy but positive drive from Australia. . . . Australia conscientiously if not over-enthusiastically, played its part."[47] It played no part in the decolonization of Pacific territories except for Papua–New Guinea. After the change of government in 1972, Australia became more actively interested in welfare policies of the South Pacific Commission and, along with New Zealand, increased its voluntary contributions to its budget. In 1971 the Liberal government had accepted an invitation to participate in the South Pacific Forum, and Whitlam strongly supported closer cooperation between Australia and the new independent and fully self-governing island states. But, despite an increasing Australian interest in the islands and their welfare, they remain low in the priorities of Australian foreign policy. Southeast Asia, Japan, and the United States are much higher on the totem pole.

To sum up, since 1919 the major change in Australian foreign policy has been the shift from dependence, almost total dependence, on the United Kingdom in matters of defense and foreign policy to a close relation with the United States. It would be an exaggeration to speak of an attempt to develop a new umbilical cord to Washington to replace the old one to London. What the Whitlam government attempted to do was to introduce a new perspective into relations with Washington and to avoid the shadow cast by the United States. Australia ceased to be a British outpost: relations with Britain were conceived of as "being based less on kin and more on kind."[48] Satellites belonged to the heavens but not to the Australian earth. Australia became a robust middle power with new contacts in Africa, Asia, Latin America, and Eastern Europe. The danger in its new outlook lay in an overexpansion of Australian diplomatic interests and commitments and in the possibility of confusing gestures about foreign policy with its substance, in mistaking image making with international reality. The element of continuity is very strong.

Notes

1 T. B. Millar, *Australia's Foreign Policy* (Sydney: Angus and Robertson, 1968), 7.

2 W. M. Hughes, *Politics and Potentates* (Sydney: Angus and Robertson, 1950), 241n.; cf. W. Farmer Whyte, *William Morris Hughes* (Sydney: Angus and Robertson, 1957), 393.

3 J. R. Poynter, "The Yo-yo Variations," *Historical Studies* (Melbourne: University of Melbourne), 14 (April 1970), 231–250.

4 See W. Hudson, "The Yo-yo Variations: A Comment," *Historical Studies*, 14 (October 1970), 424–429.

5 W. G. K. Duncan (ed.), *Australian Foreign Policy* (Sydney: Angus and Robertson, 1938), 51.

6 Paul Hasluck, *The Government and the People, 1939–41* (Canberra: Australian War Memorial, 1952), I, p. 551.

7 Hudson, op. cit., 429.

8 Jay Pierrepont Moffat, "Diaries," cited by Norman Harper (ed.), *Australia and the United States* (Melbourne: Nelson, 1971), 97–98, 104–108.

9 F. Alexander, *Australia since Federation* (Melbourne: Nelson, 1967), 171–173.

10 Lionel Wigmore, *The Japanese Thrust* (Canberra: Australian War Memorial, 1957), 177.

11 Dixon Wecter, "The Aussie and the Yank," *Atlantic Monthly*, 177 (May 1946), 52.

12 John Oliver Killens, *And Then We Heard the Thunder* (London: Cape, 1964). Part IV discusses the experiences of American troops in Brisbane during the war from the point of view of a Negro soldier.

13 Norman Harper and David Sissons, *Australia and the United Nations* (New York: Manhattan Publishing Co., 1959), 47–60; Paul Hasluck, "Australia and the Formation of the United Nations: Some Personal Reminiscences," *Journal and Proceedings, Royal Australian Historical Society*, 40 (1954), 133–178.

14 C. Hartley Grattan, *The United States and the Southwest Pacific* (Cambridge, Mass.: Harvard University Press, 1962), 202.

15 Percy Spender, *Exercises in Diplomacy* (Sydney: Sydney University Press, 1969), 120; Alan Watt, *The Evolution of Australian Foreign Policy, 1938–65* (Cambridge: Cambridge University Press, 1967), 179–181; T. B. Millar (ed.), *Australian Foreign Minister: The Diaries of R. G. Casey, 1951–60* (London: Collins, 1972), 18 (hereinafter cited as Casey, *Diaries*). Casey suggests that agreement about the treaty was finalized just before General Douglas MacArthur reached Washington after being relieved of his command on April 11.

16 Spender, op. cit., 133; Watt, op. cit., 176–185; Casey, *Diaries*, 18.

17 Text in Department of External Affairs, *Current Notes*, 22 (Canberra, 1951) 243–245.

18 Gordon Greenwood and Norman Harper (eds.), *Australia in World Affairs, 1950–55* (Melbourne: AIIA and Cheshire, 1957), 162–163 (hereafter cited as *Australia in World Affairs*). Casey commented that ANZUS was the surest

means of interesting the Americans more and more in the Southeast Asian mainland, *Diaries*, 95.

19 *Australia in World Affairs*, 163; Watt, op. cit., 178, 180; Selwyn Lloyd complained to Casey of the "stubborn exclusion" of the United Kingdom. Casey, *Diaries*, 108.

20 Casey said at the conference that "the real purpose of the Treaty is to present a concerted front against aggressive Communism, which presents the free world with immediate problems of security. Our own defense policy is directed to this dominant purpose." *Diaries*, 185.

21 *Current Notes*, 34 (June 1963), 5; New York *Times*, June 4, 1963.

22 Norman Harper, "Australia and the United States," *Australia in World Affairs, 1961–65* (Melbourne: Cheshire, 1967), 340–342.

23 Alan Watt, *Vietnam: An Australian Analysis* (Melbourne: Cheshire, 1968), 112–117; *Australia in World Affairs, 1961–65*, pp. 353–356.

24 H. Holt, *Commonwealth Parliamentary Debates* (House of Representatives), vol. 57, p. 1857 (hereafter cited as *C.P.D.* [*H. of R.*]); Clark Clifford, "A Viet-Nam Reappraisal," *Foreign Affairs*, 47 (July 1969), 607.

25 See Henry Albinski, *Politics and Foreign Policy in Australia: The Impact of Vietnam and Conscription* (Durham, N.C.: Duke University Press, 1970); Norman Harper, in *Australia in World Affairs, 1961–65* 358–60; and ibid., *1966–70* (Melbourne: Cheshire, 1974), 291–297, 303–307.

26 Trevor E. Reese, *Australia, New Zealand and the United States: A Survey of International Relations, 1941–68* (London: Oxford University Press, 1969), 332.

27 Norman Harper, "Australia and Suez," in *Australia in World Affairs, 1950–55*, pp. 341–357; Casey, *Diaries*, 249–257.

28 *Australia in World Affairs, 1956–60*, p. 234.

29 Hobart *Mercury*, March 24, 1968.

30 J. G. Crawford and Nancy Anderson in *Australia in World Affairs, 1961–65*, p. 223, and ibid., *1966–70*, pp. 129 et seq.

31 Heinz Arndt, "Foreign Investment," in *Australia in World Affairs, 1966–70*, pp. 145–59; also D. T. Brash, *American Investment in Australian Industry* (Canberra: Australian National University Press, 1966).

32 See Norman Harper in *Australia in World Affairs, 1956–60*, p. 195; ibid., *1961–65*, p. 231; and ibid., *1966–70*, pp. 313–314. For a discussion of the impact of American culture in Australia, see Grahame Johnston, "Literature"; Wal Cherry, "Theatre"; Robin Boyd, "Mass Communications"; and John Buchan, "Architecture"; in Norman Harper (ed.), *Pacific Orbit* (Melbourne: Cheshire, 1968), 123–167.

33 Sydney *Morning Herald*, December 6, 1972.

34 Richard Nixon, *A New Strategy for Peace*, Report to the Congress of the United States, February 18, 1970, pp. 6, 55–56.

35 Bruce Grant, *Crisis of Loyalty* (Sydney: Angus and Robertson, 1972), 17; Hedley Bull, "From Evatt to Whitlam," Evatt Memorial Lecture, August 9, 1973 (mimeographed).

36 *Australian Foreign Affairs Record*, 44 (1973), 199 (hereafter cited as *A.F.A.R.*).

37 Ibid.

38 E. G. Whitlam, "Australian Foreign Policy," *A.F.A.R.*, 44 (1973), 31.

39 E. G. Whitlam, August 22, 1973, *C.P.D. (H. of R.)*, vol. 85, p. 200; *Australian*, July 28, 1975.

40 Whitlam, op. cit.

41 Whitlam, November 20, 1973, *C.P.D. (H. of R.)*, vol. 87, p. 3500.

42 *A.F.A.R.*, 45 (1974), 40; Norman Harper, "The American Alliance in the 1970s," in J. A. C. Mackie (ed.), *Australia in the New World Order* (Melbourne: Nelson, 1976), 43–44.

43 Melbourne *Sun*, August 1, 1970.

44 Whitlam, Address to National Press Club, New York, July 30, 1973, *A.F.A.R.*, 44 (1973), 529.

45 Mackie, op. cit., 23; cf. J. A. C. Mackie, "Australian Foreign Policy from Whitlam to Fraser," *Dyason House Papers* (Melbourne: AIIA), August 3, 1976, pp. 1–4.

46 E. G. Whitlam, *Australia's Foreign Policy: New Directions, New Definitions*, 24th Roy Milne Memorial Lecture, Brisbane, November 30, 1973 (Melbourne: AIIA, 1973), 19.

47 W. D. Forsyth, "The South Pacific Commission," in *Australia in World Affairs, 1961–65*, p. 494.

48 *A.F.A.R.*, 44 (1973), 394.

GEOFFREY SAWER

The Australian Commonwealth
and the Australian States

Since the First World War, a frequent cry of Australian state political leaders, especially those from the non-Labor parties, has
been that the power of the Commonwealth, as it was always called
until 1972—the center government in the federal system—has increased, is increasing, and ought to be diminished. The methods
and rate of increase have varied a great deal and have depended
partly on parliamentary politics, partly on judicial politics, and
partly on the occurrence of economic crises, wars, and the threats
of war substantially outside any Australian control. All federal
parties and governments have contributed to the increase—the
non-Labor parties more than Labor. Because of the demands of
office, they have increased it pragmatically, sometimes in the teeth
of official party policy. The Australian Labor party (ALP), on the
other hand, while likewise much influenced in the timing of particular federal expansions by immediate needs and demands, can
gracefully yield to such pressures because in any event it has a
long-standing commitment to strengthening the central authority;
in the minds of ALP federal leaders, the creation of a powerful
single "national" parliament, government—and since 1972 judici-
ary as well—has long been an ideological imperative, whereas the
concessions to state-rights sentiment and the preservation of a
federal devolution have been seen as the pragmatic requirement.
Prime Minister Gough Whitlam, leader of the ALP government
which achieved power at the center in December 1972 and the
most sophisticated and aggressive "centralizer" in the country's
political history, illustrated the trend when he insisted on replacing, as far as he could, the expression "Australian" for the expression "Commonwealth" to describe the institutions of the center—
"Australian" Parliament, government, and so forth; it is a usage
which leads to ambiguity in some contexts, however, so in this

essay the older "Commonwealth" is retained. In any event, the Fraser Liberal-Country government which succeeded the ALP in late 1975 has since been—slowly, as one might expect—restoring "Commonwealth" to official use. Regardless of labels, the course of constitutional development has been irregular and in many details surprising.

In 1919 Australia's constitutional system could still be described with substantial accuracy as complying with the vision of coordinate federalism set out in James Bryce's *American Commonwealth*;[1] that work had been the bible of Australia's federal fathers, including the first chief justice (Samuel Griffith) and the first two puisne judges (Edmund Barton and Richard O'Connor) of the High Court of Australia. Probably Bryce's book underestimated the extent of federal cooperation in America even when he originally wrote it, and certainly the Australians had by 1919, through Premiers' Conferences and other extraconstitutional measures, started to develop in a cooperative direction. As far as judicial interpretation was concerned, however, there were no fundamental differences between the view of federalism entertained on the U.S. Supreme Court in 1919 and that entertained on the High Court of Australia, even though the characteristic "federal implications" doctrines developed by the three original High Court justices had been coming under increasing attack by subsequent appointees, notably Isaac Isaacs and H. B. Higgins, who were also federal fathers.

It was characteristic of the Australian legal and, in particular, the judicial establishment, so much closer to the outlook of British nineteenth-century legal traditions than were the Americans, that in Australia the generalized political theory of coordinate federalism had been transmuted by the first High Court into two specific constitutional principles: the doctrine of "immunity of instrumentalities" (corresponding to the looser set of U.S. rules concerning "intergovernmental immunities") and the doctrine of "implied prohibitions" (similar to but wider than the U.S. doctrine of state "police powers"). The Australian immunities doctrine prohibited the Commonwealth government and the states from interfering with each other's governmental activities, and the "prohibitions" doctrine required Commonwealth powers to be narrowly construed so as to preserve a substantial area for state residual power under s.107 of the constitution.[2] As late as June 1919, the High Court in *Australian Workers' Union v. The Adelaide Milling Co. Ltd.*[3] applied the immunities doctrine so as to prevent the Commonwealth Court of Conciliation and Arbitration, operating under s.51 (xxxv) of the constitution, from settling an industrial dispute between two state wheat marketing authorities and their employees; the majority included Isaacs, one of the leading critics of federal implications as a means of constitutional interpretation.

By the end of 1920, an American observer of the Australian scene—such as Hartley Grattan—might well have prophesied that the future of Australian federalism was going to be markedly different from what in fact occurred. He might have prophesied that there was going to occur in Australia, largely through changes in judicial interpretation, a broad expansion of Commonwealth legislative and corresponding administrative competence and activity. On the other hand, he might have forecast that by an irony of history this accretion of normative power to the Commonwealth, would be accompanied by a growth of fiscal resources available to the states, tending to make them less subject to center influence, based upon fiscal superiority, than the Australian founders had anticipated and feared. Looking at the then contemporary political situation, he would have noted that the Nationalist party government under Prime Minister William Morris Hughes, although formed in 1917 by merging a small leaven of former ALP, Commonwealth-rights "bolters" with a large mass of state-rights Liberal party supporters, still possessed a certain amount of the Commonwealth-aggrandizing impetus of the Fisher-Hughes ALP government of 1910–1914; that government had fostered a slowly growing electoral support for constitutional change to expand Commonwealth powers, until absorption in the First World War ended such activities. Hence, it would have seemed not improbable that a Hughes-led Nationalist government, inclined to make use of opportunities for Commonwealth self-assertion, might coincide with encouragement to such activity from High Court decisions. Since the coincidental growth in state fiscal resources involved no diminution of Commonwealth fiscal resources, this need not have deterred our prophet from foreseeing for Australia something like the revolution that occurred in the federalism of the U.S. between 1936 and 1945.

This forecast about the course of constitutional interpretation would have been based on the following details. In 1920 the High Court embarked on what then appeared to be a decisively new course in constitutional construction, one predicated not on coordinate and reciprocal stasis but on "progressive" development, tending in practice to encourage the growth of central power.

O'Connor died in 1912 and Barton in January 1920. Chief Justice Griffith retired in 1919; he was succeeded by Chief Justice Sir Adrian Knox. In general terms, Knox was if anything a more conservative man that Griffith. But he had not been a founding father, had no special set of theories about the nature of a federal polity, and had achieved eminence at the Sydney bar as a competent legal technician who was at home with traditional Anglo-Australian methods of statutory interpretation. He presided over a Court containing no survivor of the original three justices. Of this Court, Isaacs (appointed in 1906) had an ideological commitment to the "nationalist" view of the constitution as a stage in Australian development; Charles Powers (appointed 1913) had similar inclinations but little reputation as a jurist; Higgins (appointed 1906) was specifically committed to a maximum expansion of central power in industry and commerce, though in some respects he had state-rights inclinations—an ideological schizophrenia later exemplified by H. V. Evatt; George Rich (appointed 1913) and H. E. Starke (appointed 1920), like Knox, had played no part in federation and were inclined to regard constitutional interpretation as mainly an exercise in statutory construction. Ironically, the principal state-rights voice now on the court was that of Gavan Duffy, who had been appointed in 1913 by the Fisher-Hughes Labor government under the pathetic illusion that because of his radical Irish background he might favor broad constructions of central power.

Hence, it was not a matter for undue surprise when in the *Engineers'* case (1920)[4] a strong majority of the Court (only Gavan Duffy dissenting) made a frontal attack on the "federal implications" doctrines hitherto followed and substituted the principle that the constitution should be interpreted by the positivistic and literal methods usually applied to statutory construction in Australian and English courts. The practical effect of this was to require reasonably broad interpretations of specific grants of power and to avoid implications (whether of restrictions on power or of grants of power), or at least implications based not on textual analysis but on some general theory about the structure and purposes of federations. This pronouncement was made the more dramatic because it was not at all necessary for the Court to take such a course in order to determine the case. The only question was whether the Commonwealth Court of Conciliation and Arbitration could settle a dispute between the Western Australian government and employees in state-owned sawmills and engineering works; a plain answer would have been (applying both Australian and American doctrine) that the function was trading, not governmental, and accordingly "implied immunity" restrictions on the federal competence had no application. Instead, the Court dealt with the "immunity of instrumentalities" doctrine as a whole; it went even further by criticizing as well the "implied prohibition" doctrine which was not involved in the case at all.[5] Then, in *McArthur's* case (1920),[6] a similarly strong majority of the Court held (Gavan Duffy again dissenting) that s.92 of the constitution, guaranteeing freedom of interstate trade, did not bind the center at all but applied to the states in a very stringent fashion, so as virtually to exclude them from any power to regulate interstate commerce as such—an approximation to the U.S. position on this topic. These two decisions provided a solid foundation for a possible course of decision leading to a predominance of Commonwealth authority in the commercial life of the country, comparable to that achieved by the U.S. Congress after 1936.

On the other hand, our 1920 observer would have been optimistic about the fiscal future of the states chiefly because the Australian people, after strong initial resistance, had become accustomed to the payment of income tax. By 1907 every state had introduced this form of taxation; the Commonwealth followed in 1915; and by 1920 a pattern had been established in which the states imposed tax at higher rates than the Commonwealth and the Commonwealth regarded itself as the residuary claimant to this form of revenue. For example, the Commonwealth treated state tax payments as deductions for its purposes—not vice versa. Discussions between Commonwealth and states with a view to achieving some uniformity in assessment principles and some sharing of administration had already begun, and in 1932 a royal commission appointed by the Commonwealth recommended both a uniform assessment act and joint administration, and the latter was actually achieved in 1936. This was a notable exercise in cooperative federalism. Insufficient attention has been paid, however, to the fact that it was a cooperation in which the states bargained from strength, because no one had as yet contended that the Commonwealth could by any means short of constitutional change exclude the states from the income tax field (as they were excluded from customs and excise by s.90 of the constitution).

The declining importance of Commonwealth grants to the states was an important factor in the successful negotiation of the 1927 agreement on public loan raisings, given constitutional blessing in 1928 by the insertion of s.105A in the constitution and the consequent establishment of the Australian Loan Council. That agreement had the effect, among others, of converting the Commonwealth per capita payments to the states, introduced in 1910, to a payment via the Loan Council toward interest and sinking funds for state indebtedness, thus freezing this kind of Commonwealth subsidy at its 1927 level. This freezing operation was accepted by the states with comparative equanimity, precisely because of the declining importance of what used to be considered their "share" of the customs and excise revenue in their budgets. The "claimant states" (Western Australia, South Australia, and Tasmania) in effect still needed to obtain transfers from the three wealthier states (New South Wales, Victoria, and Queensland) via the Commonwealth Treasury. The ad hoc system for insuring this (begun in 1910) was stabilized and rationalized by setting up the Commonwealth Grants Commission in 1933, and this added to the fiscal strength of the states as a whole by removing the special grievances of the poorer states from the regular attention of federal politicians.[7]

The same American observer might now look back and ask "where did my prophecy go wrong?" He would have had to reply somewhat as follows: first, the story of judicial interpretation did not follow the course suggested by the *Engineers'* and *McArthur's* cases, and it failed to do so for a mixture of judicial and political reasons.

Politically, the Bruce-Page, Nationalist-Country party coalition government which held office from 1923 to 1929 was quite prepared to extend Commonwealth powers to their limit in defense of capitalism. Indeed, their long-drawn-out war with the trade unions was the eventual cause of their downfall; but they were not so keen on the business of regulating capitalism and were happy enough to leave to the states the major share of economic development and such meager expansion of welfare services as occurred.[8] The absence of frequent occasions for testing the validity of Commonwealth legislation in the sphere of commercial and industrial control, apart from controls over industrial strife, contributed materially to what occurred in the area of judicial decision. Although the language of the *Engineers'* and *McArthur's* cases was adopted by strong majorities of the High Court, its implications needed to be developed by prompt legislative and administrative action on the part of the Commonwealth and given subsequent judicial blessing so as to convert what could be regarded as mere obiter dicta into accepted constitutional jurisprudence.

On the judicial side, the basic difficulty was that only Sir Isaac Isaacs was committed without qualification to the principles of the majority judgments in the *Engineers'* case and *McArthur's* case—as a program for making the Commonwealth both the main instrument of an emerging Australian nationhood and the commercial policy leader for both external and domestic purposes. Higgins had reservations about Commonwealth supremacy, probably accentuated by his bad personal relations with W. M. Hughes. Knox, Rich, and Starke preferred an *Engineers*-style approach mainly for technical reasons—it saved them from speculations about the general nature of the constitution, which to them smacked of politics, and it avoided the apparent logical trap of treating the "residual" gift to the states under s.107 as if it contained a "specific" gift as well. Gavan Duffy rejected the *Engineers* approach. There are grounds for thinking that Isaacs alone fully understood the reasoning and implications of the *McArthur* judgment; certainly, that decision was never squarely applied in its own particular field, namely, the meaning and application of s.92, the guarantee of interstate free trade. In such contexts, the case was habitually cited with unctuous respect and then was ignored. The proposition that the Commonwealth was not bound by s.92 was repudiated by Evatt soon after his appointment in 1930, abandoned by the Commonwealth itself in *Vizzard's* case (1933),[9] and pronounced bad law by the Privy Council in *James* v. *Commonwealth* (1936)[10]; thus the possibility that the Commonwealth would not only be empowered but in practice be compelled to provide a national code of commercial law for interstate commerce accordingly disappeared. Critics of the *Engineers'* case appeared. Owen Dixon (appointed 1929) soon established a reputation as the greatest Australian jurist of all time and one of the greatest common law judges of this century; he disliked its style even more than its contents. But even as to its contents, he joined Evatt in the view that literal interpretation could not solve all problems and that some general conception of federalism ought to enter into judicial reasoning about the Australian federal constitution.[11] It was not surprising that Justice Dixon should have criticized the *Engineers'* case and sought to narrow its application, since he was a conservative, brought up in a Victorian atmosphere which accepted almost without thinking the state-rights view of the constitutional structure, and he had never regarded the views of the first three justices as manifestly wrong.

It seems today more surprising that Evatt should likewise have regarded the *Engineers'* case with suspicion. Indeed, on some subjects, generally speaking the construction of positive Commonwealth powers, Evatt accepted an *Engineers'* case approach. Even before going into Commonwealth politics, he supported the extension of Commonwealth competence, especially in the international field. Like many middle-class socialists of his generation, however, Evatt had grown up in an atmosphere of state politics. He expected more immediate and positive results from social reformers at state levels than he did from the Commonwealth—partly because of the Commonwealth's restricted competence in social welfare fields and partly because of the relatively conservative bias of Commonwealth politics, which was derived from the political demography of the continent as a whole. It was that attitude that had caused the Labor parties in general to oppose federation in the first place. My personal impression of Evatt was that he remained a politician, in the narrower sense of "politics," even while on the High Court. It seems that his opinions on constitutional matters were guided more by the immediate contemporary trend of politics than by any long-term views about the structure and working of constitutional systems. Through the 1920s he had seen the dominance of the right-wing parties in federal politics, while at the same time Labor had a fair share of government in New South Wales and Queensland and a respectable record of carrying out social reforms. His appointment to the High Court in 1930 was entirely due to the ALP federal election victory of 1929. It was already apparent by 1930, however, that James Scullin's ALP government was in deep internal trouble and was not prepared for frontal battle with the overwhelmingly hostile Senate. Thus by 1931 Evatt had good reason to suppose that the future pattern of Australian politics was going to be much like what it had been ever since the break-up of the ALP under Hughes in 1916. Therefore, he did not change the outlook which dictated a desire to preserve a considerable degree of power and autonomy for the states. It was also an Evatt characteristic that in constitutional matters he appeared as advocate for cases in which he believed, not readily changing the views which he had developed as advocate. He had been on the losing side in the *Engineers'* case, and it was probably of more than symbolic significance that his successful opponent was R. G. Menzies.

Dixon and Evatt were the outstanding intellectual influences on the Court between 1930 and 1936, when Sir John Latham was appointed chief justice. Latham may not have been of quite the

same caliber as a jurist, but he had far greater experience and
understanding of politics and the conduct of government. Moreover, he had a positivist bent of mind which inclined him strongly
toward the *Engineers'* case viewpoint. On constitutional questions, he had an influence comparable to that of Dixon and Evatt.
On the other hand, Latham was also a conservative in his general
political outlook and was not disposed toward the construction of
Commonwealth powers in such a way as seriously to abridge the
position of the states.[12]

The consequence was that after 1936, and even after the departure of Evatt from the bench in 1940, the Court as a whole pursued
a somewhat wavering path. The *Engineers'* case continued to be
the basis for interpreting Commonwealth powers in a more generous spirit than they had been interpreted before 1920; but the
defense power was treated in a less generous way than Isaacs had
treated it in 1916;[13] and the ghost of "federal immunities" continued to appear in some of the wartime decisions.[14] The *Uniform
Tax* case (1942)[15] beautifully illustrated these clashing influences
and provided a bridge from the judicial to the fiscal theme, which
was the second one to develop in ways not easily predictable in
1919.

The fiscal autonomy which income taxation and economic
expansion were bringing to the state through the 1920s did not
appear to be immediately prejudiced by the financial agreement of
1927, even though the Loan Council machinery for handling the
public debts of the seven governments to a considerable extent
bypassed all seven parliaments. This was because the agreement
gave the states a voting majority on the Loan Council. Although at
the time a revolutionary step in cooperative federalism, it was
again the sort of cooperative federalism which rested upon at least
equality of bargaining power between center and regions. It was
accepted from the first that Loan Council decisions would be
carried into effect by the Commonwealth, but even this was not
seen at the time as a special threat to the states. However, the
circumstances of the world depression, already apparent in Australia by late 1929, rapidly produced conditions under which the
Loan Council system became in practice an important instrument
of financial domination by the Commonwealth as against the
states.

Through 1930–1931, the politics of this was seen in the "battle
of the plans." Premiers' Conferences and Loan Council meetings
(almost indistinguishable in personnel and responsibilities) settled

for deflationary policies which in turn brought about even greater fissions in the ALP than those caused by military conscription in 1916–1917.[16] The Scullin government was defeated at the polls in 1931, and the Lyons-Latham Commonwealth government which succeeded it proceeded at once to make vigorous use of several Commonwealth powers—including those created by s.105A of the constitution—to coerce and drive from office the only remaining Labor government prepared to defy the "premiers' plan." That was the Lang government in New South Wales; when it endeavored to suspend debt servicing, its revenues in banks were frozen or seized by the Commonwealth—a course held constitutionally valid by the High Court in the three *Garnishee* cases (1931).[17] Those decisions were in a sense logical applications of *Engineers'* case principles. Gavan Duffy, now chief justice, dissented because he was a genuine state-righter, and Evatt dissented because he disliked coercion of this particular state by this particular Commonwealth government. Dixon went with a majority against the general trend of his constitutional thinking, ostensibly because of the overriding effects of s.105A and probably also because of a sense of national emergency. Thus the economic, political, and judicial events of 1929–1932 established that the Loan Council system was likely in practice to be an instrument of Commonwealth ascendancy in this aspect of public finance. The Commonwealth's position was strengthened by the financing of the Second World War, by the banking policies initiated by the Curtin-Chifley governments in 1941–1949, and, in basic principles, continued by subsequent Liberal-Country party governments. These insured that the Commonwealth government could exercise a veto on Loan Council decisions because it could prevent the council from establishing any direct relations with the loan market, domestic or overseas.

Having thus collared the field of loan finance, the Commonwealth proceeded to obtain a *de facto* monopoly of income tax by a combination of legal and political pressures and a *de lege* monopoly of indirect taxation, mainly through judicial decision.

The income tax monopoly obtained in 1941–1942 was immediately occasioned by the fiscal consequences of the Second World War, in particular the enormous expenditures made necessary by the Japanese entry into that war and the real threat of a Japanese occupation of north and northwestern Australia. Even before December 1941, however, it had become apparent that some means for equalizing the tax burden in Australia had become essential because of the increasing magnitude of that burden. The technical obstacle was the requirement in s.51(2) and s.99 of the constitution that federal taxation should be uniform. State income taxes were at many different levels. In particular Victoria had become a low-tax, low-expenditure state, while New South Wales was a high-tax and high-expenditure state. Those states had the bulk of population and industry. The only radical solution to the problem was to end state income taxes and substitute a uniform Commonwealth tax at a very high rate. The Menzies-Fadden governments of 1939–1941 had not been prepared to face up to the politics of this. The Curtin-Chifley governments of 1941–1945 did have the necessary political fortitude and expressed it in four interlinked acts. Four states immediately challenged the acts in a High Court of five—Dixon being absent as minister in Washington— but they were all held valid by varying majorities. The main basis was the Commonwealth's ability to make conditional grants under s.96, applicable in peace as in war. By 1945 the so-called uniform tax scheme— which should have been called the Commonwealth monopoly of income taxation scheme—had become so well entrenched and so much liked by the electors and by some of the state governments that Ben Chifley had no difficulty in carrying it on through postwar reconstruction to 1949. The Menzies-Fadden government elected in 1949 was pledged to an attempt at returning income tax to the states. From the point of view of legal theory, there was nothing to stop the states from reimposing income taxes at any time, at least after 1957 when the High Court, while dismissing a further challenge to the scheme,[18] held invalid during peacetime the tough priority-in-collection provision that had been upheld in 1942. In 1959 the Commonwealth even removed the provision in the Grants Act imposing a condition of abstention from income taxes on its reimbursement payments to states. The obstacles to state resumption of income taxes were by then wholly political, economic, electoral, and fortitudinal. Nonetheless, they were effective.

Meanwhile, the High Court, initially under the mischievous influence of Dixon, had gratuitously embarked on a course of expanding the scope of the "excise duties" which by reason of s.90 of the constitution were denied to the states. This development was completed by 1970, when it was held that all sales and purchase taxes were outside state competence.[19] From 1966 on, several states had been endeavoring to build up a tax system based on the notion of a "stamp duty" on various kinds of receipts, and some of these were undoubtedly valid, in particular the taxes on the receipt of salaries and wages. However, it was difficult to manage such taxes without approaching in substance a sort of income tax, which successive Commonwealth governments increasingly resisted after the retirement of Menzies in 1966. It was also difficult to avoid regressive incidence. In 1971 the states finally abandoned these attempts and accepted instead another installment of reimbursement offered by the Gorton Commonwealth government. As a result, the states have come to rely on Commonwealth grants for more than half of their current revenues. Through the Menzies regime (1949–1966), less than 30 percent of these Commonwealth grants were conditional, and less than 20 percent were conditional in a sense tending to reduce state policy autonomy. Thereafter, the number of conditional grants steadily increased, and their terms and the kinds of administrative oversight developed by the Commonwealth made them increasingly restrictive of state autonomy. In 1972 the Whitlam ALP government adopted a systematic strategy for developing this aspect of "cooperative federalism" as an instrument of Commonwealth policy control. In 1974 the proportion of conditional grants had risen to over 40 percent of all Commonwealth revenue grants to states. In 1973 Whitlam made an offer to the states to cede them some powers of imposing sales taxes, which would have required constitutional amendment; it was an amendment most unlikely to be endorsed by the electors. In 1974 the High Court held valid a form of state consumption tax suggested by the present writer, but by a majority of one this was accompanied by crippling conditions on the mode of administration.[20] The same decision validated a form of state franchise tax by states in order to tax petrol and tobacco sales. However, it was characteristic of state behavior in this field that Tasmania, which pioneered the taxes just mentioned, abandoned them in 1974 in return for a special federal grant. By 1975 the possibility of the states' recovering anything like fiscal autonomy seemed to have disappeared. The Fraser New Federalism of 1976 offered once again a limited state competence in the personal income tax field, but the constitutional and political obstacles to its successful application appeared in 1977 to be formidable. The states will do anything to get more money, except to take the responsibility for imposing fresh taxes.

However, it remains characteristic of Australian federalism that the center has to struggle to get its way—by a combination of fiscal pressure and political persuasion—because it remained true in

1977 that the High Court was, on American standards, niggardly in its approach to central powers. We should mention that, from the beginning, the High Court and not the Judicial Committee of the Privy Council has been the chief judicial instrument for interpreting and adapting the constitution. Privy Council decisions have been important on only one topic—the guarantee of freedom of interstate trade under s.92 of the constitution—and in 1968 the possibility of further constitutional appeals to the Privy Council was removed.[21] Even on s.92, the Privy Council has but palely reflected the course of doctrinal change in the High Court. It is sufficient to say that the course of decision on that topic since *McArthur* in 1920 has produced a doctrine, binding Commonwealth and states alike, which permits "reasonable regulation" of interstate trade but no more—making it a Herbert Spencerian sort of due-process clause which benefits only interstate trade, on a fairly narrow understanding of both "trade" and "interstateness."[22] The section killed the Chifley bank nationalization scheme in 1947–1950 but provided no restraints at all on the plans of the Whitlam ALP government. More serious for that government was the narrow High Court reading of the Australian interstate trade power—constitution s.51(i)—compared with the meaning given interstate commerce by the U.S. Supreme Court. The paradigm decision is the *Airlines of New South Wales* case (1965),[23] in which the High Court unanimously declined to treat a feeder airline in New South Wales as a part of interstate trade for constitutional purposes. The Supreme Court of the United States would have treated this service as interstate, long before the adventures of 1937, under the doctrine of the "interstate journey," and since then in cases like *Wickard* v. *Filburn*,[24] under the theory of a passage or throat through which interstate commerce moved.[25]

The great constitutional possibility of the future in Australia, as far as judicial interpretation is concerned, arises not under the interstate trade power but under the corporations power—s.51(xx). This is because in the *Concrete Pipes* case (1971),[26] the High Court, in an unaccustomed burst of judicial enterprise and inventiveness, overruled an old decision which placed a very narrow construction on that power. It treated the power to make laws with respect to "foreign corporations, and trading or financial corporations formed within the Commonwealth" as adequate to support Commonwealth regulation of restrictive trade practices and monopolies in corporate business. The Whitlam government relied heavily on this power for much of its legislation in the economic field, but in 1977 the limits of the power remained to be drawn by the courts.

Another power which the High Court has interpreted with some generosity is that with respect to "external affairs"—s.51(xxix). The main expansive interpretation occurred in 1936,[27] and subsequent references in the cases have been guarded. The Whitlam government endeavored to use international agreements as a basis for legislation on human rights and other matters otherwise beyond Commonwealth power. Senate obstruction hindered the program, however, and no decisive cases reached the High Court. On one matter, the High Court has given the Commonwealth a very wide freedom of action: when international agreements and s.51(xxix) might, between them, have been expected to create restrictions on its competence—namely, policy with respect to territories held under United Nations trusteeship agreements or otherwise subject to UN surveillance as colonies. The High Court held that such territories were controlled by the Commonwealth, not under the external affairs power (the view which Evatt, as justice and as politican, preferred), but under the power in s.122 of the constitution to provide for the government of territories.[28]

A corollary of this decision was that Commonwealth legislative and executive acts in relation to Papua–New Guinea were from the domestic point of view quite unaffected by the UN Charter or by trusteeship agreements. This assisted conservative Commonwealth governments to pursue policies of gradualism in the political development of Papua–New Guinea through the 1950s. In the early 1960s Prime Minister Menzies announced that the winds of change must blow in those parts as well. In one sense, therefore, Australia's position as a colonial power has had virtually no influence on its domestic constitutional law. In another sense, however, once Canberra under Labor had decided to use every effort to rid itself of the Papua–New Guinea colonial appendage, the lack of constitutional inhibitions made the process, legally speaking, extremely easy and smooth. Papua might have raised the objection that since it was part of Australia—and its people both British subjects and Australian citizens—there was no way of compelling it to accept independence. But its indigenous politicians chose to follow the different course of trying to get either separate independence or better terms for its inclusion in an independent Papua–New Guinea, which was finally set up in 1975.

Although the corporations power provides the only striking

example of judicial interpretation especially favorable to the Commonwealth during the period since the *Uniform Tax* case, there have been subsidiary developments in that time advantageous to the Commonwealth—at least if one takes as a point of comparison the other choices argumentatively open to the High Court. The Dixonian revolt against *Engineers* reached its maximum development in the *State Banking* case (1947),[29] when a majority held that the Commonwealth could not require states to bank with a government (as distinct from a privately owned) bank. In so doing, it appeared to revive the doctrine of immunity of state instrumentalities from Commonwealth regulation, at least in a modified form. But there has been no clear later application of that decision. The *Payroll Tax* case (1971),[30] which upheld the application of Commonwealth payroll tax to states in respect of the employment of public servants, went some distance toward "distinguishing" the *State Banking* case out of existence. In the *Professional Engineers'* case (1959),[31] even Dixon, then the chief justice, joined in a ringing reaffirmation of the rejection of "implied prohibitions" as an approach to constitutional interpretation. In *Victoria v. Commonwealth* (1957),[32] the second uniform tax case, the Court declined to permit any implied restrictions, implied by federalism or anything else, on the kinds of conditions which the Commonwealth might impose on grants to the states under s.96 of the constitution.

The net result of the decisions of the period has been to encourage Commonwealth use of its fiscal dominance in order to coerce or at least persuade the states to accept its policy leadership, both by upholding its fiscal dominance and by declining to construct doctrines which might have restricted the use of its dominance as a weapon against the states. On the other hand, the Court has also tended to force the Commonwealth into using the states as an instrument for administering its policies—by raising doubts as to the Commonwealth's capacity to spend directly on purposes outside its other powers (*Pharmaceutical Benefits* case [1946])[33] and by its cautious handling of positive Commonwealth legislative powers.

The course of cooperative federalism thus judicially indicated suited reasonably well the political policy and style of the Liberal-Country party governments which held federal office from 1949 to 1972. It was less well suited to the plans of the Whitlam ALP government which took office in December 1972. That government attempted to reconstruct Australian federalism by four parallel strategies. The first was to appoint to the High Court judges who might be prepared to take a fresh look at constitutional interpretation. Two opportunities occurred and, consequently, Kenneth S. Jacobs and Lionel K. Murphy add an occasional radical voice to High Court discourse. The second was legislation designed to test at their limit the heads of power which might yet be capable of expansion by judicial decision, such as the external affairs, corporations, and spending powers. The third was to try to build up a new type of federal structure, to some extent exemplified by U.S. practice, in which the Commonwealth establishes direct relations with local government, particularly in the metropolitan cities where about 70 percent of Australians live, thus removing the need for mediating its urban social policies through state governments with different views on goals and priorities. This would probably require formal constitutional amendment to be completely effective. The fourth was to launch proposals for formal amendment of the constitution by referendum pursuant to s.128, including proposals for amending the amendment procedure itself to make amendment politically easier. Four such proposals put to the electors in 1974 were defeated, partly because they were related to immediate political issues rather than to any long-term constitutional restructuring.

Perhaps more promising from the point of view of Labor policy was a development in 1974 concerning relations between the two federal houses. Since the introduction of proportional representation for the Senate by the Chifley Labor government in 1949—a disastrous error for such a government—it had become very difficult for any major party to gain decisive control of that house, and especially difficult for the ALP. The Whitlam government was continually frustrated by adverse Senate voting, and in 1974 it obtained a dissolution of both houses under s.57 of the constitution. This was only the third such dissolution in federal history, and for the first time the government obtained it in respect, not merely of one bill which the Senate had rejected, but of several. Whitlam was returned to power, with a reduced majority in the House of Representatives and still no majority in the Senate, but with sufficient numbers in both to have an overall majority at a joint sitting of the two houses, which was promptly convened under the terms of s.57 of the constitution—the first such meeting ever held. The procedure was duly challenged in the High Court, which held valid both the double dissolution and the holding of a joint sitting in respect of more than one deadlocked bill.[34] Thus the way was opened for a government based on a reasonably reliable popular and hence House of Representatives majority to save up a batch of measures rejected by the Senate (with appropriate accompanying financial measures) and put the lot to the people at a double-dissolution election under s.57, which will also be in effect a plebiscite on those measures, followed by enactment at a joint sitting under s.57. In 1974, however, the batch of measures was not well planned nor was it accompanied by financial provisions.

In the end, the Senate destroyed the Whitlam government, aided by the unanticipated intervention of Governor General Sir John Kerr. By October 1975, electoral opinion was running strongly against the government, and the Senate majority against it had increased as a result of the fact that two departed ALP senators[35] were replaced, contrary to long-observed practice, by non-Labor temporary appointees chosen by non-Labor state governments. The Senate majority deferred supply on October 16, 1975, in order to compel Whitlam to dissolve one or both houses—there being ample deadlocked bills to justify a double dissolution as in 1974. Although questioned by some eminent lawyers, the Senate's legal power to pursue such a course is not open to reasonable doubt; the most that could be said, as with the casual vacancy episodes, is that long-continued practice to the contrary was ignored. After a period of bluff and counterbluff, the governor general on November 11, relying on his "reserve" or residuary legal power to appoint and dismiss ministers and obtain different advice, dismissed Whitlam and his cabinet and appointed the opposition leader, J. M. Fraser, to lead a caretaker government pending the holding of a double-dissolution election. At the election on December 13, 1975, Fraser won a landslide victory in both houses.

In the commotion and bitterness that followed, the main stress was on the exercise of the reserve power of the governor general. His action was without direct precedent. In the opinion of some (including this writer) but by no means all constitutional commentators, it was based on a wrong principle and was taken prematurely and without observing fair procedure. It is beyond question, however, that a crisis had arisen and that failure to obtain lawful appropriation acts authorizing government expenditure would have compelled Sir John Kerr's intervention within a short time, unless one or other of the contestants had meanwhile weakened or a compromise had been reached.[36] Kerr's action, however, had no connection with the federal nature of the constitution; it flowed from the principles of Westminster—that is, the system of monarchical-democratic, responsible, cabinet government as transplanted to Australia. So far as the result has led to cries for a republic—more strident and widespread than at any time since the 1890s—it may turn out in the long run to be the chief consequence of the Whitlam regime.

In the shorter run, however, the Kerr episode is less important than what caused the crisis—the Senate's action—and that was a consequence of the federal structure. The Senate derives its considerable political power base and legislative competence, including power as to money bills, from its theoretical position as the protector of the states. Federation would not have occurred in the 1890s if the Senate had not been given such a position. Actually it has always been primarily an extension of the politics of the lower house, used as such by all parties having control in the Senate, most particularly when they lacked a majority in the lower house. The ALP has been the most consistent sufferer from the electoral basis of the Senate—equal representation for all states. Nevertheless, the ALP has obtained majorities in that house, and Whitlam's trouble basically was political, not constitutional. He failed to gain sufficient political following in the states, other than New South Wales and Victoria. The Australian federal system, because of the electoral basis of the Senate, requires a radical reformer to carry both an electoral majority for the House of Representatives and separately an electoral majority for the Senate in four states. That is the same sort of double majority as that required for amending the constitution.

The pervasive conservatism of Australian politics has been a matter of concern and curiosity to scholars over a long period. The above sketch demonstrates how well the Australian scene illustrates A. V. Dicey's views on the relation between conservatism and federalism. In many respects, Australia's major political parties and their platforms are well to the left of corresponding parties in the U.S. Certainly "socialism," if only as a myth or symbol, figures much more largely in Australian political debate than it does across the Pacific. Correspondingly, the constitutional law and the institutional structure based on it in Australia have played a greater and more continuous role in restraining or obstructing political plans than has been the case in the U.S. since the great reversals of Supreme Court doctrine in the 1930s. Central power has increased greatly in Australia, absolutely and relatively, but the states have been able to put up rearguard actions, hold chosen positions, bargain, and at times simply obstruct—and this often more from positions of constitutional strength than because of the sort of political demand for the preservation of local influence and autonomy that has remained powerful in the U.S. After the surges of central initiative in 1928–1934 and 1942–1949, it proved impossible to return to the status quo ante, and it will probably prove equally impossible to do so after the Whitlam-led surge of 1972–1975. In each such instance, however, the new federal relationship is found to be less new than reforming leaders wanted or than the mass electorate was prepared to endorse, and that is chiefly because of the constitutional structure.

Notes

1 James Bryce, *American Commonwealth* (2 vols., London, 1888); see especially vol. 1, p. 432.
2 The logical effect was like that achieved by the Canadian listing of exclusive dominion and exclusive provincial powers in *British North America Act,* 1867, ss.91 and 92.
3 26 Commonwealth Law Reports 460.
4 28 CLR 129.
5 R. G. Menzies, later Sir Robert Menzies, prime minister 1939–1941, 1949–1965, appeared for the trade union seeking center arbitration; Dr. H. V Evatt, later a justice of the High Court, minister in ALP governments (1941–1949) and leader of the ALP in opposition (1951–1960), appeared for the government of New South Wales to resist the plaintiff union and uphold state rights.
6 28 CLR 530.
7 A. H. Birch, *Federalism, Finance and Social Legislation* (Oxford: Clarendon Press, 1955), chap. 4.
8 G. Sawer, *Australian Federal Politics and Law, 1901–1929* (Melbourne: Melbourne University Press, 1956), vol. 1, chaps. 10–12.
9 50 CLR 30.
10 55 CLR 1.
11 G. Sawer, *Australian Federalism in the Courts* (Melbourne: Melbourne University Press, 1967), 132 ff.; L. Zines, "Mr. Justice Evatt and the Constitution" (1969), 3 Federal Law Reports 153; idem, "Sir Owen Dixon's Theory of Federalism" (1965), 1 FLR 221.
12 See the forthcoming notice of Latham by G. Sawer in the *Supplement* to the (U.K.) *Dictionary of National Biography.*
13 E.g. in *Gratwick* v. *Johnson* (1945), 70 CLR 1.
14 E.g. in *R.* v. *Commonwealth Court ex Victoria* (1942), 66 CLR 488.
15 65 CLR 373.
16 G. Sawer, *Australian Federal Politics and Law, 1929–1949*, chap. 1.
17 46 CLR 155.

18 *Victoria* v. *Commonwealth*, 99 CLR 575.

19 *W.A.* v. *Chamberlain Industries* (1970), 44, Australian Law Journal Reports, 93.

20 *Dickinson's Arcade Pty. Ltd.* v. *Tasmania* (1974), 48 ALJR 96.

21 Partly by the *Privy Council (Limitation of Appeals) Act 1968* and partly by High Court policy, on which see *W.A.* v. *Hamersley Iron (No. 2)*, 120 CLR 42. In 1975, all appeals from High Court to Privy Council were abolished.

22 Sawer, *Australian Federalism*, 185–194.

23 113 CLR 54.

24 (1942) 317 U.S. 111.

25 E.g. *Stafford* v. *Wallace* (1922), 258 U.S. 495.

26 124 CLR 486.

27 *R.* v. *Burgess*, 55 CLR 608.

28 *Fishwick* v. *Clelend* (1960), 106 CLR 186. See also *Tau* v. *Commonwealth* (1969), 119 CLR 564. Dr. Evatt wanted trust territories to be regarded as held under the external affairs power so as to insure that Australia gave effect to the terms of the mandate.

29 74 CLR 31.

30 122 CLR 353.

31 107 CLR 268.

32 See note 18.

33 71 CLR 237. The question was again left in doubt by the sole decision on the point in the Whitlam period—namely the *Australian Assistance Plan* case (1975), 50 ALJR 157.

34 *Cormack* v. *Cope* (1974), 131 CLR 432; *Victoria* v. *Commonwealth* (1975), 7 Australian Law Reports 1; *W.A.* v. *Commonwealth* (1975), 7 ALR 159.

35 One by appointment to the High Court, one by death.

36 The many legal and conventional points involved are discussed in Geoffrey Sawer, *Federation under Strain* (Melbourne: Melbourne University Press, 1977).

JOSEPH JONES

Provincial to International: Southwest Pacific Literature in English since the 1920s

To writer and reader alike, the prospects for indigenous literature in the Southwest Pacific just after the First World War could not have appeared very roseate. Following a cultural resurgence in both Australia and New Zealand during the 1890s, hopes had dwindled during wartime, and new strength ready to take over was in short supply. "Colonial" writing was in fact for the most part still just that, despite a large measure of political self-determination already achieved, and was to remain colonial for some time to come. No single poet, novelist, or playwright of undoubted stature could be counted on either side of the Tasman Sea. There were no local literary reviews or other such journals; newspapers took note of whatever might occasionally venture into print, continuing to serve this function so faithfully that some of them are still sources of respectable criticism. As a result of assignments falling to the lot of the Anzacs during the First World War, a catastrophically high percentage of the best young men were sacrificed in the costly attempt upon Gallipoli and in the scarcely less savage campaigns on the Western Front. What incipient authorship there was among them, never to develop, cannot be known, but it is not unreasonable to surmise that the scarcity and mediocrity of literary production in the 1920s must have been related to so much slaughter of talent among the generation that otherwise would have survived to be given its chance.

At the same time, both Australians and New Zealanders were among the more assiduous readers whom British publishers took special pains to keep supplied with books from "home." All together, there were fewer than seven million such antipodean customers in 1920, about five and a quarter million Australians and a million and a quarter New Zealanders—a good subsidiary market, to be sure, but one that could scarcely be expected to produce for itself even if the talent were to appear. No one would seriously have disputed in 1920 the continuing preeminence of English literature, meaning of course the literature of England. Although Americans (Canadians too) had been writing and publishing for well over a hundred years, American literature was still no better than a country cousin, receiving only nominal attention in American schools, none at all in universities, and very little from critics. From an even more remote quarter like Australasia, then, what could have been expected?

From the days of Captain James Cook and other explorers, there had been a European fascination with Pacific islanders and other primitive peoples, and during the nineteenth century Australian and New Zealand writers—not to mention visitors and indeed a few who had never set foot in the area—used natives and what passed for native culture as poetic themes or occasional decorations for fiction. A few, especially in New Zealand, where the Maori wars of the 1860s and later years attracted wide attention, left enduring records of both conflict and peaceful intercourse between natives and Europeans,[1] but neither islanders nor Australian mainland natives were able to speak for themselves, at least not in the intruder's language. Up to the period with which we are here concerned, little enough had appeared that would direct attention to what, nevertheless was already a substantial literary effort.

At the end of the 1920s, C. Hartley Grattan wrote a survey for *The Bookman* (August 1928), subsequently published as a pamphlet-type volume (one of the University of Washington Chapbooks) called *Australian Literature*—the first such study to appear in the United States. His conclusion was that "Australia is getting what it demands—only a tiny trickle of worth-while native literature."[2] The foreword to that volume was provided by Nettie Palmer of Melbourne, a vigorous and loyal partisan who had already published *Modern Australian Literature (1900–1923)*. When she first came across Grattan's account in *The Bookman*, she reports, it surprised her "with its sincerity and insight." All the more surprising—"incredible" was the word she used—was "that such a study could be written by an American visitor, when most of our own pundits were uninformed on the matter, and not much interested in it." As for European attention, "No English critic has done this for our growing literature. The usual reviewers have persisted in regarding us as still 'colonials' of the nineteenth century."[3] At most there was not very much to be said.

A generation earlier the prospect had not seemed quite so bleak. During the late 1880s and 1890s, a numerous and lively band of Australian–New Zealand writers began appearing in the Sydney *Bulletin*—shepherded, exhorted, and quite often severely copyedited by an inspired editorial staff which included J. F. Archibald, A. G. Stephens, and (somewhat later) David McKee Wright of New Zealand. There was, however, no long-term local audience of sufficient strength to sustain such effort, and overseas audiences all too soon were caught up in the First World War. *The Bulletin* survived (and still appears) but for various reasons—the war not least among them—the promise of a golden age it had helped generate in the 1890s died away, somewhat in the manner of a played out gold rush. In 1920 those who might at the time have seemed leftovers from the earlier days included Henry Lawson, Mary Gilmore, Christopher Brennan, Bernard O'Dowd, Miles Franklin, C. J. Dennis, "Banjo" Paterson, and Shaw Neilson. (Stephens had long since separated from *The Bulletin*.) A few of these still had contributions to make, and taken together they formed a distinguished set, but they were in no position to sustain and enlarge upon the sort of movement they had begun. In a sense they had made up what Jessie Mackay of New Zealand called the "gray company." Her poem of that title points out that the pioneers after their "weary sowing" at least lived to see a green harvest, whereas

> . . . the gray, gray company
>   Stood every man alone
> In the chilly dawnlight;
>   Scarcely had they known
> Ere the day they perished
>   That their beacon-star
> Was not glint of marshlight
>   In the shadows far.[4]

Much of the "bush" poetry from this group and much of the fiction as well would have seemed local or provincial to a great many critics, some of them Australian critics, although at least two out of the company—Brennan and Neilson—were first-class poets by any general standard, and Lawson's stories at their best were superb. But no level of achievement had yet been reached to suggest that writers in Australia and New Zealand could expect, in any foreseeable future, any sort of career outside local bounds. Nor was there at this time any viable conception of English as a world language, destined—long before the century was out— to produce a world literature embracing a multitude of races and nationalities, capable of being read by hundreds of millions. The achievements of the past fifty years should be viewed, therefore, as taking place not only within single national groups (or combinations of national groups within related areas) but also within a reorientation rapidly widening to world proportions.

A few minds in the 1920s were already beginning to feel such stirrings, and a generation gap, as between the bush bards and a city-bred group trained in the new universities, soon became apparent. Pioneering young poets like Kenneth Slessor, R. D. FitzGerald, and Kenneth Mackenzie knew and respected the work of Gilmore, Brennan, and Neilson (and some of Lawson's), but in the 1920s they responded more readily to the influence of Norman Lindsay as exerted through the periodical *Vision*. Sydney and Melbourne were still as yet content with a largely self-imposed isolation from one another, and the other centers—Adelaide, Hobart, Brisbane, and Perth—were of little consequence.

In fiction, the most memorable impact in the 1920s came from two expatriate women who wrote using the pseudonyms "Henry Handel Richardson" (whose Australian trilogy, *The Fortunes of Richard Mahony*, 1929, is a towering landmark) and "Katherine Mansfield" of New Zealand. A second New Zealander, Jane Mander, returned after a season abroad in which she developed her talent; the others remained permanently overseas. With respect to New Zealand writing during this period the chief literary historian, E. H. McCormick, said:

> Reasons for the poetic *malaise* of the nineteen-hundreds and nineteen-twenties are not far to seek. As the most delicately constituted members of the community, poets were more sensitive than others to the dominant emotion of their time, an emotion that was strengthened by their almost complete dependence on English literature. For the dangers inherent in New Zealand's colonial status were most noticeable in the very period when the country became a Dominion and acquired an indeterminate measure of nationhood. That the Bowens and the Dometts should read and write as Englishmen was natural, indeed inevitable; though they had set up homes at the antipodes, they were, after all, still Englishmen. For New Zea-

landers, sometimes of the second colonial generation, to visit in their literary excursions solely a region of scenes, images, and ideas not merely foreign to them but, in some respects, contrary to the facts of their experience—this was different and more dangerous. The most serious consequence was not, however, the occasional confusion of seasons in the minds of young readers but the creation of an abstract, idealized, often sentimentalized "literary" world, remote from both poles of reality, the English writer's and the colonial reader's. This was the imaginative world of all but a few of New Zealand's versifiers and poets in the years under review.[5]

In the 1920s (and earlier) expatriation seemed to some writers to offer the only means of recognition—as it still does to many writers in English from the Caribbean, say, or parts of Africa or Asia. The usual destination was London, though from New Zealand it might be Sydney or Melbourne. The problem was never exclusively or even predominantly a literary one; scientists, doctors, lawyers, journalists, politicians, academics, and others sought or came to be offered careers overseas as regularly as did writers, and usually with better financial reward. At any rate, leaving was sometimes made—either subsequently or at the time of departure— a dramatic gesture tinged with bitterness. This sort of traumatic response occurred more frequently and survived later among New Zealanders (as for example D'Arcy Cresswell and "Robin Hyde" in the 1930s) than among Australians, but in both homelands expatriation, or alienation if one remained, was not uncommon. Now, by contrast, an overseas residence seems not so much a cutting of home ties as an act of choice, made perhaps for achieving perspective (which may mean obtaining the right degree of isolation needful to get on with the work)—Hal Porter, for instance, writing his recollections of early Melbourne in Earl's Court, London, or Patrick White working at various places. Mobility, at the same time, has much reduced the sense of separation with its attendant tensions.

But let us look back about half way to 1920—to the years immediately following the Second World War—and see what evidence of literary hope and confidence may or may not have been present after a second imperative military demand had been made upon both countries, this time much closer to home. During the 1950s, in the official view at least, Australian literature was still struggling. In September 1950 a Commonwealth Office of Education bulletin called "Literature in Australia" predicted a continuation of lean days for Australian writers facing overwhelming competition from abroad. Most of them, this account concludes, "will have to write merely for the love of writing—and earn their bread-and-butter in more profitable but less congenial occupations."[6] In 1955 another agency, the Australian News and Information Bureau, felt much the same:

> Australian writers, handicapped by being last in the field, still conduct an unceasing struggle against the appeal of the works of famous overseas authors. However, the Australian public, whose interests are mainly material and whose cultural tastes are still in the formative states, is now taking a wider interest in the work of Australian writers.
>
> It is gratifying to note that while developing, however slowly, a sophistication and interest in things beyond Australian horizons, Australian writing still retains its freshness, virility and love of action.[7]

These observations would hold true for most writers anywhere, but by 1955 it was becoming clearer that size of audience, not intrinsic worth of the writing, was the major drawback. So it still is in most of the Commonwealth literatures, but exceptions to the rule—the authors good enough (or perchance good enough and lucky enough) to make the grade in any literary culture—have become more numerous. No writer in Britain or the U.S. could with any grace complain of a public reception as generous as those given in the past few years to Patrick White, Morris West, or Thomas Keneally of Australia or Janet Frame of New Zealand. The same can be said for the plays of Ray Lawler and the poems of A. D. Hope (both Australians).

Despite such stringently qualified estimates as were still being made in the 1950s, however, the Australian public conscience was commencing to stir, influenced at least in part by events in Canada, where the Massey Commission of inquiry into the state of the arts (1951) led to the formation of the Canada Council, at the same time emphatically calling attention to a situation that might be found in other parts of the British Commonwealth. The principle of public support for the arts in Australia goes all the way back to the first decade of the commonwealth, to 1908, when Alfred Deakin established the Commonwealth Literary Fund "to provide a few pensions for impoverished writers."[8] In the late 1930s the CLF began to widen its activities to include two or three writers' fellowships, and subsequently came annual lectures by prominent writers and critics along with increasing grants-in-aid for publication. Since 1960 there has been a measure of state support, supplemented locally, for arts festivals in Adelaide and Perth. In 1968 a "new era of governmental patronage" arrived with the creation of the Australian Council for the Arts and a grant of $1,660,000. In 1972 the grant had risen to $5,700,000.[9]

Something of the new hope inspired by the increased activity which perhaps the CLF helped to create, but to which it was also a response, was expressed by the veteran editor of *Meanjin Quarterly*, C. B. Christesen, writing in the early 1960s. During the quarter century of approximately 1935–1960, he felt, "increased 'social density' has been at least one important factor which has aided the Australian writer to produce work of a more varied and complex character, of higher quality, more perceptive of the human condition here." Summing up, he observed:

> It is true to say that during this period more poetry of quality has been written, more plays, novels, stories, literary and art criticism, more painting, sculpture, and musical composition of genuine value have been produced than during any other period of our history. And all this has been achieved under conditions which (not to put too fine a point on it) have been far from propitious for a flourishing artistic and intellectual life. The contrast between the Australia of 1940, when the first issue of *Meanjin* appeared, and the Australia of today, is nothing short of amazing.[10]

An indication of how New Zealand authors regarded themselves, and of what their actual strength was prior to the mid-1940s, may be gained from the records of the P.E.N. New Zealand Centre, which came into being during the depression, at Wellington in 1934. For the first few years it "operated quietly, but effectively," reported a historical survey published in 1947, "establishing closer bonds between New Zealand writers, assisting young writers and holding a series of social gatherings"[11] at the old Turnbull Library. Another early achievement was the inauguration of a Jessie Mackay Memorial Prize for Verse, with Douglas Stewart as winner of the first competition.

In 1936 there was organized in each of the four centers a New Zealand Authors' Week. As a result, the *P.E.N. Gazette* recalled in 1955, "the N.Z. book emerged from the back shelves of the booksellers' shops and became a window display item; it evolved from the poorish school-book format to one of adequate comparison with the overseas article. Best of all, though, the writing inside improved. Soon a mort of new poets commenced to loom on the horizon." After twenty-one years, the same account states, "we have won a measure of respect," whereas before the advent of the P.E.N. New Zealand Centre in 1934 "our writers were the poor relations of the publishing world."[12]

P.E.N.'s 1947 account marked, in fact, a watershed in New Zealand literary geography in that it came at the same time as the New Zealand Literary Fund was being established—at the recommendation of the P.E.N. Centre. Three of the initial advisory committee to the fund (including the chairman, Sir James Elliott, also president of the New Zealand Centre) were nominated by P.E.N. Thus the New Zealand government became, and has remained, the single most important patron of local authors. At this time the P.E.N. membership, which may be taken to have represented serious pretension to authorship throughout most of the country, numbered fifty-seven. Of these, not many more than a dozen are still to be recalled in the annals of New Zealand literature; the others were historians, academics, librarians, and the like. The P.E.N. Centre continued to be active and influential, nominating advisory committee members into the 1960s.

A twenty-five-year history of the New Zealand Literary Fund, 1946–1970, conveniently ties in with the P.E.N. accounts just cited, to call attention to later developments. While the list of its grants is not precisely a full history of New Zealand literature, dates and names appearing in it form a sort of working outline guide. For instance: 1948–1949: John Mulgan (posthumous: republication of book), John A. Lee, Allen Curnow; 1949–1950: Helen Wilson, D'Arcy Cresswell, A. E. Woodhouse; 1950–1951: John Pascoe, Ruth Park, Roderick Finlayson, and the new journal *Landfall*; 1951–1952: Robin Hyde, John Reece Cole; 1952–1953: Maurice Duggan, Mary Stanley, *Landfall* again (as regularly thenceforward); 1953–1954: R. M. Burdon (and by this time the NZLF was subsidizing the Mackay and Church literary awards); 1954–1955: J. R. Hervey, O. E. Middleton, Ruth Gilbert; 1955–1956: James McNeish, Charles Doyle, Janet Frame; 1956–1957: Keith Sinclair, Helen Shaw; and 1957–1958: A. R. D. Fairburn, James K. Baxter. These are only some of the authors appearing in the records during the first ten years. The following decade yields such others as R. A. K. Mason, Noel Hilliard, Gloria Rawlinson, Hone Tuwhare, C. K. Stead, J. E. Weir, Olaf Ruhen, Frank Sargeson, Renato Amato,

Charles Brasch, Vincent O'Sullivan, Ruth Dallas, Marilyn Duck-worth, Gordon Dryland, and Bill Pearson. Records of the Austra-lian CLF would reveal similar emergences of talent, and the histo-ry of various Australian authors' societies is of course multifaceted and far more complex, with current memberships running into many hundreds. When we recall the slender basis upon which P.E.N. New Zealand Centre was launched in 1934, or even its membership in 1947 (all of which would fit into one very modest-sized cocktail party), we can gauge with some accuracy the growth of New Zealand writing during the quarter century that followed.

The quickest way to discover what has been happening during the past thirty years would be to consult a chronological bibliog-raphy of works in English which, while listing poetry, fiction, drama, and so forth, would identify countries of origin. Such a list is not available in comprehensive yet analytical form, but if it were it would show—in the later 1940s and throughout the 1950s—a number of writers only just beginning to emerge who in another fifteen to twenty years (even less in some instances) would be well established and a few who would be quite outstand-ing figures. While this would be true of any ongoing literature, it has special significance for the Southwest Pacific: in the postwar period, for the first time in the literary history of either Australia or New Zealand, literary reputations begin to appear steadily and in cumulative numbers rather than sporadically, as before.

For Australia, the following publications would loom especially large: in 1940 Patrick White, *Happy Valley*; in 1941 Eleanor Dark, *The Timeless Land*, and Kylie Tennant, *The Battlers*; in 1944 Peter Cowan, *Drift*; in 1946 Judith Wright, *The Moving Image*, and James McAuley, *Under Aldebaran*; in 1954 Vincent Buckley, *The World's Flesh*; in 1956 Hal Porter, *The Hexagon*, and Randolph Stow, *A Haunted Land*; and in 1958 Thea Astley, *Girl with a Monkey*.

In New Zealand one would note in 1940 Frank Sargeson, *A Man and His Wife*; in 1941 Allen Curnow et al., *Recent Poems*; in 1944 James K. Baxter, *Beyond the Palisade*; in 1945 Dan Davin, *Cliffs of Fall*; in 1948 Charles Brasch, *Disputed Ground*; in 1949 John Mulgan, *Man Alone*; in 1954 James Courage, *The Young Have Secrets*; in 1958 Sylvia Ashton-Warner, *Spinster*; and in 1959 Errol Brathwaite, *Fear in the Night*, and Maurice Shadbolt, *The New Zealanders*. The ten names in each of these lists might readi-ly be extended to fifteen or twenty.

During the 1960s, as another evidence of literary maturity, we encounter among the older poets several collected or other comprehensive volumes of their work: for Australia, in 1961 Hugh McCrae, *Best Poems*; in 1963 Mary Gilmore, *Selected Poems*; in 1965 R. D. FitzGerald, *Forty Years' Poems*; in 1966 A. D. Hope, *Collected Poems*; in 1967 Douglas Stewart, *Collected Poems*; in 1968 David Campbell, *Collected Poems*; for New Zealand (where the "new" poets were somewhat younger), in 1962 R. A. K. Mason, *Collected Poems*; and in 1965 A. R. D. Fairburn, *Collected Poems*. It should also be kept in mind that whereas in both Australia and New Zealand the native peoples of the Southwest Pacific were being written about—often sympathetically and perceptively[13]—titles by the indigenes themselves do not appear before the 1960s.

In the earlier 1970s the most important event was the award of the 1973 Nobel Prize for literature to Patrick White. Although this undoubtedly has called attention to Australian literature as "new," it should be clear from the record we have just been exploring that there was very considerable preparation, during which White was no solitary figure in a Vossian literary wilderness. Work on both sides of the Tasman Sea, during the past fifty years, has brought to World English (English regarded as a language of global currency, which has produced a literature of commensurate scope) a large new sector in the Southwest Pacific. Throughout the whole region, there has lately been a quickening among Polynesian and Melanesian writers alike, adding a Third World dimension. All this, as it becomes progressively an accustomed part of English literary study, will help create new perspectives and contribute an impressive share to the richly textured final unity.

Enough has been said to show that, from a geographically vast but not as yet densely populated area of the English-speaking world, there have come literary achievements over the past fifty years, culminating chiefly in the past twenty or twenty-five, that have been truly remarkable. Nor have these gone unheralded: over the past decade, recognition on the international scale has been apparent in book-length studies of single authors (New Zealand and Australian) published both in Britain and the U.S. Also an extensive series of shorter biocritical works on Australian writers has appeared.

Understandably, attention has been drawn chiefly to poetry and fiction (to Judith Wright, for example, or A. D. Hope, Patrick White, Sylvia Ashton-Warner, and Janet Frame), but what has been happening in poetry and fiction has been paralleled in drama, more notably (for reasons of larger potential audience) in Australia. Geoffrey Serle reports:

> In recent years the number of promising plays being written has outstripped the resources of theatres and professional companies available to present them. Overall attendances at theatre, opera and ballet have been steadily increasing. A new professionalism is evident in companies like the Melbourne Theatre. The number of professional actors who may now fall back on a booming entertainment industry in pubs, clubs, restaurants and discos, has also grown considerably. The National Institute of Dramatic Art about 1970 could accept only some 40 of 400 applicants, and nine out of ten of its graduates were professionally employed.[14]

With the Melbourne Theatre and the Sydney Opera House both flourishing, one may be permitted a question or two about the present situation in the hinterland, which would include so remote-seeming a place as New Guinea. In both Australia and New Zealand, the primitive cultures of the native populations have interacted—belatedly, to be sure, and after protracted estrangements of varying intensity—with those of the European settlers. The "Jindyworobak" movement of the 1940s and 1950s, for instance, centering in but not confined to South Australia, laid heavy stress on indigenous folklore, culture, and even vocabulary (not easily manageable, by reason of the many differing tribal languages); the name chosen to identify the group, for example, means "to join" or fuse—looking, ideally, to a synthesis of native and European traditions. Interpreted as a back-to-the-ancient-origins gesture, it attracted some attention but even more ridicule, and after the premature death in 1955 of its spokesman, Rex Ingamells, it subsided. The "Jindys," nevertheless, had made a start in Australia toward the kind of sympathy and understanding that had been confined largely but not exclusively to anthropologists and sociologists, some of them gifted amateurs. A work of quite a different sort, and out of a special set of circumstances, was R. D. FitzGerald's *Between Two Tides* (1952), a long narrative poem about Tonga. The author was a surveyor in Fiji from 1931 to 1936, learning the native language along with much folklore and local history. Katharine S. Prichard's *Coonardoo* (1929) and Xavier Herbert's *Capricornia* (1938) were relatively early examples of serious attention to the Aboriginal situation, to be followed by the work of such later novelists as Mary Durack, Donald Stuart, and Randolph Stow. In 1965 came Colin Johnson's *Wild Cat Falling*, marking the entry of the Aboriginal writer into Australian fiction. The poetry of Kath Walker emerged at about the same time.

Australians in New Guinea encountered the native problem in even more acute terms, complicated by the Japanese invasion during the Second World War. There, and then, certainly, Herman Melville's taunting question in *Moby Dick*—"In fact, did you ever hear what might be called regular news direct or indirect from New Guinea?"—was answered: emphatically yes! After the war, developments in and around Port Moresby led at length to the establishment of the University of Papua–New Guinea, where a literary upsurge has begun to take place. It was prompted in large measure by a short residence in the latter 1960s of Professor Ulli Beier and his wife, on loan as it were from Nigeria. Consequently, there is somewhat of an African format to what has emerged, but the examples of Nigeria, Kenya, Ghana, and other African states would in any case have figured prominently in the minds of young intellectuals thinking in terms of political and cultural independence.

One of the Beiers' early discoveries was a man named Albert Maori Kiki, and it was not pure coincidence that on first encounter he reminded them of their African friend Ezekiel Mphahlele—they had come to New Guinea seeking another version of what they had already experienced in Nigeria and had found what they hoped for. The brief time the Beiers remained in New Guinea was spent working as catalysts to focus and bring to publication the beginnings of a new national literature. Kiki's autobiography—*Kiki: Ten Thousand Years in a Lifetime* (New York: Praeger, 1968)—was edited by Beier from a series of tape recordings made by the author, who by the time the book appeared had already become more the political man of affairs than the pioneering writer. His book, nevertheless, is fundamental in a number of ways. The first three chapters are pre-European; the remaining seven may be categorized in three principal ways: (1) the ethnic—continuing the account of native life and customs already begun and widening the contrast between New Guinea servant and Australian master; (2) the administrative—describing the author's experiences as a health and welfare officer; and (3) the political—explaining how Kiki the public servant found himself gradually drawn into newspaper polemics as well as private arguments, then into trade unionism and work with cooperative groups (some of them highly unorthodox from the governmental point of view), and finally into formalized politics and membership in the House of Assembly as a leader of the Pangu Pati (the last of several attempts to form an effective native Opposition).

Fiction and drama contain much the same material and reflect the same tone. The novel *Crocodile* (Brisbane: Jacaranda, 1970) by Vincent Eri illustrates transitional confusions through the experience of the Papuan villager Hoiri Sevese, who serves the Australian military during the Second World War (finding the Australians completely incomprehensible) and is torn between mission Christianity and the ritual traditions of his tribe. Two other recent novels by Caucasian authors, *The Wire Classroom* (Sydney: Angus & Robertson, 1972) by John Bailey and *The Stolen Land* (Brisbane: Jacaranda, 1970) by Ian Downs, contain sharply contrasting pictures of colonial experience. In the first story an Australian schoolteacher, under satirically presented circumstances, disintegrates and finally absconds; whereas, in the second, a young New Guinean befriended and sponsored by a white man succeeds brilliantly for a time as a reform politician, only to be tragically destroyed.

Formal study of this limited production has already begun. At a conference on the teaching of literature, held at the University of Papua–New Guinea in the summer of 1972, the poet Apisai Enos speaking on "Niugini Literature"[15] reviewed both traditional and contemporary literature and went on to discuss the conditions of creativity. Enos recognizes that much of what is already being created, principally in English and emerging from the university, will be "unpopular" because the transitional period has not yet been long enough to bring the masses into appreciation of the art of reading, "which took the Europeans hundreds of years to develop so that reading is a part of their culture." He goes on to say:

> It all boils down to the fact that we are in fact creating an unpopular literature for an elitist culture in which it functions. . . . [I]n recognizing and preserving our traditions we come up with the same dilemma of moving in the same direction of elitist culture. What we are creating is a tradition which is neither traditional nor popular in the sense that oral literature in the villages is appreciated and shared by a large audience. We are in fact replacing more elaborate and ritualistic literature and art with a kind of literature which is idealistic, and artificial. This is to me, neither traditional nor new. Occasionally it has been painfully imitative of European traditions because this University is, and it is where the creation of

such a literature is taking place, in an environment the very opposite of that in the village where everyone shares in the performance, and creation. In other words, poetry, drama, novel have become adjuncts of Niugini culture rather than an integral part.

The countertendency needed, he believes, is for authors to realize that "we have a rich proud tradition and we are not in some vacuum"; that "materials and ideas are there for us to use and manipulate in creating our modern tradition." To the charge that popular culture may be low in quality he replies with a question, "Isn't this what is happening all over the world, to return literature and art back to the people and make it functional again?"

The knowledge that such a conference was held, and that critical questions of the sort that Enos and others raised there were discussed, gives us an inkling of a situation in which cultural extremes are emphasized all over again. Another participant remarked, using Eri's novel *The Crocodile* as a reference point:

> Finally, in the innocence/experience structure of the novel can be seen a model for understanding the plight of Hoiri's Papuan generation. The traditional way of life represents the innocent period of modern man's development. The growth of civilization and materialism brought man, over a long period of time, into the world of experience. Hoiri and his fellows have been forced to make this dreadful crossing in the space of one generation. All the problems of re-orientation are heaped on Hoiri's shoulders. It is hardly surprising that he fails to cope. Something is always lost in the transition from innocence to experience, and in the modernisation of the Papuan race it was Hoiri's generation which was sacrificed.[16]

The impression one gets from surveying the limited amount of English fiction and drama so far produced by Niuginian writers is that their transitional experience, understandably enough, has been a traumatic one; that colonial administration has been far too often a recapitulation of long-outmoded British-sahib paternalism laced with an equally outmoded Australian squattocratic despotism. Nor were New Zealanders notably more skillful or successful in their handling of Samoa following the First World War. Perhaps the conclusion to be drawn is that administrators of colonies learn by doing, mostly the hard way, and that by the time they have developed whatever finesse is possible the colonies are "ready" for self-determination. The hope is, as expressed by Judith H. McDowell, that

Deprived by colonialism of the sustaining power of traditional culture, the talented writers of New Guinea may turn this deprivation to an advantage, for, liberated from tradition yet subtly influenced by it, they are free to express their native insights in new forms which might be very exciting.[17]

In New Zealand, the Maoris were so different in temperament and in political ability (which included no little sophistication in the art of warfare, coupled with a fine tradition in oratory) that the adversary relation between them and the Europeans compelled attention and a measure of respect never accorded the bush dwellers of Australia and New Guinea. These people were far more than confused paleolithics or mere nuisances; they had to be taken seriously. There was, moreover, a virtually uniform Maori language, marked by a few dialectal differences of no great importance. Many early New Zealanders, missionaries and traders alike, learned and used Maori as part of the natural condition of daily life, especially in the North Island. "Pakeha Maoris" (non-Maori traders attaching themselves to a specific tribe) were not uncommon in the early nineteenth century. The great early governor, Sir George Grey, became an eminent student of Maori folklore, as his *Mythology and Traditions of the New Zealanders* (1854) and other volumes notably attest. Thus there was never any extended hiatus in the attention given Maoris and Maori affairs by the Pakeha (white) New Zealanders. While the national reputation for enlightened native policies may not always have been unequivocally deserved, it can be justly claimed that for the better part of a hundred years, since the aftermath of the tragic Maori wars, New Zealand can be credited with at least a few good deeds in a chronically naughty colonial world. The Maori wars in themselves constitute a variety of heroic age, up to now principally for non-Maori writers. Maoris as subjects for poetry, fiction, and drama have a well-defined literary history of over a hundred years and have always been more visible and more usable to the writer than have Australian Aboriginals. Had a Maori poet or novelist, writing in English, appeared at any time during this period, he or she would have been welcomed, albeit as something of a curiosity (a parallel is the African slave-poetess Phyllis Wheatley, whose work was published out of the American colonies in 1773).

Other portions of the Pacific are showing similar signs of activity, although under less promising circumstances by reason of comparative isolation and smallness of population. From Samoa, an exceptionally well written novel by Albert Wendt, *Sons for the Return Home* (Auckland: Longman Paul, 1973), appeared the same year as Witi Ihimaera's *Tangi*. *Sons* is a study of expatriation, or the threat of the loss of Samoan identity, through a family residing in New Zealand during the education of the children. Samoa has poets, too, as do Fiji, Tonga, and the Cook Islands. The New Zealand scholar-poet K. O. Arvidson, who has given extended attention to Polynesian writing, says:

> Most writing is done in close proximity to an oral tradition and yet, like the poetry of Hone Tuwhare, reveals a completely contemporary awareness on the moral-political level; most writing displays a fineness of regional detail which can only enrich the consciousness of the non-Polynesian reader; and most writing embodies dialectal variants of English which are stimulating well beyond their linguistic curiosity value. Above all there is an air of juvenescence coupled with a maturity of viewpoint consistent with the antiquity of Polynesia.[18]

Closer home, New Zealanders found themselves suddenly on a new plane of Maori-Pakeha relations at the funeral service in October 1972—a *tangi*—for James K. Baxter (1926–1972) of the Jerusalem commune. Baxter had assumed the name "Hemi" (Maori for James), had been adopted into the Ngati Hau, and in the final phase of his poetic career had adopted Maori equivalents for Christian phraseology in the *Jerusalem Sonnets* (1970) and other works. The impact of his passing, together with the circumstances of his leadership-servantship at Jerusalem (the name originally given to a Catholic mission, Hiruharama, on the Wanganui River), created a response unexpectedly widespread and profound throughout the whole country. The media covered events in a manner far transcending the usual obituary of a literary figure, almost as if in realization that Baxter had become—after an uneasy career—a kind of St. Francis figure whose Pakeha-Maorihood (or Maoritanga)[19] was in most respects an antithesis to the kind of tensions his ancestors had encountered upon immigrating to nineteenth-century New Zealand.[20] Thus Baxter achieved in New Zealand some of the objectives that the Jindyworobaks of Australia had striven for, ineffectually, a generation earlier.

Throughout the whole Southwest Pacific, then, the "poor relations," as the New Zealanders modestly considered themselves a generation ago (Australians have never seen fit to challenge their neighbors' surpassing humility), not only long since have achieved literary recognition and respectability—they have now reached the level at which, henceforward, their literature must be reckoned as forming part of a world-sized pattern which we may call, most directly and easily, World English. Serle's analysis, in this context, is especially indicative, and the terms by which he describes Australia may be applied, generally speaking, to the whole Southwest Pacific area. Australian culture, he believes, "must not be seen as an isolated growth" but rather as developing "Australian versions of English or European or world trends." Moreover, "an international movement or a change in the parent culture sometimes precipitated a breakthrough of a specifically Australian creative kind." Whereas Brennan and White, for example, "probably owed nothing to any Australian literary tradition or to earlier Australian writers," they nevertheless took inspiration from the general culture. Thus artists increasingly become a product of their Australian predecessors; they discuss their craft with their fellows and are part of movements which, even if foreign in origin, develop local emphases. More immediately stimulated by new local work of original power, they are likewise influenced by the particular tendencies of their Australian audience. Even if they would, they cannot escape being a product of the Australian cultural climate; necessarily, their inspiration comes, in part, from their particular experience in Australia and from their thinking about the problems of their art in an Australian context of discussion. Those who do not choose to use "the giant springboard of the past," including their particular past, court failure.[21]

The "giant springboard" grows larger all the while as any one special area's past becomes enmeshed with that of the whole earth, to which willy-nilly it is exposed. To Serle's caveat might well be added another, directed not so much at writers as at critics and scholars. What does all this mean? When shall we expect mutative changes bringing us the enlarged conception of a unified language and literature to which developments everywhere in the world of English so clearly point? What can we learn from viewing the enlargements suggested in the earlier pages of this essay? Or was the exercise no more than a mildly pleasurable tourist's cruise into exotic regions and back out again?

In the future, it would appear, students of English must come to view Southwest Pacific literature as one segment of a great world unity, whose constituent parts interrelate in numerous ways. Regional characteristics need not be lost through such an approach; indeed, they will be more clearly evident through comparisons. Paradoxically, literature and history will be found to be enlarging their bounds as they draw more closely together. Scholarship has just begun to look in these new directions.

Movement toward the formal study of World English began during the 1960s in Britain, in several other European centers, and in North America. This development had to do, basically, with a great increase in international exchanges following the Second World War. Before long, societies or groups within societies came into being: at Leeds the Association for Commonwealth Literature and Language Studies and, in North America, Group 12 (World Literature Written in English) of the Modern Language Association—both sponsoring publications and holding periodic meetings of their membership.

To what may these societies and other agencies principally concerned with the study of English look forward? They can observe, already, that the English language, in its international context, is one of the most powerful instruments for maintaining peace available in the world today. Literature in English, concomitantly, is internationally useful to a high degree. Examined by itself, however, and by its own producers, each of the several literatures in English has at most only a limited social value; it may be regarded, within its country of origin, as merely something "nice to have"—standard equipment in any national culture kit—and treated with benign neglect, or on the other hand it may be forced into active alliance with chauvinistic politics. But, if through systematic study the whole world constellation of these literatures can be brought into a comparative relationship, very desirable insights will begin to emerge, possibly for the first time. Evidences of both variety and unity can be explored; relations with Europe on the one side and North America on the other (not only as looked at by the Southwest Pacific but by Africa and Asia as well, and by the Caribbean as a special case) will become apparent. Literature then will link more readily with geography, anthropology, and other social studies—all this and more, above and beyond the pleasure readers take in finding whole new vistas of authorship they did not realize existed.

Along with deserved recognition long deferred, the emergence of the "new" literatures into world status will bring problems, both local and general. So long as the works of local writers were clearly minority productions (colonial or otherwise), not much noticed, there was no compelling obligation to keep them in print, write criticism (apart from initial reviews), publish extended studies of their authors, or make them part of literary education in schools and universities. Such obligations may still not be very keenly felt among most of the population, but they are being taken into account by some of the more energetic among the literary community, academic and nonacademic alike. Founded within comparatively recent years, and still being founded, are new journals, new societies both local and international (as noted above), active branches of established publishing houses, or whole new ventures, new series, and formal exchanges—all efforts toward linkage.

If it is already evident, then, that Southwest Pacific literature can no longer be regarded as the sole or even primary concern of Australia and New Zealand and their erstwhile colonial dependencies—that, with other striking developments in English, it is already part of World English—what are the implications of this dawning realization for teachers and students, for publishers, for librarians and general readers? First, what can be done, should be done, for the teaching and professional study of World English? The traditional method of teaching, through classroom lectures laced with required textbooks, is still the only generally accepted procedure. When one stands aside and attempts to view the situation without academic prejudices, it is difficult to tell why so disjunctive and wasteful a method should be continued. Certainly for full-strength English instruction it can no longer serve; the subject is simply too big, too complex, to be sliced up. The teaching of British-American literature (all that the student commonly encounters) is itself so fragmented into specialties that a comprehensive view is more and more rarely attained.

Teaching, inevitably, has strong impacts on publishing, with English textbook publishing forming one of the largest divisions of the industry. What would be the result of drastically curtailing English course offerings with their tailored textbooks, in favor of a wider, more genuinely exploratory, approach? One can readily imagine dislocations and protestations of hardship within the present scheme, where the ideal is that everyone be given the opportunity of "teaching their specialty." But, if there are no more than, say, fifty or sixty teachers (and that is a department of considerable size) for at least five or six hundred specialties (see any recent annual bibliography), what becomes of the vast silent majority of writings in English not provided with available specialists? The absurdity of such territorial imperatives within a discipline alleging itself to represent broad aesthetic culture—the humanities, the liberal arts—is painfully clear. Quite possibly librarians, along with serious general readers whom they serve, are currently better aware of literary enlargements than are a great many busy English specialists. Whereas English has indeed become irreversibly international, scholars and teachers, nevertheless, must remain provincial as long as they refuse to comprehend and accept this exciting change of affairs and enlarge their practice to meet it.

How can we manage to absorb so much rapid new development into a tradition which, until day before yesterday, we had thought was rich and varied, of course, but still comfortably defined? Now that it is so precipitately redefining itself, how can we possibly "teach" it all? Quite obviously we can't, but we, nevertheless, should face up to our dilemma. With demands for the widening of academic horizons long since upon us, the question of "teaching" has to be rephrased. How can we do justice to a set of claims that are worldwide and at the same time of high quality? Unless the scandal of a discipline unaware of its own perimeters is to be allowed to grow even more notorious, some fairly drastic restructuring will have to be undertaken—and soon. The most hopeful forecast at this time is that, when the day of decision comes, traditional classroom presentation will be obliged to give place to a greatly expanded and extended pattern of self-directed study, assisted by frequent contact with faculty members and by a highly flexible system of seminars, special lectures, and other modes in a wide variety of presentations. That is the only kind of curriculum that, for the study of English in the latter twentieth century and beyond, will fit reality. Whatever we do, our aim should be to guarantee that students will be put in touch with the full resources of this English literature; that they will be induced to think of their mother tongue as a great continuum within which, together with hundreds of millions of others all round the globe, they will spend their life.

A recent volume from India, *Powre above Powres*,[22] serves to underline much of what has just been said as well as to bring together once more the ramifications of literary development in the Southwest Pacific. Subtitled "Essays in South Pacific Literature," this collection contains critical survey-essays—"Recent Australian Poetry" (in which twenty-one poets figure) and a companion piece on recent New Zealand poetry, "Painfully Upright among Lost Hills"; "Women in Australian Drama"; "One of Those Islands" (on the special relation of New Zealand literature to New World literature in English); and so forth—in addition to poems by Australians, New Zealanders, and various Pacific islanders. Finally, of special interest in the immediate context, there is a comprehensive list of references for South Pacific literature: new writing from Papua–New Guinea, New Zealand (Maori writers), Samoa, Indonesia, the Cook Islands, New Hebrides, Fiji, and other places.

The contributors to *Powre above Powres*, understandably, hail chiefly from the South Pacific itself, but there are others from India, Canada, the United States, the Philippines, and Denmark. One sees clearly in such a gathering the movement outward toward localities which only a few years ago would have been largely ignored in any search for serious writing in English. Along with this goes an evident scholarly and critical readiness among New Zealanders and Australians—now already in the parental role though not long out of leading strings themselves—to welcome the newcomers as part of the growing complex. It all emphasizes the attitude expressed in a passage which the author of the essay on New Zealand poetry quotes from Charles Brasch:

> I do not know the shape of the world.
> I cannot set boundaries to experience.
> I know it may open out, enlarge suddenly,
> In any direction, to unpredictable distance,
> Subverting climate and cosmography,
> And carrying me far from tried moorings.

Notes

1 Bernard Smith's *European Vision and the South Pacific* (Oxford: Oxford University Press, 1960) has much to say about the early years of European penetration into the Pacific, as does also Alan Moorehead's *The Fatal Impact* (London: Hamish Hamilton, 1966). Examples of Pakeha writing about Maoris include F. E. Maning's *Old New Zealand* (1863), uncommon for its humorous and at times satiric approach; J. E. Gorst's *The Maori King* (1864); and A. A. Grace's *Tales of a Dying Race* (1901), whose title suggests an attitude typical of its period. Samuel Butler's *Erewhon* (1872) uses a Maori guide, Chowbok, in the Southern Alps of the South Island; in *Erewhon Revisited* (1901) this humble personage has become a professional churchman, Bishop Kahabuka. Australian Aboriginals, unapproachably different from the islanders in almost every way ("All they seem to want is for us to be gone," Cook observed), were not to

appear as believable characters or subjects of serious literary attention until much later. As J. J. Healy says in "The Treatment of the Aborigine in Australian Literature from the Beginning to the Present Day" (Ph.D. dissertation, University of Texas, 1968), "Interest in the mythology and general culture of the aborigine had been a continuing one from the first contact. The logic of this material being made available should have been the greater accessibility of the aborigine as a genuine, rather than a spuriously romantic, field for the fictive imagination" (p. 10).

2 C. Hartley Grattan, *Australian Literature* (Seattle: University of Washington Book Store, 1929), 39. Alongside this early survey may be placed, for comparison, Grattan's chapters on literature in *The Southwest Pacific* (2 vols., Ann Arbor: University of Michigan Press, 1963). It should be recalled, as well, that in the early 1920s Grattan was already quite actively interested in American literature—as later evidenced in his books—at a time when academic concern had not yet developed. One may presume that such concern with American literature as an emergent subject of serious intellectual attention may have had something to do with Grattan's recognition of Australian literature as tending, however slightly at this early point, in similar directions.

3 Ibid., 7–8.

4 W. Murdoch and A. Mulgan (eds.), *A Book of Australian and New Zealand Verse* (4th ed., Melbourne, London, Wellington: Oxford University Press, 1950), 266. (This book has an interesting publication history: in 1918 it appeared as *The Oxford Book of Australasian Verse*; then in 1923 a second edition shifted the title to *A Book of Australasian Verse*, reprinted in 1928 and 1936; the third edition, 1945, was reprinted in 1949 as *A Book of Australian and New Zealand Verse*; and the fourth edition appeared in 1950, by which time each of the two literatures had begun taking its own path.)

5 E. H. McCormick, *New Zealand Literature* (London: Oxford University Press, 1959), 102–103.

6 Commonwealth Office of Education, "Literature in Australia," *Current Affairs Bulletin* 6, 13 (September 11, 1950), 222.

7 Australian News and Information Bureau, *Literature* (Canberra: Department of the Interior, Reference Paper no. 19, June 1955), unpaged.

8 Geoffrey Serle, *From Deserts the Prophets Come: The Creative Spirit in Australia, 1788–1972* (Melbourne: Heinemann, 1973), 218.

9 Ibid., 218–219.

10 C. B. Christesen, "The Twenty-One Lives of *Meanjin Quarterly*," *Texas Quarterly* V, 2 (Summer 1962: special issue, "Image of Australia"), 85.

11 *The P.E.N. New Zealand Centre* (Wellington: P.E.N., 1947), 7.

12 *P.E.N. Gazette*, December 1955, p. 5.

13 For Australia, in this context, the names of Eleanor Dark, Mary Durack, Xavier Herbert, Rex Ingamells, Ian Mudie, Katharine Susannah Prichard, Randolph Stow, and Donald Stuart have special importance; so in New Zealand do those of Sylvia Ashton-Warner, James K. Baxter, Roderick Finlayson, Noel Hilliard, and Bill Pearson.

14 Serle, op. cit., 222–223.

15 Apisai Enos, "Niugini Literature," paper at the Conference on Teaching Literature in P.–N.G., July 31 to August 2, 1972. Mimeographed, 3 pp.

16 Nigel Krauth, "Towards a Balanced Approach in the Study of Modern Papua–
New Guinean Literature," paper at the Conference on Teaching Literature in
P.–N.G., 1972. Mimeographed, 6 pp.

17 Judith H. McDowell, "The Embryonic Literature of New Guinea," WLWE (World
Literature Written in English), 12, 2 (November 1973), 303. With luck, we
should have a good deal more Niugini writing within the next few years. It
is revealing to compare the scattering, totally "foreign" literary items included
in W. A. McGrath's *New Guineana, 1942–1964* (Port Moresby: Author, 1965)
with productions of the later 1960s and early 1970s as shown in McDowell's
survey.

18 K. O. Arvidson, "The Emergence of a Polynesian Literature," WLWE 14, 1 (April
1975), 113. Arvidson's article (pp. 91–115), with the notes following, provides
a useful survey as well as an indication of how quickly local criticism is approaching the scene. Arvidson thinks that Niuginian writers, with whose work
he compares Polynesian writing, may for reasons largely economic have a better
chance of survival and/or recognition than do Fijians, Samoans, Cook Islanders,
et al. It will be interesting to see, some years from now, the literary response
in the Marianas under American auspices.

19 For the meaning of "Maoritanga" see the essay by M. P. K. Sorrenson on "Maori
and Pakeha," elsewhere in this volume.

20 See W. S. Broughton, "A Discursive Essay about Jerusalem," WLWE 14, 1 (April
1975), 69–90. Baxter's work is treated at length in a recent study by Charles
Doyle, *James K. Baxter* (Boston: Twayne, 1976).

21 Paraphrased from Serle, op. cit., 230–231.

22 H. H. Anniah Gowda (ed.), *Powre above Powres, 1: Essays in South Pacific Literature* (Mysore: Center for Commonwealth Literature and Research, University of Mysore, 1977), 245 pp.

W. E. H. STANNER

The Australian Aborigines

A case might be made for a view that for several decades after 1788 the damage done to Aboriginal society by the British colonists of Australia was not willful and was not seen as a necessary effect of their own presence. A hope persisted that a way might yet be found to assimilate the Aborigines agreeably into European society or to insulate them from it while giving them the benefits of civilization and Christianity.

It would be hard to sustain any such thesis for the 1820s and impossible from the 1830s onward. By then the colonists were becoming aware, and their understanding grew ever stronger, that they were in deadly struggle with the Aborigines for scarce life-space. During the next sixty or seventy years, the colonists broke imperiously away from the Colonial Office plan for a concentrated settlement and dispersed into the interior, reaching by the 1890s the farthest limits set by the market of the time as the economic margin. They dispossessed the Aborigines of all land of good pastoral potential and brought hundreds of tribes to ruin. Europeans not only had an awareness of what they were doing but also had a comfortable assurance that a fusion of political authority, law, morals, religion, and rationality supported their self-interest. The situation stayed more or less stable until after the depression of the 1930s. By then a third period had begun; that period, which is the particular concern of this essay, was characterized by a slow but persistent change in the ethos of Australian society. Aboriginal problems began to come to the forefront of national attention and emerged finally as a leading issue of politics and public policy. That led to a far-reaching reorientation of policy and practice and a marked if lagged rise in the political self-consciousness of the Aboriginal people themselves. In the 1970s a fundamental issue, always immanent in the life of Australian society but not manifest for more than a century, was disclosing itself. The issue was whether European Australians would accept the fact that Aboriginal society has a personality and, therefore, a claim and right to a future of its own.

The Years of "Fatal Consequence"

Our thesis concerning the first few decades of settlement may seem too charitable in the light of the conflict and bloodletting that did occur. But it, nevertheless, has merit and avoids anachronism. The early colonists—totally ignorant of the systematic aspects of Aboriginal society, culture, and ecology—could make little sense of the visible degradation that came upon every tribal group in touch with the settlements; nor could Europeans foresee the long chain of similar effects in events that had yet to happen. It is consistent with the mentality of authorities who, left without guidance and having no precedent, yet were bound by an idealistic imperial policy to bring old principle and new circumstance together in a bastard military-civil polity in a strange country where in many eyes ". . . nature is reversed, and if not so, she is nearly worn out."[1] It suggests how occupation could become irreversible before anyone had a clear understanding of the dilemma intrinsic to and continuous in the whole undertaking. A persistently bifocal vision distracted eyes from the evidence (and minds from the appraisal) of the destruction of Aboriginal society. And it provides part of the paradigm of the political and public issue again becoming manifest in the 1970s.

In 1819 a French visitor to Sydney—repelled by the squalor of Aboriginal life in the capital and by the unseeing and unfeeling attitude of the European populace—had noted, nevertheless, that natives "from the interior" were coming into the settlements. He rightly thought them driven to do so because of interference with, or destruction of, their natural food supply.[2] The new Aboriginal mobility was widely noted.[3] Events near the coast were thus making clear what would become more obvious in the future. Knowledge gained by personal acquaintance with Aborigines was growing quite rapidly and was better understood both by travelers and by pastoralists on the transmontane slopes and plains. That knowledge was that a society of hunters and foragers could not coexist within the same boundaries with a pastoral and agricultural society.[4] The basic postulate of European society in Australia thus established, its structure and ethos developed consistently over the next century.

The settlers, whether bond or free, did not seem to have been notably worse or better than others of their kinds and times. Also they were like all people in needing to justify their actions to themselves. Many self-exculpatory formulas were used among them: "needs must," ethnic dogma, God's design, the laws of nature and of history, and the supposed social correlates of biological evolution. We need do no more than mention briefly some of the things said by a few men who, assuredly representative of their day, may be thought to have expressed well the ruling mentality and moral sentiments. The instances cover roughly but adequately the period from the 1840s to the 1890s, a period of most fatal consequence for the racial situation in Australia up to the end of the First World War.[5]

In 1843 a man of piety and exemplary balance came to believe after an agonizing struggle of conscience that ". . . upon the whole, it is a gain to the cause of truth and virtue for Christian England to possess those wilds which lately were occupied by miserable natives," of whom he thought "we may safely speak . . . in terms that are suitable to their degraded state."[6] In 1860 an English traveler who apparently ranged widely in Australia saw the Aboriginal scene as one of gross darkness and misery, physical and moral: "Their God is their belly; their will, or rather their passions, are their law, as long as they are able, through violence and cruelty, to maintain their point; and the testimony of Scripture, that 'the dark places of the earth are full of the habitations of cruelty,' finds in their case an awful verification."[7] In 1873 an eminent novelist, contemptuous alike of "savages of the lowest kind" and of what he called "negro-philanthropy," said that ". . . an increasing number of aborigines in the land, – were it possible that the race should increase, – would be a curse rather than a blessing"; that ". . . their doom is to be exterminated; and the sooner that their doom be accomplished, – so that there be no cruelty, – the better will it be for civilization."[8] A few years later a historian removed the question from the plane of actuality: "Whether the interests of civilization are better served by the destruction of the race than they would have been by its preservation or redemption, is a question for philosophers to settle."[9] At that time, possibly seventy thousand or eighty thousand Aborigines of the full blood may have been alive.

What can have made such sentiments credible and tolerable among a civilized and Christian people? They were moving toward a life hardly to be surpassed anywhere in the world for vitality, spaciousness, security, and prosperity; and they were already distinguishing themselves by the quality of their effort to generalize democracy, equality, and justice. It is possibly more a paradox than a question. With hindsight, one can see a moral dilemma being "thought away" so as to become irrelevant to its conscious social morality. There was no conscious plan, conspiracy, or agreed intent, no process under rational control. Rather, what Alfred North Whitehead called "senseless agencies" were effecting two things at the same time. They were so disvaluing the scruples of our man of piety and exemplary balance that it came to seem an unbelievable thing for anyone to have said: "... true, indeed, these despised Australians may, hereafter, rise up in judgment against Europeans to condemn them."[10] And they were replacing it by a mythology of self-perception such that, in the same year (1889) as the historian G. B. Barton wrote, the poet Percy Russell could say:

> Her shield unsullied by a single crime,
> Her wealth of gold and still more golden fleece,
> Forth stands Australia, in her birth sublime,
> The only nation from the womb of Peace.[11]

Certain circumstances enabled that regression to take place. Over the period of most fatal consequence the Aboriginal numbers fell at a catastrophic rate. By 1901, according to the best estimate yet made,[12] there were a scant 67,000 as against the 251,000 in 1788. Those who were left were, unless located far beyond the economic margin, either institutionalized on government or mission settlements or allowed to form camps on the fringes of up-country towns, pastoral properties, farms, and mines, which were usually tucked away well out of sight of the busier centers of colonial life. Over the same period, the European populace became predominantly urban. The transition from a rural to an urban majority (metropolitan and provincial) came in the 1880s. Thus, in the ordinary course of life, a steadily declining number of Europeans were placed where they could see or meet or get to understand the circumstances of a steadily declining number of decadent Aborigines. The decade of the 1880s was also that of the highest net immigration of the nineteenth century, so that the newcomers who saw, met, or heard about Aborigines tended to receive the now conventional impression of that gross darkness and misery, physical and moral. It was just at that time too that—largely because of foreign stimulus—the first truly scholarly study of Aboriginal society began. Much of the work has put moderns in a permanent debt to these old-time scholars, but unhappily much of it magnified the supposedly prehistoric status of the Aborigines, so much so that more than a generation later they seemed "poor, naked cannibals" even to the genius of Sigmund Freud.[13] On the level of popular portraiture, the derision and contempt expressed in the mid-century years deepened toward a malevolent vilification at the end of the century. The member of the South Australian parliament who saw the detribalized Aborigines of Port Darwin in 1882 as "degraded specimens of humanity . . . some less manlike than a grinning and chattering monkey . . ." and questioned ". . . whether, on the whole, any beings bearing the semblance of humanity could be found more low-sunk than these . . ."[14] may be bracketed with the member of the new Commonwealth Parliament in 1902 who said: "There is no scientific evidence that [the Aboriginal] is a human being at all."[15] And, of course, the hypothesis of the 1840s had become the axiom of the 1890s: the Aborigines were a dying race. Sir Baldwin Spencer, the greatest of authorities, remained of that opinion in 1926: "It is inevitable that the full-blooded aboriginal must disappear. The difference between the white race and the black one is so great that it cannot be bridged. All that can be done is to treat those who remain as generously as possible."[16] Although at that time the curve of depopulation was almost certainly starting to flatten out before starting to climb, the fact was unsuspected.[17] The imminence of a demographic explosion was barely credible even in the 1950s.

Those circumstances may help us understand what was negative—the incognition, the indifference, and the neglect—in Australian attitudes and conduct over a full century. What would be needed for the rest—the irrational positive—is an anthropology of the structure and ethos of transplanted British society in the imperial days of palm and pine. It is not our intention to try to account in such terms for this part of "the paradox." We can but point to some of the attendant circumstances that paved the way for a reversal by the third quarter of this century of most of the situations and attitudes that were assumed to be constants when the colonies federated in 1901.

The "Third Period"

The six colonies had more in common than not in their treatment of and attitude toward Aborigines.[18] The constitution which made them into a Commonwealth contained only two specifically relevant provisions. One (sec. 127) said that "in reckoning the numbers of the people of the Commonwealth, or of a State or other part of the Commonwealth, Aboriginal natives shall not be counted." The proffered explanation has always been that to count the nomads would not have been feasible. It is less than fully convincing. At that time only a minority of the full bloods were truly nomadic, and with each year enumeration become more practicable. A better explanation has been given. The provision "was probably not an expression of racist sentiments . . . but a recognition of the fact that full-blood Aborigines were outside the political and social system: to include them in the operation of determining electoral boundaries and parliamentary representation would have given states with large Aboriginal populations a fortuitous advantage." [19] The second provision (sec. 51, xxvi) gave the federal Parliament power, though not exclusive power, to make laws with respect to "the people of any race, other than the Aboriginal race in any State, for whom it is deemed necessary to make special laws." The proffered explanation has been that, because the Commonwealth at foundation "held no territory in the continent and therefore had no direct responsibility for Aborigines, it gave no thought to the possibility of such responsibility arising in the future." [20] The provision was not, in truth, aimed at the indigenous race but at non-European peoples such as the Chinese and Melanesians who had been introduced in considerable numbers in the second half of the nineteenth century. However, the fact of its adoption tends to confirm what we have suggested. At the turn of the century, not even the most farsighted statesmen, alert as they were to the need to provide for all political contingencies, foresaw a need of special laws for a vanishing race.

The three notable developments in what we have called the third period—the shift of white attitudes to Aboriginal problems, the reorientation of policy and practice, and the rise of Aboriginal political consciousness and activity—have been attributed to "forces," "trends," and "causes," which as often as not only reify what happened and, more dangerously, help generate a mythology about what happened. There is virtue in saying simply that ideas, interests, and situations changed and that people changed with them. Some essential facts of background and chronology certainly need to be considered.

It is almost forgotten that the Australian Commonwealth might have been an Australasian Commonwealth (that is, including New

Zealand) but for a fear that it would treat the Maoris as it had treated the Aborigines. After the First World War, when the fate of all native peoples under the new system of mandates became a matter of international concern, Australia's administration of New Guinea received unusual attention simply because of its record concerning the Aborigines. Its credit fell still further when within Australia between 1926 and 1934 there were:

> two Commissions of Inquiry into atrocities perpetrated against the Aborigines; a Departmental inquiry into a serious allegation of the same kind; a general investigation by a special Commissioner into the conditions of the Aborigines in the Northern Territory; a Commission of Inquiry in Western Australia arranged in response to dissatisfaction about the conditions and treatment of Aborigines in that State; and a successful protest against an official suggestion to send a punitive expedition to 'teach the natives of East Arnhem Land a lesson' following a series of killings of some Japanese, two prospectors, and a police constable in 1932–33.[21]

The official paper from which this excerpt is taken referred also to "unsatisfactory" ("discreditable" would have been a more apt adjective)[22] aspects of court proceedings in the Northern Territory and to "telephone conversations at a high level" between London and Canberra, "showing that England was concerned with the general position of the Aborigines." The facts of the conversations have never been disclosed. But there seems no need for so oblique a description. The British government was embarrassed by the revelations and felt its own international reputation affected. At that time Australia had no foreign representation of its own, and its foreign policy, insofar as it had one, was hardly distinguishable from that of the United Kingdom. There was a tacit assumption that Australia would act (as it almost always did) conformably with Great Britain. In those circumstances it was not unusual or inappropriate for the Dominions Office to make representations to the Australian high commissioner in London and for him in turn to do so to the government in Canberra.

But domestic as well as external considerations made a contribution. The old isolation of the Australian bush was now at an end. The motorcar, the airplane, and the wireless had improved the flow of information as well as the transport and communication patterns. The treatment of Aborigines in the outback and deep bush may not have been any more inconsiderate than before, but more about the situation became known, and known more quickly, in the cities. At that time the news media, entering on a new phase of sensationalism, exploited the revelations and in particular the justifiable suspicions of official hugger-mugger. The outcome was a public agitation, without parallel since the 1830s, for a more considerate treatment of Aborigines.

The demand was for a radical change from a negative policy of protection to a positive policy of welfare and citizenship. The first distinct signs appeared of a swing of public sentiment away from the old depreciation of Aboriginal culture toward a new appreciation. But the effects were formal and notional rather than actual and concrete. It soon became clear that people and organizations of the kind which had been dismissed contemptuously in the nineteenth century as "Exeter Hall philanthropists" still had insufficient force against the inertia of governments and their instrumentalities. An immense amount of enthusiasm, indignation, and hard work therefore had few practical results, though there were some. Commonwealth and state officials concerned with the administration of Aborigines met together in 1937 for the first time in Australian history. In 1938 Professor A. P. Elkin, who had played a leading part in the public agitation, cleverly negotiated with the Commonwealth a set of proposals for application in the Northern Territory, which had been a federal responsibility since 1911. The proposals were referred to and became known as "A New Deal for Aborigines." They had a strong and positive welfare component and were assimilationist rather than simply protectionist in concept. Little had come from them by the time the Second World War broke out. The same was the case with formative ideas put forward by other authoritative persons, including Donald Thomson, Pearson Chinnery (both anthropologists), Theodore Strehlow, Charles Duguid, and the many devoted people who are too numerous to mention. During the war and for several years afterward Australian attention concentrated overwhelmingly on the claims of the natives of Papua–New Guinea. Aboriginal problems did not again come under serious consideration until after the Commonwealth had accepted substantial responsibilities toward other racial populations outside Australia. A disproportionate concern for non-Australian "natives" continued to characterize policy for many years.

The sequence in which new departures in external and domestic "native policy" occurred clearly suggests, therefore, that foreign considerations had much to do with the first softening of Australian attitudes toward the Aborigines. We do not suggest that this is more than a part of the truth or that it was as true of the second part of the third period (from the 1950s to the 1970s) as of the first. But what truth it has may well be set against a myth in the making: that Australian virtue, always there but now newly discovered by its own motion, alone accounts for the attempt to reverse so much that disfigured the record from the 1830s to the 1930s.

It is also fanciful to suggest that the discovery that the Aborigines were not after all a vanishing people had a great deal to do with the change of attitudes. The discovery postdated the shift. The increase in the number of part-Aborigines probably began in the 1920s. Some anxious mention was made of it at the 1937 conference, but there was no such anxiety over the number of full bloods. Indeed, their number was not known with any certainty to be increasing until the middle 1950s although, as we have already pointed out, the turning point was probably near at hand a good quarter of a century earlier. The qualification "with any certainty" is important. In the census of 1947 only half the estimated number of full bloods were enumerated, and a relatively complete enumeration was not obtained until 1966.[23] It is one of the open secrets of Australian public life, so little had the fact of a demographic explosion registered, that even in 1972 Commonwealth advisers and officials were hard put to persuade authority that funds and plans were still dangerously incommensurate with a rate of increase in the total Aboriginal population of about 3.4 percent per annum—". . . one of the highest rates of natural increase in the world and almost four times the figure for non-Aborigines in 1966."[24]

The third development—the rise or at least the organized public expression of Aboriginal political attitudes—is popularly supposed to have been the prime cause of the first, the changed European outlook, and of the second, the reorientation of policy and practice. The actual relations seem to have been very nearly the opposite until perhaps the 1960s, but even then the door on which Aboriginal activists began to hammer was already unlatched and opening. Of course, resentment and open or covert opposition to Australian rule had animated the Aboriginal people since 1788, silent though the history books may be about it—as they are of the scale and pattern of resistance by arms against the spread of settlement. But apart from a few very exceptional incidents little has been recorded of organized Aboriginal political activity. In the 1870s and 1880s the remnants of the five great tribes of the Kulin

Nation persistently lobbied the government of Victoria. In 1937 exactly 1,814 Victorian Aborigines sought to petition King George VI through the prime minister to prevent their extinction and to be represented in the federal Parliament by an Aboriginal or a sympathetic European. In 1938 a New South Wales body known as the Aborigines Progressive Association celebrated the 150th anniversary of Australia's foundation by "A Day of Mourning and Protest" and issued a public manifesto extraordinarily like statements to be made thirty-five years afterward. A few days later a deputation of the same protestants went to Canberra to ask the prime minister and the minister for the interior to bring all Aboriginal affairs under a federal ministry. (In the upshot the petition never reached the king. The petitioners were advised that both federal and state governments believed themselves to be doing everything in their power to prevent the extinction of Aborigines and fully appreciated their responsibilities for Aboriginal welfare.) But it would be unwise to deduce from the infrequency of such protests, or from the paucity of the record, that the Aborigines lacked political capacity. Another and probably better explanation can be found in the decimation of numbers, the destruction of social organization, the scattering of tribal remnants, and the consuming misery of their circumstances, without even referring to the systematic suppression or removal of outspoken or aggressive men who, being regarded as trouble-makers, may in many instances have been natural political leaders. It is a fact, however, that when in the reformist atmosphere of the 1930s an increasing number of new voluntary societies began to form around older societies, such as the Association for the Protection of Native Races and the National Missionary Council of Australia, there was little Aboriginal membership or movement toward leadership. Not for some years were attempts made by Aborigines to achieve exclusive control of new societies by members of their own race. With a few notable exceptions[25] the first generation of leaders were preponderantly men and women of mixed descent drawn mainly from urban and provincial groups, and that has remained largely the case down to the late 1970s.

The Search for a Policy

The reformist movement in the second half (1948–1973) of the third period began with a step of decisive importance. The officials who had met in 1937 had clearly recognized the needs of part-

Aborigines but not those of the full bloods. This was now correct-
ed. Because later much was to hang on the failure at the time of
transition to effect more than a partial reversal of the past, the
events leading to the correction need summarizing.

The 1937 conference had recommended that "half-castes," as
they were then called, should be educated for employment at
white standards so as to facilitate their absorption into the Australian populace. But it did not make any such recommendations
concerning the full bloods. It suggested that they be categorized
as "detribalized," "semicivilized," and "uncivilized." It appeared
to favor something like apartheid in inviolable reserves as an appropriate way of dealing with the last two categories but suggested
that this should be done as far as possible without damage to the
needs of employers of Aboriginal labor. The idea of the absorption
of part-Aborigines took hold of the official imagination, though
under the new rubric of assimilation, which then came quickly
into general currency. Several states began to legislate or to adapt
administrative philosophy and practice accordingly. The Commonwealth went a step farther. It developed an outline plan to
apply the new concept in an expanded form to the whole Aboriginal population of the Northern Territory. For its time, that was
a signal advance.

The design of the plan obviously owed much to Chinnery's New
Guinea experience as well as to Elkin's and Thomson's[26] recommendations. There were to be a Department of Native Affairs,
special courts to deal with Aboriginal offenders, an Aboriginal con-
stabulary, and a field staff trained in law and anthropology. The
basic assumption was that Aboriginal culture had collapsed, or
would soon do so everywhere, and that assimilation into a European mode of life was the one rational possibility. The basic postulate was that Aborigines were of right entitled to eventual citizenship in a full sense. Therefore, they should be trained for a settled
life and useful occupation; taught to recognize authority, law,
and the rights of property; given religious training to "replace the
stability of character which has been lost by the destruction of
their ancient philosophy and moral code." The uncivilized were
to be left alone until progress had been made with the semicivilized and detribalized categories.

The war came before the plan could be followed through to
effect, although between 1940 and 1946 some useful preparatory
steps were taken. When in 1948, after a lapse of eleven years,
Commonwealth and state officials (now drawn from a wider range

of administrative, welfare, and social service agencies) again met, they recommended a policy of assimilation for the whole Aboriginal population of Australia. The recommendation was formally adopted after further meetings (with ministers meeting at the same time) in 1951 and 1953. A watershed of philosophy, attitude, and practice thus seemed to have been crossed. But, in spite of a more generous provision of funds, legislative and administrative acts of excellent intention, and hard work by a new breed of dedicated officials, controversy over attitudes and purposes persisted.

The new policy soon came under attack by Europeans who sympathized with the Aborigines and eventually by many Aborigines. The reasons are not hard to state. A new ideology was taking hold of influential sections of the Australian public, especially the young, the educated, and the well-to-do in the cities and provincial towns. It was founded in part on a belief that Aboriginal culture, being of significant value in itself, should be preserved. But governments were plainly acting as if Aboriginal preferences were unimportant and as if religious, land, law, marital, and family customs were no longer worth saving. The early forms in which the policy had been stated were also ambiguous. Certain words and phrases seemed to imply an eventual intent to compel Aborigines to become wholly Europeanized or at least appeared to assume their consent to the abandonment of their own social forms and culture. The authorities made patient and sincere efforts to find neutral words to express what seemed at that time a commonsense proposition, namely, that ". . . the native people will grow into a society in which, by force of history, they are bound to live."[27] But the studiously careful version finally adopted[28] did not still the disquiet or end the controversy, even though it represented a quantum jump from the past. Certain facts deepened the antagonisms. The new policy seemed to become for governments and many officials a superior conventional wisdom which could be criticized only for irrational reasons or from dubious motive.[29] The more it was criticized, the more it had to be defended. Evidence accumulated that the habilitation of the Aboriginal people continued to lag behind the now explosive growth of their numbers. No appreciable improvement appeared to be taking place in their standards of health, housing, employment, wages, educational performance, legal status, or civil liberties. Many legal and social discriminations remained unchanged. There appeared to be no intention in the official program to rectify the gut grievances over Aboriginal land and law. Situations multiplied to show that one consequence of assimilation would be that Aborigines might well lose their effective right of choice between Aboriginal and European ways. In the Northern Territory and Queensland especially, there appeared to be a public policy of fair words and an inner policy sharply different from them. One could hear in the Northern Territory the slogan of "assimilation through individualism," which, as far as it was understandable, seemed to imply that a bureaucracy had the skills to dismember a society and its culture and then to fit the human pieces together again in a new social order with new values. The scene was thus set for the 1960s, the most turbulent decade of European-Aboriginal relations.

The New Aborigines

The writer has kept a running record of parliamentary, government, mission, academic, and general public events affecting Aborigines over many years. About fifty such events were noted in the 1950s. The total for the 1960s was nearly two hundred, and there were four times as many in the first four years of the 1970s. The disparities illustrate quite well the rapidly growing visibility of Aboriginal affairs on the Australian scene. They also illustrate the growth of Aboriginal restiveness.

Whereas, in the 1950s, only one event initiated by Aborigines seemed sufficiently important to note, there were at least twenty-five in the 1960s, and the high rate of increase has continued into the 1970s. Some matters of large consequence were substantially of Aboriginal origin in the 1960s. They included (1) the presentation to Parliament by Yirrkala Aborigines of a petition of protest against an excision of land from the Arnhem Land Reserve for mining leases; (2) litigation by the same Aborigines against the Commonwealth and a mining consortium; (3) a walk-out by Gurindji tribesmen at Wave Hill cattle station and the transformation of an industrial dispute into a land rights struggle; (4) freedom rides to towns in New South Wales where racial relations had caused offense; and (5) a marked growth of militant demands for the restoration of land, for the recognition of Aboriginal law, for legislation against discrimination, for compensation for alienation, and for a massive attack on poverty and ill health. In these and other matters European activists and sympathizers no doubt played a part. Both the language and the forms of protest certainly carried this suggestion, but the grievances were unquestionably Aboriginal. It was a recidivist blunder for authorities to attribute the growth of restiveness to the influence of "stirrers." Impercipience of this kind did much to reduce the yield of a notably productive decade.

The record is far too complex to summarize, nor is it central to our purpose to try to do so because, among other reasons, the effects are still working themselves out. But valuable advances were made in the extension to Aborigines of social service payments (including pensions and unemployment allowances), the electoral franchise, and imaginative educational benefits. Productive technical inquiries into education, housing, health, and wage policy questions were initiated or encouraged. Perhaps there were seven major events: (1) the establishment of the Australian Institute of Aboriginal Studies (1961); (2) the decision by the Social Science Research Council of Australia to undertake a study of the whole Aboriginal situation (1964); (3) the national referendum which by an overwhelming majority changed the constitution so as to free the Commonwealth Parliament from statutory restrictions on its power to deal with Aboriginal problems (1967); (4) the establishment of a Commonwealth Council for Aboriginal Affairs and an Office (which in 1972 became a Department) of Aboriginal Affairs (1967); (5) the first meeting in Australian history of Aboriginal spokesmen drawn from every part of the Commonwealth (1969); (6) the unprecedented intrusion of Aboriginal affairs as a policy issue into the federal elections of 1969; and (7) the subsequent appointment of a minister in charge of Aboriginal Affairs. It would be injudicious for the writer, who was personally much involved in these events, to attempt any very specific account of the results they produced, so the following remarks about the 1970s are very general indeed.

By the end of the 1960s, it became clear that the old, self-serving "fusion of political authority, law, morals, religion, and rationality" which had allowed an utterly discreditable racial scene to develop and persist was breaking up, and had to do so. Each of the five elements underwent independent challenges which jointly became virtually impossible to withstand.

A South Australian government under Don Dunstan experimented with the legal recognition of Aboriginal claims to land and with legislation—with real teeth—against racial discrimination. Soon, Aboriginal questions became irreversibly politicized throughout Australia. By the time of the 1969 federal election, three of the five main contesting parties had recognized Aboriginal questions as explicit issues. A fourth party did so at the next federal election in 1972. Thereafter, the fifth, the Country party—made up largely of extreme and unquiet rural conservatives and their followers—now in a coalition opposition, by stages softened its policy toward Aborigines until by the 1975 election it stood alongside the other parties.

The first step by a Commonwealth government toward a new kind of federal policy can hardly be dated before April 1971, when Prime Minister W. M. McMahon, with the advice of his Council for Aboriginal Affairs, pledged his government to move actively toward five objectives: (1) to assist Aborigines as individuals and as communities to attain and hold "effective and respected places within one Australian society" and to preserve and develop their own culture as "a living element within a diverse Australia"; (2) to allow them to choose the degree and pace of their identification with "one Australia"; (3) to take into account their expressed wishes in forming policy and programs; (4) to follow, in collaboration with the states, a strategy that would encourage Aboriginal self-management; and (5) to base all measures on the need of individuals and groups for special care and assistance, not upon a theory of racial needs or according to a plan for separate development. The prime minister formally restated the policy on Australia Day (January 26) 1926 but for party reasons gelded the statement of the kind of promises that would satisfy the now clamorous "land-rights" claimants. By the 1972 election, at which McMahon's Liberal-Country party coalition was defeated, the land-rights issue had precipitated two causes célèbres—Wattie Creek and Yirrkala. The first had been so mishandled by the coalition that it had turned into a kind of public torment. In the second the Commonwealth had opposed the Aborigines in a most partisan way. Justice Blackburn had found against the Aborigines on the matters actually in question—whether they had any kind of sustainable claim for relief against the mining consortium—but at the same time could easily be read as regretting that the law was indifferent to far deeper questions of a moral, social, and political order. Insofar as public feeling could be judged, the preponderant response was summed up to the writer by an Aboriginal at Yirrkala: "If that is the law then the law must be changed." And changed it was, though not by McMahon's government. It is fair to add, however, that the McMahon government did pass some formative measures to improve, in particular, the education of Aborigines at all levels, including the posttertiary, and to provide capital grants and loans to the more enterprising.

The legislative record of all Commonwealth and state governments, with the possible exception of Queensland, in the 1960s and 1970s was impressive. More than fifty new laws were passed, or old laws repealed or amended, to liberate Aborigines from restrictions or discriminations, to guarantee them independence and equality as far as laws could do so, and to provide them with assistance to overcome their legacy of social handicaps as an ethnic minority. The pace of change increased remarkably with the advent of the Whitlam ministries in and after December 1972 and was well maintained by the Fraser ministry, which came to power three years later.

The fusion thus fell apart under the direct impact of political and legal measures and under the indirect influence of a vast sea change in moral sentiment, which now moved unmistakably behind the Aboriginal cause. The many religious bodies which for years had been in the van of the protest and reform movements shared but did not dominate the leadership, which was at times essentially secular.

It may well appear in the light of history that the Aborigines had won what they saw as the substance of their struggle when the first Whitlam ministry moved, immediately after election, to halt the further grant of leases and mining licenses in the Northern Territory Aboriginal Reserves. The second ministry, early in 1973, appointed Justice A. E. Woodward as Aboriginal land rights commissioner to report on means to effect the government's decision to recognize Aboriginal land rights. The final report was made in 1974. It was a work of remarkable penetration and productivity. It demonstrated that a coherent plan could be made to give Aborigines, at first in the Northern Territory and later perhaps elsewhere, titles over land that would be valid, safe, and unquestioned. The titles would freely allow the owners, whether individuals or communities, to use and enjoy their land in their own way, while not neglecting the possible national interest or abrogating any existing interest. A bill was prepared and actually introduced into the Parliament, but it lapsed with the defeat of the Whitlam government. The privilege of having a changed bill passed as an act fell to the Fraser government in 1976. But an interim land commissioner had been appointed in 1975 to begin hearing claims for land by Northern Territory Aborigines. And an Aboriginal Land Fund Commission had already begun to buy properties for, or to fund the purchase by, Aboriginal communities throughout much of Australia, again except Queensland.

The collapse of the rationalist basis of the older attitudes—that Aborigines for genetic reasons lack capacity; that their culture and society have no potential for development; that European culture and society are intrinsically superior; that modern life is morally and materially richer; and that the weak and inferior must go to the wall—through exposure to skepticism and in some cases actual disproof, left Australian opinion a ready victim of a new cult. A new appreciation of "Aboriginality" has been immensely stimulated by some contemporary ideologies, in particular those of the "third world," "the quality of life," antiurbanism, antipollution, and "the national estate." An unprecedented number of competent inquiries into Aboriginal capacity and conditions by parliamentary, scientific, scholarly, and church bodies has brought a truly prodigious flow of hard information where previously there had been little or none. The facts of the Aboriginal standards of living have been shown to be so appalling and scandalous that white imagination, however unwillingly, has been compelled to respond. At the same time Aboriginal leaders and spokesmen have been presented with a large and soft area of public sympathy ready for cultivation. In the late 1970s, they are cultivating that sympathy ingeniously and for the most part with patience and moderation. Nevertheless, within white Australia, there are some unreconciled oppositions which fly new flags in front of old attitudes and are ready to make much of many continuing and new problems for which no credible and practicable answers have yet appeared. Perhaps "solutions" will prove to be the beginnings of new "problems," but more joint wisdom, black and white, is now being called upon to consider them than at any time since 1788.

Much may now depend upon the joint effects of three ventures of policy, one being almost wholly Aboriginal in conception, the second and third being of European inspiration with some Aboriginal support. The first is a "homeland" or decentralization movement by Aborigines away from government settlements, mission stations, and other centers of white population and influence, in favor of small bush centers usually, but not invariably, in clan or tribal territory to which a claim of traditional association or ownership is made. This movement has accelerated in recent years but is of long standing, and it would have drawn notice much earlier had there been anything like the flow of government money that for some years now has freed Aborigines from their former almost absolute dependence upon the nearest European. The viability of many of the new, small settlements is not yet established. Much thought is being given to the means of maintaining health, educational, and other standards. The apparent belief of many Aborigines that they can cobble their old settlement pattern, social organization, and to some extent ecology to a new technology of motor and air transport, hardware, firearms, and radio in a system dependent on an unfailing flow of government money must clearly be put to a severe test.

That law of human affairs which brings multiple effects from the most single-minded intention or action invites attention to the second and third ventures: the creation of a National Aboriginal Advisory Committee and the passage through Parliament of an act to allow the incorporation of Aboriginal associations of whatever kind. Both measures appeared in 1977 to be essential to the Aboriginals' search for true identity and to their capacity in law to manage their own affairs. But many questions abide. Whereas the first venture may perhaps be regarded as an attempt by an ill-used people to escape from the hectoring solicitude of white authorities, the second and third are based rather on the logic of European lifestyles. Nevertheless, they are the best efforts of Walter Bagehot's "hard-worked men at the end of the earth" to give reward and security to a people who lost them two hundred years ago. Exactly how they will fit in with an intention to permit and assist Aborigines to preserve and develop their own culture as a "living element within a diverse Australia" remains to be seen.

Notes

1   Extract from a letter from Major Robert Ross, Sydney Cove, November 16, 1788, to Sir Evan Nepean, Under-Secretary for the Home Department, London. Quoted by G. B. Barton in *History of New South Wales from the Records* (Sydney: Government Printer, 1889), 500.

2   Ward and Olive Havard, "A Frenchman Sees Sydney in 1819" (trans. from the letters of Jacques Araga), *Royal Australian Historical Society, Journal and Proceedings*, xxiv, pt. 1 (1938), 24.

3   R. H. Cambage, "Exploration between the Wingecarribee, Shoalhaven, Macquarie and Murrumbidgee Rivers," *Royal Australian Historical Society, Journal and Proceedings*, vii (1921), 219–288.

4   W. K. Hancock, *Australia* (London: E. Benn, 1930), 33. See also his *Discovering Monaro* (Cambridge: Cambridge University Press, 1972).

5   See Geoffrey Blainey, *The Triumph of the Nomads* (Melbourne: Macmillan, 1974); R. H. W. Reece, *Aborigines and Colonists: Aborigines and Colonial So-*

ciety in New South Wales in the 1830s and 1840s (Sydney: University Press, 1974); and W. E. H. Stanner (ed.), *Australian Aboriginal Studies* (Melbourne: Oxford University Press, 1963).

6   The Rev. W. Pridden, *Australia: Its History and Present Condition* (London: J. Burns, 1843), 73.

7   Alexander Marjoribanks, *Travels in New South Wales* (London: Smith Elder & Co., 1847), 92.

8   Anthony Trollope, *Australia and New Zealand* (London: Chapman and Hall, 1873), ii, 87.

9   Barton, *History of New South Wales from the Records*, 130.

10 Pridden, *Australia*, 73.

11 Percy Russell, *A Journey to Lake Taupo and Australian Tales and Sketches* (London: E. A. Petherick, 1889).

12 Leonard Broom and F. Lancaster Jones, *A Blanket a Year* (Canberra: Australian National University Press, 1973), 43.

13 Sigmund Freud, *Totem and Taboo*, James Strachey (trans.) (London: Routledge & Kegan Paul, 1950), 2.

14 W. J. Sowden, *The Northern Territory As It Is* (Adelaide: W. K. Thomas, 1882), 28.

15 *Commonwealth Parliamentary Debates*, House of Representatives, ix (April 23, 1902), 11930.

16 Quoted by J. Lyng, *Non-Britishers in Australia* (Melbourne: Macmillan, 1927), 204.

17 W. E. H. Stanner, "Aborigines in the Affluent Society: The Widening Gap," paper delivered at 45th ANZAAS Congress, Perth, August 1973 (typescript, 8–9).

18 The similarities and differences may be explored in E. J. B. Foxcroft, *Australian Native Policy* (Melbourne: Melbourne University Press, 1941); Clive Turnbull, *Black War* (Melbourne: Cheshire, 1948); S. C. McCulloch, "Sir George Gipps and Eastern Australia's Policy toward the Aborigine," *Journal of Modern History*, xxxiii (1961), 261–269; and Robert Travers, *The Tasmanians* (Melbourne: Castle, 1968).

19 Broom and Jones, *A Blanket a Year*, 7.

20 Department of Territories (pub.), *The Australian Aborigines* (Canberra, 1967), 48.

21 Ibid., 33–35.

22 See C. D. Rowley, *The Destruction of Aboriginal Society* (Canberra: Australian National University Press, 1970), 290–297.

23 Broom and Jones, *A Blanket a Year*, 41.

24 Ibid., 43.

25 For example, Pastor (now Sir) Douglas Nicholls, the first Aboriginal to have been knighted by Her Majesty the Queen.

26 The late Dr. D. F. Thomson in 1935–1936 and 1936–1937, for a total of twenty-six months, made two expeditions into Arnhem Land to assist the federal government to understand the Aboriginal situation, which at that time was very disturbed. See his *Interim General Report of Preliminary Expedition to Arnhem Land, Northern Territory of Australia, 1936–1937* (Canberra: Government

Printer, 1936). See also his "Recommendations of Policy in Native Affairs in the Northern Territory of Australia," *Commonwealth Parliamentary Papers* (1937–1940), iii, 805–812. As regards the similarity with the New Guinea experience, see W. R. Jacobs, "The Fatal Confrontation," *Pacific Historical Review*, xl (1971), 283–309.

27 Department of Territories, *Australian Aborigines*, 43.

28 Ibid., 44.

29 W. E. H. Stanner, "Continuity and Change among the Aborigines," *The Australian Journal of Science*, xxi (December 1958), 103–104.

M. P. K. SORRENSON

New Zealand: Maori and Pakeha

It has been a common assumption, in this century if not the last, that New Zealand's race relations have been better than those of Australia, the United States, or South Africa. Indeed a recent article by a leading New Zealand historian accepted this as an axiom and simply went on to ask why.[1] As has often been pointed out, there has been since the turn of the century, and especially since 1920, a Maori renaissance marked by considerable improvements in the demographic, social, and economic status of the Maoris. Such improvements have provided the opportunity for much self-congratulation. New Zealand's "success" in handling the "natives" at home was used by Premier Richard J. Seddon at the beginning of the century to justify demands for empire in the South Pacific. More recent foreign policy statements relating to racial conflicts abroad have commonly been prefaced by complacent reference to amicable race relations at home.

There is substance in all these assumptions, but they need to be qualified. Visiting observers, who have taken rather more trouble to discover Maori attitudes than the average Pakeha (European) New Zealander takes in a lifetime, have commonly found considerable friction and unease. In 1937 Dr. S. M. Lambert, representative in the South Pacific of the Rockefeller Foundation, observed that "the general conception that New Zealand is tolerant of coloured races, in my opinion is not true. The average N.Z.er rarely sees a Maori; in the large centers he rarely appears. When one goes out in a Maori district one finds the same racial antagonism as is found in other countries when a coloured race becomes familiar and competitive and has a lower standard of living."[2] More recent visitors like Robin W. Winks and David P. Ausubel have made similar comments.[3] In a qualitative situation of considerable complexity, it is not possible to make definitive judgments. New Zealand race relations are not necessarily better than those in other countries, though they do have some different characteristics.

This essay, like most discussions of race relations in New Zealand, is confined to the indigenous Maori and immigrant Pakeha communities, and even in this context it is far from exhaustive. Owing to a rigid—and successfully disguised—white New Zealand immigration policy, non-European immigration has been severely restricted, except for a slight influx of island Polynesians since 1945.[4] The insignificance of non-Polynesian ethnic minorities within the total population is clearly revealed by table 1.[5] The fact that New Zealand has admitted, though scarcely encouraged, immigration from existing and former colonial territories of the South Pacific has enabled it to escape some of the opprobrium heaped on Australia for continuing to operate a white immigration policy; but New Zealand's policy can hardly continue unmodified. The European preponderance within the New Zealand population is slowly decreasing and will continue to do so.

Nineteenth-Century Heritage

New Zealand began its history as a British colony on a wave of humanitarian idealism.[6] This was reflected in the Treaty of Waitangi of 1840, with its promise to respect the Maoris' rights to land and to grant them the rights and privileges of British subjects. It was hoped that the rights of the Maoris could be reconciled with the needs of colonization and that the two races could be amalgamated—in effect, that the Maoris could be assimilated into European civilization. The ideal was in many ways naive and overoptimistic. Rapid European colonization soon provoked bitter disputes over land, with sporadic fighting in the 1840s and more widespread war in the 1860s. British troops were needed to break the back of Maori resistance, though after 1865 it was possible to rely on colonial militia supported by Maori auxiliaries. The colonists were granted a representative constitution in 1852, a large measure of internal self-government in 1856, and control over native affairs in 1861. They lost no time in turning this power, and the fruits of military victory, to their advantage. Under the New Zealand Settlements Act of 1863, they confiscated some three million acres of land belonging to "rebel" tribes (subsequently about half of this was paid for or returned). Under the Native Lands Acts of 1862 and 1865, they abolished the Crown's right of

TABLE 1. RACIAL PERCENTAGES IN NEW ZEALAND POPULATION

Census	Race	Numbers	% of Population
1921	European	1,207,763	95.09
	Maori	56,987	4.50
	Island Polynesian	331	.03
	Chinese	3,241	.26
	Indian	605	.06
1976	European	2,693,183	86.10
	Maori	270,035	8.60
	Island Polynesian	61,354	2.00
	Chinese	14,860	.50
	Indian	9,247	.30
	Other	80,704	2.50

SOURCE: New Zealand census returns.

preemption, laid down in the Treaty of Waitangi, and allowed settlers to purchase land directly from Maori owners, after a Native Land Court had adjudicated and individualized the Maori titles. The land acts initiated an era of "free trade" in Maori land in which the greater part of the North Island passed into European hands.[7] By 1900 the Maori estate in the North Island had been reduced from some twenty-eight to seven million acres, and this area was to be halved in the twentieth century. The confiscation and "free trade" in Maori lands were carried out in an often unscrupulous manner that has left a legacy of bitterness.

Though the land legislation of the 1860s was designed primarily to facilitate the needs of European colonization, it was also regarded as an essential part of a larger policy, the amalgamation of the races—the colonial legislators remained heirs to the imperial civilizing mission. Anxious to bring Maoris and their land within the authority of colonial law, they were willing to concede in return that Maoris should have the rights and privileges of British subjects, including the right to appeal to the courts (clarified in the Native Rights Act, 1865) and the right to elect four members of Parliament (the Native Representation Act, 1867). Provision was made for village schools in 1867, and there were spasmodic attempts to provide medical assistance. But this was about as far as nineteenth-century politicians, wedded to laissez faire principles, would go in providing aid. They assumed that European civilization would catch on like a benevolent infection.

In fact, contact with Europeans was proving to be a mixed blessing, indeed was very nearly fatal for Maoris. The alienation of their land was often accompanied by prolonged social dislocation and dissipation. There was little opportunity and no assistance to farm the land that they retained. And European diseases continued to reduce the Maori population. It was not until the turn of the century that the trend was reversed (see table 2).

The twentieth-century revival was facilitated by improved living conditions, the development of resistance to disease, increased government assistance especially in the field of health, a slowing down of land acquisition, and vigorous new Maori leadership.[8] Notable here was the work of James Carroll, the half-Maori minister of native affairs from 1899 to 1912, and several young Maori graduates he brought into public life, including the medical graduates Maui Pomare and Peter Buck, who led the Maori hygiene division of the newly created Department of Health, and Apirana Ngata, a graduate in arts and law, whose main work lay in land development and tenure reform. On their entry into Parliament, these men formed what has been called the Young Maori party. Their work in promoting a Maori renaissance is well known, but it is worth adding that they could hardly have succeeded without the sympathetic support from Maori communities in which the old leadership, still smarting under nineteenth-century grievances, was giving way to younger, better educated men and without at least some support from a European legislature rather more sympathetic to Maori welfare than it had been in the past.

Yet the Maori revival had hardly got under way when New Zealand became involved in the First World War. Pomare and Ngata organized a contingent of Maori volunteers, and Buck resigned his seat in Parliament to accompany it as medical officer. Nevertheless, there was strong resistance to volunteering in Maori districts that had been involved in the wars of the 1860s, and just before the war ended conscription was introduced to catch Maori draft dodgers. Here was a reminder that racial animosities of the nineteenth century were still alive. But the fact that many Maoris had answered the call and fought with distinction at Gallipoli and in France meant that they could not be ignored in the postwar years.

TABLE 2. MAORI PERCENTAGES OF NEW ZEALAND POPULATION

Census	Maoris	Maori % of N.Z. Population
1858	55,049	48.6
1874	47,330	13.7
1881	45,141	8.6
1896	42,113	5.7
1901	45,549	5.6

SOURCE: New Zealand census returns.

Between the World Wars

The interwar years were marked in New Zealand, as elsewhere, by economic uncertainty, giving way in 1929 to acute depression and in the late 1930s to a slow recovery. In the circumstances race relations were bound to come under strain, though the Maori people were not sufficiently integrated into the economy to offer serious competition with unemployed Europeans for jobs and benefits. During the worst of the depression, Europeans suffered a fall in their standard of living, but some Maoris achieved an advance as a result of land development. Indeed, there was such an improvement in the Maori condition that one historian has felt inclined to describe the interwar period, not the years before the First World War, as the time of the Maori renaissance.[9]

At the beginning of the period, however, the Maori revival suffered a severe check. The influenza epidemic of 1918–1919 caused far more Maori than Pakeha casualties: among the Maoris a death rate of 22.6 percent compared with 4.9 percent for Europeans.[10] To add to their disillusion Maori exservicemen found that they were not provided with the generous rehabilitation assistance that was granted European exservicemen.[11] Disgruntled and bewildered, many Maoris began to turn away from the Young Maori party to the faith healer and prophet, T. W. Ratana.

Despite the setback of the influenza epidemic, Maori population recovery was rapid: from about 1926 Maoris were increasing more rapidly than Europeans and becoming a slightly larger segment of the total population (see table 3).

Prewar census figures had been greeted with some skepticism. Some held that the Maori populations was not really increasing, merely that the enumeration was becoming more effective. But

TABLE 3. MAORI PERCENTAGES OF NEW ZEALAND POPULATION

Census	Europeans	Maoris	Maori % of N.Z. Population
1921	1,214,677	56,987	4.5
1926	1,344,469	63,670	4.5
1936	1,491,484	82,326	5.2

SOURCE: New Zealand census returns. The 1931 census was abandoned as an economy measure.

by 1926 there was no doubt that the numbers of Maoris were on the rise. As one senior official patronizingly remarked, "It is satisfactory to know that such a noble race is not dying out as we feared."[12] In the circumstances it was no longer possible to justify continued acquisition of Maori land. By 1920 the land in Maori ownership had been reduced to about nineteen acres per head—much of this was remote, rugged, and bush-clad—and there was a danger of Maori paupers becoming a burden on the state. It was indeed a good time to call on the state to assist Maori land development. And this time there was likely to be a more sympathetic European response, since J. G. Coates, who had taken over the portfolio of Native Affairs in 1921 and retained it when he became prime minister in 1925, was more ready to heed Maori demands than his predecessor had been.

Equally important, Coates was prepared to investigate Maori grievances resulting from nineteenth-century acquisition of Maori land. In the 1920s several commissions of inquiry were appointed; the most important was the royal commission appointed in 1926 to examine the confiscations of the 1860s. This commission's powers were limited because it could recommend only monetary compensation, not the return of unjustly confiscated land. The commission reported in 1928[13] that all the confiscations except one (at Tauranga where most of the land had been returned) had been unjust or excessive. It recommended that the government pay in perpetuity the sum of $NZ 10,000 per annum to the Taranaki tribes, $NZ 6,000 per annum to the Waikato tribes, and $NZ 600 per annum (plus a lump sum of $NZ 40,000) to the Whakatohea of Whakatane. The recommendations were accepted by the Coates government and by all the tribes except the Waikato, who, after prolonged negotiations, eventually accepted an offer by the Labour government in the 1940s to raise the compensation to that

paid to the Taranaki. At the time the compensation seemed reasonable enough, though inflation has long since eroded its value.
Yet it was not so much the money that counted but the final
admission by Pakehas that the confiscations had been unjust; this
considerably improved the climate of race relations and facilitated
cooperation over land development.

There had already been considerable progress in land development, much of it inspired by Ngata.[14] Working first among his
Ngatiporou tribe of the East Coast, he had started two major land
reforms before the war. First, there was the system known as incorporation, whereby large blocks of land still in multiple ownership were taken over and farmed as single units by committees
of owners who in turn employed an experienced manager (often,
for a start, a European) and used Maori labor, selected from those
who had an interest in the block. The incorporations had many
of the characteristics of a limited liability company and could provide more security for credit than the individual holders would
have been able to offer. The system proved particularly effective
on the East Coast, where most of the land was suitable for extensive pastoralism and needed to be farmed in large units, but
it also could be applied to other activities like forestry. Ultimately,
some three hundred incorporations were formed.

Ngata's other land reform was known as consolidation; it was
a gathering together in contiguous holdings of an individual's fragments of land which hitherto had been dispersed throughout tribal
lands. Consolidation of land into individual family holdings was
desirable where the land was suitable for dairying. At first Ngata
used a laborious process of mutually exchanging fragments. That
could be effective with his own tribe but was unlikely to work
with others. After the war the procedure was simplified by merely
listing on paper the value of each individual's land rights and ap-
portioning these as consolidated holdings. To be effective this new
system had to be operated on a large scale; if possible, all tribal
lands needed to be consolidated in one operation. The new system
was first applied to the Urewera tribe in 1922 and then, as Ngata
was able to assemble teams of consolidators, to other tribes later
in the 1920s.

Incorporation and consolidation needed to be accompanied by
the development of land and effective farming. State resources had
long been used to assist European farmers, notably in the use of
cheap credit; therefore, Ngata was determined that Maoris should
have a similar benefit. In the mid-1920s he promoted dairy farming

on the consolidated holdings in the fertile Waiapu valley of the Ngatiporou country. He established a cooperative dairy factory, owned by the farmers, to process and market their produce. In 1926 he invited Coates to inspect the farms; the prime minister was so impressed that he agreed to advance Maori Land Board funds for land development before titles had been consolidated.

In 1928 Coates's Reform party lost office. In the new United government, Ngata became minister of native affairs. He used state funds for a rapidly expanding Maori land-development program and continued to increase expenditures, despite cutbacks in spending in other departments in response to the deepening depression. By the end of 1931, when the economy was in dire straits, Ngata had commenced thirty-nine land-development schemes, covering over half a million acres. In 1929–1930 $NZ 13,022 was spent on Maori land development; by 1935–1936 the sum had increased to $NZ 558,020.[15] In his haste to press ahead, Ngata took personal control of most of the schemes, cut through departmental red tape (even if it meant ignoring set procedures of accounting), and did not hesitate to fire European farm supervisors who could not get on with local Maori leaders. There was much press criticism of Ngata's "high-handed" methods and, when this was joined by the Departments of the Treasury and the Auditor-General, Prime Minister George Forbes gave way and set up a commission of inquiry. The commission reported in 1934 to the effect that Ngata had ignored proper civil service procedures, had used state funds in the interests of his tribe, and had allowed departmental supplies and vehicles to be used for private purposes. The report also stated that some of his subordinates had been involved in fraud.[16] Ngata accepted responsibility for the disclosures and resigned office. His colleagues were forced to follow suit a year later, having suffered resounding defeat at the polls, and the Labour party, which had relentlessly criticized Ngata, took over.

Labour, however, was content to accept, indeed to expand, Ngata's land-development schemes. By 1939 some 840,000 acres had been put under development at a budgeted cost of $NZ 1,350,000 for Maori land development. Some 1,900 farmers had been established on holdings, and another 3,000 were employed as farm workers.[17] But it had now become evident that Maori land development could no longer provide a livelihood for the bulk of the rapidly increasing Maori population. Already there was a significant urban movement—by 1936 11.2 percent of the Maori population was described in the census as living in urban areas—and this process was to be accelerated during the Second World War. Labour had also begun to deal with the urgent problem of Maori housing—according to the 1936 census 71 percent of Maori houses were either inadequate shacks or grossly overcrowded[18]—by making loans available on easy repayment terms or building rental houses. The comprehensive free medical and social security benefits which Labour introduced in 1938 were, with the exception of some pensions and widows' benefits, made available to Maoris on the same basis as to Europeans. These, with the fuller employment which followed from the returning prosperity in the late 1930s, meant a considerable improvement in the Maori standard of living.

Such improvements in the conditions of the Maoris seemed to indicate that they were being steadily integrated into the European economy and that the two races were gradually being amalgamated. The trend seemed to be confirmed by several studies of acculturation which were carried out in this period. F. M. Keesking's *The Changing Maori* (1928) and the penultimate chapter of Raymond Firth's *Primitive Economics of the New Zealand Maori* (1929) are typical examples. Firth's applied anthropology tended to regard acculturation as a unilinear process of Europeanization. The discussion of recent Maori history—Firth called this latest period "The Acceptance of European Standards"[19]—was confined mainly to Maori material progress and the work of the Young Maori party. But that was somewhat misleading, since the renaissance was as much a revival of Maori culture as it was an adaptation of European standards and economic techniques. Ngata certainly wanted Maoris to adopt European methods of farming; but they were to do so within a Maori context and, wherever possible, under Maori leadership. And, far from allowing modernization to promote detribalization, Ngata wanted to transform the old tribal animosities into peaceful competition in land development, cultural activities, and sport. Beyond the tribe there was a rather vague concept of a Maori nation, variously expressed as the Maori people, the race, the *iwi*,[20] and the oft-repeated exhortation, first voiced by Carroll in 1920, "to hold fast to Maoritanga." Carroll said that it would be for others to define this term—"to give it hands and give it feet"[21]—and it has generally been equated with "Maoriness." Maoritanga has been promoted in various ways: by the preservation of Maori language; by the performance, recording, translation, and publication of Maori myths, legends, songs, poetry, and dances; by the perpetuation of arts and crafts; by the construction of meetinghouses and the preservation of *marae*, as focal points for ceremonial; by the continuation of *tangihanga* (funeral wakes), *hui* (feasts), and *korero* (speechmaking). Leaders of the Young Maori party, particularly Ngata, were active in promoting all these kinds of Maoritanga.

Yet it would be misleading to concentrate solely on the work of the giants of the Young Maori party, as tended to be the case with books and articles published in the interwar period. It was common to ignore other groups, notably the Ratana movement.[22] Founded by the faith healer, T. W. Ratana, in 1918, the movement soon began to attract adherents from the established, European-controlled churches, though these, with the exception of the Methodists, were soon to break with Ratana on doctrinal grounds. Unperturbed, Ratana went on to found his own church, which was duly registered in 1925. The Anglicans quickly conceded Maori demands for a Maori bishop by appointing F. A. Bennett, a member of a prominent Anglo-Maori family, as bishop of Aotearoa in 1927, and other churches began to devote more attention to Maori mission activities. The Ratana spiritual tide was stemmed; though formal membership in the Ratana church continued to increase until about the mid-1930s, it did not exceed 20 percent of the Maori population.[23]

Ratana's political influence was to be far more profound. From the beginning, he had represented himself as the savior of the *morehu*, the dispossessed ones. In 1924 he took a petition to King George V urging the settlement of Maori land grievances and the ratification of the Treaty of Waitangi. Like previous Maori petitioners, Ratana was politely referred back to the New Zealand Parliament, a reminder that he had to enter the New Zealand political arena if he were to have any influence. Though he did not stand for Parliament, he announced in 1928 that his candidates would capture the Four Quarters—the four Maori electorates. That prophecy was steadily fulfilled: in 1932 Eruera Tirikatene captured Southern Maori for Ratana; Western Maori followed in 1935; Northern Maori in 1938; and Eastern Maori, the seat which the great Ngata had held for thirty-eight years, in 1943. Since then the Ratana hold on the four seats has been broken only once, when a Maori Mormon briefly held a seat. Ratana's political success was due largely to two factors: first, the thorough identification of his movement with the expanding Maori proletariat; second, his political alliance with the political representatives of the Pakeha proletariat, the Labour party, effected by Ratana and the Labour leader, M. J. Savage, on the morrow of Labour's victory in 1935. The alliance has remained unbroken.

The War and Postwar Developments

The Second World War did not produce the strains in race relations that had been evident during and immediately after the first war. Once more a volunteer Maori battalion was created, and the veteran Ngata, now joined by the Ratana M.P.s, played an active role in recruiting it and in organizing the Maori war effort. This time volunteers came forward freely from all tribal areas. Though the first commander of the battalion was a Pakeha, he was soon replaced by a Maori and thereafter the battalion had Maori officers. The battalion fought with some distinction in Crete, North Africa, and Italy; one of its number, Te Moana Nui a Kiwa Ngarimu, was posthumously awarded the Victoria Cross. At home the Maori communities gave generously to the war effort, and Maori labor was used extensively for producing and packing food, mainly for American troops in the Pacific, or for urban industries hastily devised to meet wartime shortages.

The opening of the war had not prevented New Zealand from celebrating its centenary in 1940. The centennial exhibition in Wellington, the numerous publications that marked the event, including *The Maori People Today*, edited by I. L. G. Sutherland, and the *hui* for the opening of the great carved meetinghouse at Waitangi were used by Maori and Pakeha leaders alike to applaud the New Zealand achievement in race relations. So too was the large *hui* of 1943, at which the V.C. was ceremoniously presented to Ngarimu's parents. Prime Minister Fraser was as eager as Ngata to make the most of these opportunities.

When the war ended there was no question of the Maori ex-servicemen's not receiving the same treatment as their fellow Pakeha veterans. Some got financial aid to start them off on farms or businesses; others were given trade training or educational assistance. In recognition of problems arising from increased Maori urbanization, some of the trade-training schemes started for ex-servicemen were continued for young Maori civilians, and the government appointed Maori welfare officers to the staff of the Maori Affairs Department.[24] In 1945 the Maori Social and Economic Advancement Act was passed. It formally recognized and provided subsidies for a network of tribal committees charged with promoting Maori welfare and the preservation of Maori culture. Significantly, Labour was moving away from the age-old policy of assimilation. Fraser, who became minister for Maori affairs in 1947, had a deep sympathy for the Maoris' attempt to preserve their cultural identity and frequently compared Maori tribalism to the Scottish clan system. In his final report as minister of Maori affairs in 1949, he proclaimed: "An independent, self-reliant, and satisfied Maori race working side by side with the Pakeha and with equal incentives, advantages, and rewards for the effort in all walks of life is the goal of the Government."[25] It is not surprising that Labour was able to retain its Maori mandate since Fraser's goal was very like that which Maoris had sought for years; Labour's only trouble was that it lost the Pakeha mandate in the 1949 election.

To some extent, however, Labour had merely been tampering with problems that were inherent in a situation caused by rapid increases in Maori population and an equally rapid Maori urbanization.[26] These demographic developments are reflected in tables 4 and 5. Since the Maori population is not spread evenly over the whole country but is concentrated largely in the northern half of the North Island, its density in some northern areas is in fact much higher than the national average.

As the pace of Maori urban migration[27] increased, overcrowding became common in the poorer tenement areas of the cities; there was a danger that these would become racial ghettos. Since the war there had been an acute housing shortage. Maoris found great difficulty in obtaining better housing since most of them had unskilled, low-paid jobs, large families, and little capital or access to credit; and sometimes they were discriminated against by landlords or land agents. There was also some discrimination against them in pubs, schools, and cinemas. By the mid-1950s there was acute tension in some inner-city districts and in one or two rural towns like Pukekohe, a market gardening area where Maoris provided most of the labor force. The exclusion of Dr. Henry Bennett, a well-known Maori psychiatrist and a son of the first bishop of Aotearoa, from a small-town pub provoked a storm of criticism which reached the overseas press. There was a danger that New Zealand's cherished reputation for amicable race relations would be tarnished.

To its credit, the National government acted speedily to avert a crisis. Acts of discrimination were publicly disavowed. The welfare and land-development policies of the Labour government were carried on. More important now there was a crash program in

TABLE 4. MAORI PERCENTAGES OF NEW ZEALAND POPULATION

Census	Europeans	Maoris	Maori % of N.Z. Population
1945	1,647,635	100,044	5.8
1951	1,825,626	115,740	6.0
1956	2,038,883	137,151	6.3
1961	2,250,153	167,086	6.9
1966	2,477,376	201,159	7.5
1971	2,635,217	227,414	8.0

SOURCE: New Zealand census returns.

providing trade training and urban housing. The Maori Affairs Department took the lead in building houses for rent or sale to Maori families. The housing program had a dual objective: first, to clear congested inner districts; second, by scattering ("pepper-potting") Maori families throughout new working-class suburbs, to hasten the process of assimilation.[28] It was hoped that Maori families, surrounded by Europeans, would soon adopt the mores of suburbia. In some respects they did so only too well. Anxious to fill their new homes with all the modern conveniences that were thought to be essential, Maori householders often became overencumbered with hire-purchase debts. The new suburbs lacked essential community facilities, and the Maori families, torn away from their rural lives and often without the steadying influence of tribal elders, were in a rootless situation. The young often became involved in petty crime and disturbances; some formed themselves into gangs. A situation all too familiar in societies undergoing rapid urbanization overseas was appearing for the first time in New Zealand.

The National government was content to press ahead with a program of assimilation, trying anxiously to eliminate remaining vestiges of legal inequality. In 1960 the Maori Affairs Department published a major statement of policy, known as the Hunn Report. It listed the remaining inequalities (most of these in fact discriminated in favor of Maoris) and recommended their gradual elimination. The report contained an important discussion and definition of policy. It rejected any form of segregation of the races. It also rejected assimilation, at least as an immediate objective of government policy, while admitting that "signs are not wanting that that may be the destiny of the two races in New Zealand."[29]

TABLE 5. PERCENTAGE OF N.Z. POPULATION LIVING IN URBAN AREAS

Census	Maori	Total N.Z.
1951	29.0	72.7
1956	34.7	73.8
1961	46.0	76.4
1966	61.1	79.3
1971	70.2	81.5

SOURCE: *New Zealand Official Year Book, 1972,* p. 63.

Finally, the report came down in favor of a middle policy called "integration," defined as an attempt "to combine (not fuse) the Maori and Pakeha elements to form one nation wherein Maori culture remains distinct."[30] The report was greeted with much Maori criticism. Even those who were prepared to accept integration as a goal were disturbed by the government's implementation of it, which they saw as nothing but the old policy of assimilation.[31] "Pepper-potting" of Maori housing was but one instance. There was also the bitterly resented attempt by the government to halt uneconomic fragmentation of Maori land by the compulsory purchase of interests of value less than $NZ 50, the abolition of the so-called Maori schools,[32] the streamlining of the judicial system, and the failure positively to promote Maori culture. There is little doubt that National governments were responding to majority European opinion, which assumed that it was sufficient to provide Maoris with equal opportunities (but no favors) in the law courts, education, housing, and employment. It was widely assumed that the government intended to abolish the four Maori parliamentary seats and include Maori voters on the ordinary rolls, but no National government proved willing to grasp this nettle. Though the National party has held office for all but six years of the period since 1949, it did not once capture a Maori seat. This was sure evidence of the electoral unpopularity of the National government's administration of Maori affairs.

Yet it was also a consequence of the continuing low socioeconomic status of the Maori people within the New Zealand community. Despite undoubted improvements in Maori health and housing and despite their fuller integration into the national economy, Maoris remained dangerously overrepresented in lower paid, unskilled forms of employment and badly underrepresented in highly skilled, professional, commercial, managerial, and administrative positions.[33] They have failed to reach the higher rungs of the establishment because not enough of them have passed a series of competitive examinations at secondary and tertiary levels of education. Dropouts from the educational system have helped populate the prisons; Maoris, according to the official statistics, have a higher rate of crime than Pakehas. But in education, as in crime, it is not so much that Maoris are failing as it is that they are being failed by an alien system ill adapted to their needs and aspirations. With its education, as with its judicial system, New Zealand is forcing a monocultural system onto a multicultural society. In consequence race relations have again come under strain.

This failure to accommodate an ethnic minority, to recognize and preserve its identity, is not unique to New Zealand. Indeed, New Zealanders have still to learn the lesson that their race relations are neither very different nor necessarily better than race relations in other countries with a similar ethnic composition. Moreover, New Zealand's race relations are being complicated by the influx of Polynesians, most of them from the former New Zealand territories in the South Pacific—Western Samoa, the Cook Islands, Niue, and the Tokelaus. The 1971 census recorded 45,413 Polynesians other than Maoris living in New Zealand, 1.6 percent of the total population. Since the islanders compete with local New Zealanders and especially with Maoris for employment, housing, and social services, there are and will continue to be stresses in race relations. But there are also advantages, so far only barely appreciated, of this recent Polynesian migration to New Zealand. The islanders bring further cultural diversity to a country that has long been characterized by a dull conformity to Anglo-Saxon cultural norms. It is from the diverse Polynesian cultures—and from indigenous developments in Pakeha society—that New Zealand will find its national identity. The real significance of race relations over the last fifty years is that Maoris, and lately other Polynesians, have begun to recover the place in New Zealand that was very nearly obliterated by a century of European colonization and all that that meant. But there is a very long way to go, for Maoris have little more than their *turangawaewae* (a standing place for the feet) and some of them not even this, in a land that was once theirs.

It was Frank Corner, later to become secretary for foreign affairs, who said in 1962 that "the renaissance of the Maori people is making New Zealand the chief country of Polynesia and restoring our moral right to take a leading part in its affairs."[34] Here was a new version of an old myth: New Zealand, by virtue of its treatment of Polynesians at home, had the right to handle them abroad. Certainly there has been an improvement in relations with island Polynesians since the hysterical imperialism of the nineteenth century with "Vogel and Seddon howling empire from an empty coast"; or even at the outbreak of the First World War when "in an atavistic flurry of imperialism, New Zealand had acquired Western Samoa";[35] or, yet again, in the later 1920s when New Zealand's heavy-handed paternalism provoked the Mau resistance in Samoa. But it was only in the latter stages of New Zealand's rule in Samoa and elsewhere that the paternal civilizing mission— so characteristic of nineteenth-century treatment of the Maoris— gave way to an enlightened appreciation of Polynesian values and aspirations, including their desire for a full or qualified form of independence. The change came in the late 1930s. It was reinforced by the high ideals of the Atlantic Charter and given direction by the Trusteeship Committee of the San Francisco Conference, which was chaired by Peter Fraser. In the islands New Zealand was well served by administrators like Guy (later Sir Guy) Powles and J. M. McEwen and by constitutional advisers like J. W. Davidson and Colin Aickman. In the two decades after the Second World War, New Zealand was to guide its main island territories to independence in a manner which won it international acclaim. But whether it will retain a moral right to exercise a leading part in Polynesian affairs will depend on its treatment of Polynesians at home and abroad. That right is by no means assured.

Notes

I have not attempted to take the discussion past 1976, the date of the last census. Maori words not in common usage are italicized with translations in parentheses. Currency figures are in New Zealand, not United States, dollars.

1 Keith Sinclair, "Why Are Race Relations in New Zealand Better Than in South Africa, South Australia or South Dakota," *New Zealand Journal of History*, V, 2 (October 1971), 121–127.

2 J. Forster, "The Social Position of the Maori," in Erik Schwimmer (ed.), *The Maori People in the Nineteen-Sixties* (London: C. Hurst, 1968), 104.

3 Robin W. Winks, *These New Zealanders* (Christchurch: Whitcombe and Tombs, 1954); David P. Ausebel, *The Fern and the Tiki* (Sydney: Angus and Robertson, 1960).

4 P. S. O'Connor, "Keeping New Zealand White, 1908–1921," *New Zealand Journal of History*, II, 1 (April 1968), 41–65.

5 Unless otherwise indicated, all figures are taken from New Zealand census returns.

6 The best of numerous discussions of early colonization and racial conflicts are Keith Sinclair, *The Origins of the Maori Wars* (Wellington: New Zealand University Press, 1957), and Alan D. Ward, *A Show of Justice* (Toronto: University of Toronto Press, 1973).

7 M. P. K. Sorrenson, "The Purchase of Maori Lands, 1865–1892" (M.A. thesis, University of Auckland, 1955).

8 John Adrian Williams, *Politics of the New Zealand Maori* (Seattle: University of Washington Press, 1969); R. T. Lange, "The Revival of a Dying Race: A Study of Maori Health Reform, 1900–1918" (M.A. thesis, University of Auckland, 1972).

9 G. V. Butterworth, "A Rural Maori Renaissance? Maori Society and Politics, 1920–1951," *Journal of the Polynesian Society*, 81, 2 (June 1972), 160.

10 J. M. Henderson, *Ratana: The Man, the Church, the Political Movement* (2d ed., Wellington: Polynesian Society, 1972), 17.

11 Butterworth, op. cit., 165.

12 Ibid., 168.

13 *Appendices to the Journal of the House of Representatives (A.J.H.R.)* 1928, G-8.

14 M. P. K. Sorrenson, "Maori Land Development," *New Zealand's Heritage*, 6, pt. 83 (1973), 2309–2315; Butterworth, op. cit., 174–178; J. B. Condliffe, *New Zealand in the Making* (Chicago: University of Chicago Press, 1930), chap. 2; F. M. Keesing, "Maori Progress on the East Coast," *Te Wananga*, I (1929), 10–55, 92–93.

15 Butterworth, op. cit., 176.

16 *A.J.H.R.* 1934, G-11.

17 Butterworth, op. cit., 180–181.

18 Ibid., 181.

19 Ibid., 457.

20 *Iwi* is usually translated as "tribe" but Buck and Ngata often equated it with "the people" or "the race." Buck-Ngata correspondence, 1927–1937, passim, Ramsden Papers, Alexander Turnbull Library, Wellington.

21 Alice Joan Metge, *The Maoris of New Zealand* (London: Routledge & Kegan Paul, 1967), 59.

22 The main study is Henderson's *Ratana*.

23 Ibid., 121.

24 Butterworth, op. cit., 187–190.

25 Ibid., 188.

26 *New Zealand Official Year Book*, 1972, p. 63. Here "urban" is described as a concentration of 1,000 people.

27 The main source is Alice Joan Metge, *A New Maori Migration: Rural and Urban Relations in Northern New Zealand* (London: University of London, Athlone Press, 1964).

28 Metge, *Maoris of New Zealand*, 80.

29 J. K. Hunn, *Report on Department of Maori Affairs* (Wellington: Government Printer, 1960), 15.

30 Loc. cit.

31 Metge, *Maoris of New Zealand,* 216.

32 These were primary schools established by the Labour government in the late 1930s in districts where there was a preponderance of Maoris. They had a special curriculum with some emphasis on Maori culture. Pakeha children could and sometimes did attend them, but there was a danger that they would become a vehicle for educational segregation—hence their abolition by the National government despite Maori opposition.

33 Department of Industries and Commerce, *The Maori in the New Zealand Economy* (1967). The report was compiled mainly by G. V. Butterworth.

34 "New Zealand and the South Pacific," in T. C. Larkin (ed.), *New Zealand's External Relations* (Wellington: New Zealand Institute of Public Administration, 1962), 150.

35 Ibid., 137.

DERYCK SCARR

Movement and Change
in the Pacific Islands

All is movement and change—political and otherwise—in the contemporary Pacific islands. It seems so especially to the generation who knew the island scene before the Second World War when economies were miniscule and dependent and when paternalists held government reins—when, for example, if "Native Regulations" were enforced, the men of the Gilbert and Ellice Islands Colony could not take their canoes to sea between November and March. The change must also seem dramatic to island leaders who were once colonial pupils and are now ministers and heads of state.

Fiji is another striking illustration of the Pacific-wide tendency toward change and progress. Ratu Sir George Cakobau, as governor general of Fiji, occupies a gubernatorial dwelling at Suva which is the successor of the one at Levuka to which his great-grandfather came a century ago to pay courtesy calls on the colonial governor. Fiji became a dominion on October 10, 1970, but the transition to independence was difficult. Of all the major Pacific dependencies, Fiji was the one most inclined to retain its metropolitan ties—for the reason that the Fijians feared that the preponderant numbers of Indians would dominate the political life of the islands as they already dominated their economic life. With the adoption of the Independence Constitution, the protection of Fijian rights has been assured, and the Indians have recognized that their physical safety depends on their accepting a second-class political position. Consequently, race relations in Fiji have been far more placid than they have been in such places as Mauritius and Malaysia. Even so, extremes of Fijian nationalism have sometimes been manifest at times of elections. In contrast, the Indian-dominated National Federation party is internally divided, and when in 1977 it won a surprise victory in the general elections, the indecisiveness of its leaders caused foreign observers to wonder whether it had the will to govern. As in other island groups, race relations in Fiji will probably be determined not only by constitutional compromise but also by the general state of the island economy, which in turn may be shaped by such imponderables as emigration and the vicissitudes of great-power politics.

Four days after independence, Fiji joined the United Nations, an appropriate step since it owed its changed status not only to its own nascent nationalism but also to Britain's anxiety from the early 1960s to be free of a potential source of embarrassment at the UN. And, in other parts of the Pacific too where Britain or its dominions have ruled, the United Nations 1960 Declaration on Colonialism had an effect. In New Guinea the pace of change perceptibly quickened after 1962, when a UN Visiting Mission advised Australia that, among other things, it should establish a House of Assembly with a large majority of elected members. The Assembly was first convened in June 1964. Elected members began to serve as quasi ministers; parties formed; and after a visit by the then Labour opposition leader in 1969–1970 the pace accelerated to the point where independence was declared in September 1975.

The emergence of "Niugini" as one of the largest island nations commanded the world's attention because of its size and also because it seemed so unlikely a prospect for independence. But it was only the most recent instance of a series of transfers of power that had been in progress in the Pacific for over a decade. In each case the circumstances of the transfer were unique. In January 1962 Western Samoa led the way by securing independence from New Zealand. Samoa was the pacesetter because, in the words of the late J. W. Davidson, "physical and social conditions made political organization on a national scale easy, and Samoan distaste for alien rule made it inevitable."[1] The Cook Islanders in 1965 chose an entirely different course—not independence but self-government in a special relationship of "free association" with New Zealand. Another type of autonomy can be illustrated in the case of Nauru, which became a republic in January 1968. Nauru is an independent state all of eight and a quarter square miles in extent, isolated in the central Pacific with a population of only 3,500. Until recently it was rich in phosphate and (unlike its companion phosphate island and nearest neighbor, Ocean) the phosphate royalties were secured to the islanders themselves.

New, articulate, and highly self-aware island nations have come into being. Until recently island leaders were often patronized at meetings of the metropolitan-dominated South Pacific Commission. They now also meet in the South Pacific Forum, where their voices have particular resonance and dominance even though Australia and New Zealand too are members. At these meetings, the heads of government of the island groups can make effective decisions that are at least binding on their own nations. And at the South Pacific Forum political discussion cannot be cut short by political or economic threat by the metropolitan governments—not even by France, the government which is most averse to political advancement in the area.

All these developments have come about since the Second World War, partly as a result of forces released locally by the war itself, but still more as part of the general worldwide movement toward decolonization.

In 1939 the Pacific islands' condition and status were much the same as they had been in 1900. The islands were footnotes to imperial pages on which the text had been mainly printed in Africa and the Orient. Except perhaps in the case of fruit shipped to Australia and New Zealand, and some Fijian gold, their produce competed in European markets already well supplied by tropical colonies closer at hand and possessed of greater productive efficiency.

When the Second World War broke out, the Pacific islands were divided politically into nineteen colonial units of varying status. These territories were governed by six metropolitan powers whose rule in many cases had been established in the last decades of the nineteenth century. In many instances the assumption of imperial responsibility had been unplanned and reluctant. For instance, the southern Solomon Islands had been made into a British protectorate in 1893 to keep the French out. The same thing had happened to the Gilbert and Ellice Islands in 1892, when the prospect of a German presence there had similarly prompted Whitehall into action which it would gladly have avoided. Both these territories were acquired with a minimum of imperial concern and outlay. The British Solomon Islands were helped to meet their administrative costs by the copra exports of Levers Pacific Plantations Ltd., which had been encouraged to come into the protectorate by the first resident commissioner. The Gilbert and Ellice Islands were sustained by the royalty they took from Ocean Island's phosphate. It was to secure extraction rights to the phosphate that Ocean was annexed in 1900, before which time the protecting power had not considered it part of the Gilbert group.[2]

In both territories the overall administrative structure was rudimentary: a resident commissioner with a small headquarters staff and a scattering of district officers. In the Gilbert and Ellice Islands, it was true, local government flourished, following traditional patterns in the island councils and—perhaps especially in the Ellice—able to evade the paternalistic hand of the resident commissioners by virtue of remoteness from the administrative center. In the Solomons there was no such clear traditional basis. There district officers and government-appointed headmen held uneasy, superficial sway over extensive populations on large, mountainous islands; and it was not until 1940 that attempts were first made to establish court systems and informal councils giving statutory sanction to existing indigenous practice.[3]

These two territories owed immediate allegiance to the high commissioner for the western Pacific, who until 1952 was additionally—and preeminently—the governor of Fiji. The high commissioner could also claim some allegiance from two curiosities of the Pacific political world, the Kingdom of Tonga and the Anglo-French Condominium of the New Hebrides.

As Hartley Grattan has written, "in an era in the Pacific when native progress toward self-government, let alone political independence, was commonly regarded as a fantasy of disordered idealists," Tonga still retained the sovereignty which had been established in the mid-nineteenth century by Siaosi Tupou I, whose dynasty rules Tonga today.[4] The kingdom's foreign relations were long conducted by Britain under a treaty of 1900, the signing of which had caused Tongans considerable anguish since it carried overtones of a protectorate; and a resident British agent and consul had some voice in internal financial affairs. The sovereignty of the islands, however, was no longer endangered once some turbulent passages in the early 1900s had been negotiated, and Tonga stands out as the only one among the several kingdoms of the nineteenth-century Pacific (Hawaii, Fiji, Samoa) which has never lost its independence.

The New Hebrides are a very different case. Joint French and British administrations have worked there along divergent lines under a Convention of 1906, drawn up as a kind of afterthought to the Entente Cordiale. The principal issue between the two sets of nationals residing in the island group—as also between Europeans and the New Hebrideans—was the fate of land allegedly purchased from the latter. Many thousands of hectares were claimed with the greater number of the deeds in the hands of a company (the *Société Française des Nouvelles-Hébrides*) which was under French government subsidy. Here as elsewhere, the future of land claims depended on the criteria laid down for testing their validity. In Fiji in the nineteenth century, Britain applied the following tests of validity among others: right of vendor to sell, adequacy of price paid, and effective European occupation. In Samoa the same tests were also applied by Britain, together with Germany and the United States. In the negotiations over the New Hebrides convention, the British representatives accepted the provisions of French law that prescriptive right was accorded by a documentary title alone even when the land had not been occupied. The result was that some 600,000 hectares of land, in French hands as far as formal title was concerned but mostly unoccupied, were put beyond effective challenge. Moreover, the common administration set up by the convention, the teeth of which was the Joint Court, was quite incapable in the early years of combating the French residency's determination to allow its nationals a free hand in pressing their trading and above all their plantation interests. No effort was spared by French officials in the protection of disputed land or in the removal by naval force of any New Hebridean who was more effective than others in local opposition to that *mission civilisatrice* of France. In this group of islands that meant the establishment of a white plantation economy.[5]

In the wholly French territories of French Polynesia and New Caledonia, the *mission civilisatrice* had free rein. The effect was to keep both colonies in a degree of political as well as cultural subjection to the metropolitan power that was unusual even for the politically lethargic Pacific. "'Nous sommes ici la France' remained and remains the doctrine," as Harold Brookfield has written.[6] And this dogma was none the less pervasive in its effect despite the fact that each colony enjoyed an active Territorial Assembly.

For French Polynesia, the policy of assimilation with the metropole was laid down by the Organic Decree of 1887, which provided for a governor, five heads of departments, a General Council of eighteen elected members with limited powers, and district councils overshadowed by direct local administration through French officers. This policy of assimilation continued substantially until the end of the Second World War, when it was reinforced by the colony's being granted seats in the National Assembly, the Council of the Republic, and the Assembly of the French Union.

In the wake of the Indochina war and decolonization in Africa, substantial authority was transferred from Paris to Papeete by the *loi-cadre* of 1957. Nevertheless, the structure of government remained centralized, substantially on the metropolitan model. There was not much room for Tahitian as against assimilationist sentiment, and little sympathy was extended to nationalist leaders—so it proved when Pouvanaa a Oopa was jailed in 1958.

Leader of the *Rassemblement Démocratique des Populations-Tahitiennes*, and deputy for French Polynesia in the National Assembly, Pouvanaa had initially sought autonomy for French Polynesia within the French Union and subsequently demanded complete independence. His cry of "Tahiti for the Tahitians" was silenced when he was imprisoned, ostensibly for having plotted to fire Papeete but more likely because in Charles de Gaulle's recent referendum he had campaigned for independence. Pouvanaa has had active successors who have sought autonomy within the French Union. While their cause has been made popular among some voters by French nuclear testing from Tahiti, so equally has France's determination to continue the tests made it the more reluctant to consider increased devolution of power. This determination has been reflected in heavy local expenditure, and the resultant boom in the Tahitian economy (inflationary and socially disastrous though it is) may have something to do with the defeat of the autonomist party at the Territorial Assembly elections of 1972.[7] However, the autonomists have recovered: in 1976 the Territorial Assembly refused to meet; and in 1977 the autonomist deputy in the National Assembly in Paris called for independence, rejecting new statutes with the claim that they tended to neutralize all political opposition in French Polynesia and give control of its natural resources to outside interests approved by Paris. Even so, internal autonomy rather than independence still appears to be the real object.

The issues raised by nuclear testing in French Polynesia were raised in similar fashion by "nickel" in New Caledonia. The history of New Caledonia under French rule, even more than that of French Polynesia, has been dominated by French concern for metropolitan problems—first to get rid of relapsed criminals, then to supply French metallurgical industries. The New Caledonian people have been relegated to the background even more than have the French Polynesians. In French Polynesia, indeed, politics has been in great part the playground of the people of mixed blood, in whose hands lies most of the economic wealth of the colony;

consequently, there is tension between them and the Polynesians, which is a potential source of conflict. Once granted, autonomy may well leave two potentially hostile groups face to face.

No such complication exists in the politics of New Caledonia, except insofar as there is tension between locally born French and metropolitans. The Melanesian population is only slightly more numerous than the European, while the other components of the population (Polynesian and Asian migrants) are transients attracted by the mines. The local assembly has wide budgetary powers and sends representatives to Paris, but nickel dominates and is so indissolubly tied to the metropole that the colony would appear to be indefinitely tied also. But, even in New Caledonia, there have appeared black nationalist youth movements whose aspirations are becoming politically important. They are Melanesian movements, and they take the hitherto despised name "kanaka" with pride. At the very least, internal autonomy is sought—though, according to Professor Jean Guiart, autonomy followed by independence would only serve to put the means of repression into the hands of the Europeans, for whose benefit the economy is currently geared. "Il n'est de l'intérêt de personne de voir se créer une mini-Rhodésie dans le Pacifique Sud."[8]

Curiously enough, the political frustrations of autonomist French Polynesians and New Caledonians find a counterpart in the islands where the compatriots of President Woodrow Wilson have ruled—and where the system of mandates forever associated with his name has long obtained. The Caroline, Marshall, and Mariana islands came into German possession in the 1880s and 1890s and were exploited by Germany for copra. At the 1919 Peace Conference, they went to Japan, which in turn lost them in 1945 to the United States. Under United Nations supervision, they are now governed by America as the Trust Territory of the Pacific Islands. Washington has proved no less tenacious of its role in these islands than Paris has proved elsewhere, with similar metropolitan considerations in view. At Bikini atoll the Americans preceded France in nuclear testing in the Pacific, and the Pentagon's continued interest in the territory for its defense value means that it is averse to Micronesia's secession from American overlordship.

Only since the late 1960s have nationalist movements become important in Micronesia, and that development can be largely attributed to Washington's establishment in 1965 of a central legislature, the Congress of Micronesia. J. W. Davidson, consultant to the Future Political Status Commission set up by Congress in 1967, wrote before his death in April 1973:

> The establishment of Congress soon made it plain that subjection to alien rule had given the people of Micronesia a measure of common purpose and that experience abroad—mainly as students in colleges or universities in the United States—had given an intellectual minority of young men and women a consciousness of being Micronesians, as well as Palauans, Yapese or Ponapeans.[9]

It is not clear that this consciousness has been altogether welcome to the administering authority. Congress proposed a form of "free association" as the basis of Micronesia's future relationship with the U.S., a form which would in some important respects restrict the latter's powers in the Trust Territory. In particular, America would be able to use land for military purposes only in agreement with the government of Micronesia, whereas hitherto it has possessed wide latitude under the UN Agreement which recognizes Micronesia as a strategic territory. One alternative to free association has been seen by some Micronesians as independence. "Though they recognised their special dependence on American aid," wrote Davidson, "many of them now envisage other—and less destructive—means of supporting their country as a separate political entity."[10] American policy, on the contrary, has been to move Micronesia "into a permanent political relationship with the U.S. within our political framework"—as a National Security Council memorandum approved by President John F. Kennedy in 1962 reportedly expressed it. The blueprint outlining the means to achieve this end was confessedly one that would see the U.S. "moving counter to the anti-colonial movement . . . and . . . breaching its own policy . . . of not acquiring new territorial possessions."[11] Once more, as in the case of French Polynesia, it seems likely that the material inducements offered by the metropole may prevail in some islands over fear of cultural dissolution; nevertheless, "Micronesian consciousness" is not proof against the sense of being preeminently a Marianan or a Marshallese.

In June 1975, a majority of the twelve thousand Marianans voted to sever their political ties with the rest of the Trust Territory and accept a relationship with the U.S. giving them their own constitution along with American citizenship and access to $150,000,000 in economic aid. The other five districts agreed on a constitution for themselves in November of that year, but secession is still

a possibility in the Marshalls and Palau. Though American officials speak of possible independence for the territories, the island
economy remains cripplingly unbalanced, the government sector
is inflated, and there are scant indigenous resources. As one observer puts it, "one wonders whether the islands might better be
called a colony in the making rather than a developing country." [12]

In the Pacific island world, the anticolonial movement had been
led by Western Samoa. There internal division in the political system—so marked in the nineteenth century—became less visible
in the twentieth, in part because of the experience of colonial
rule: fourteen years under the Germans, then rule by New Zealand under a League of Nations mandate. Moreover, Samoa had
a traditional sense of nationality. During the 1920s and 1930s an
opposition movement called the "Mau" drew wide support; people
of traditional and modern bent alike, Samoans, part-Samoans, and
local Europeans—all worked together against the New Zealand
administration. The League had scarcely been replaced by the
United Nations when Western Samoa petitioned for self-government, and during the ensuing thirteen years progress toward independence was smoother than in most colonial territories. Independence in January 1962 was thus based on stability and essential
harmony in Samoan political life, qualities that have in fact characterized it since then, perhaps in part because the government
has taken care to respect the strongly autonomous aspirations of
the villages.
    Samoan stability has been largely due, then, to a firmly tradi-
tional society and a well-entrenched sense of nationality. It has
been assisted by the attitude of New Zealand, whose long-continued nineteenth-century chauvinism gave way at last after the
Second World War to a pragmatism and generosity which gave the
country a more enviable record than some other decolonizing
powers. This has also been true of New Zealand's handling of
its other major Pacific responsibility, the Cook Islands, which,
having been given the choice, opted to follow the Samoan example
in a modified form. In August 1965 the Cook Islands achieved
internal self-government; however, since a significant percentage
of the islanders are actually resident in New Zealand, since the
islands are dependent on the New Zealand market, the new state
exists on terms which provide it with access to New Zealand citizenship, consumers, and subventions.
    Until recently New Zealand's attitude toward the islanders on

the whole has been amiable and complacent and thus in some contrast with that of Australia. A change became visible, however, with the outbreak of troubles in Auckland in 1977 over the number of illegal island immigrants, who called attention to the country's very real racial problem. Australia, on the other hand, had long kept its major Pacific responsibility, Papua–New Guinea, under a quaintly old-fashioned rule to which that much over-worked term "paternal" may be accurately applied. As recently as 1961, the Australian Department of Territories seemed to have believed it would continue its highly centralized rule until the end of the century. The emergence of an educated elite was discouraged, and indigenous participation in government was thought practicable only at the most elementary level.

Australia's other responsibility, the tiny Trust Territory of Nauru, was a classic case of economic imperialism. From 1907 the phosphate rock which covers four-fifths of the island was mined, first for the profit of Pacific Phosphate Company share-holders and then from 1919—when the company, in part German-owned, was replaced by the British Phosphate Commission—for the benefit of Australian and New Zealand farmers. The farmers were supplied with high-grade phosphate at a rate which, given the world prices normally obtaining, represented a subsidy paid by the Nauruan people.[13] From the Second World War onward, Nauruan phosphate was sold at between one-third and one-half of the open market price, while the royalty paid to Nauruans—two shillings a ton—was a mockery. It took hard bargaining with the help of outside economic experts, and directly against Australian interests, before the Nauruans' determination to secure control of their sole, and diminishing, resource prevailed. In June 1967 an agreement was reached with the partner governments (Britain, Australia, and New Zealand) by which control of the industry passed to Nauruans. Supply was guaranteed, a price acceptable to both sides was decided, and arrangements were made for the BPC's plant to be purchased by the new Republic of Nauru. This repossession of rights to the phosphate made independence a meaningful goal for the Nauruans. The alternative offered by Australia as the administering power, resettlement within the Commonwealth, had been unattractive to them. Nauruans wished to remain Nauruans.

The emergence of Nauru as an independent republic brought something like a Monaco to the Pacific. Nowhere was the Nauruan example more closely studied, nowhere more meaningful, than on

Rabe Island in the Fiji group where the Banabans—the people of phosphate-rich Ocean Island—live in discontented resettlement. Nor does anything so well illustrate the contrast between old and new in the Pacific world as the differences between Ocean Island and Nauru. While the Republic of Nauru conducts heavily subsidized air and shipping lines under its own flag, Ocean lies firmly in the colonial hands of the British phosphate commissioners. Most of the phosphate profits have gone to the revenue of the Gilbert and Ellice Islands Colony, of which distant Ocean was found to be an integral part only when phosphate had been identified there. Ocean's people, moved to Rabe after the Second World War, live in some insecurity on the proceeds of their investments and the agricultural produce of their new island which, as fishermen-born and not natural farmers, they have not been enthusiastic about developing.

They have lived in hope that the British government would provide a more just settlement of the royalties question. They are also in ever present fear of the day—likely to fall in 1979—when all the phosphate will have been worked out. Perhaps, above all, they have sought vindication of their stand in order to reoccupy their original island homeland with a token community under a flag of their own. At the time of this writing, however, their claim for a greater share and their argument that the Gilbert and Ellice Islands Colony is not properly their financial responsibility have been before the courts, which have found for them morally but in one instance at least have awarded only derisory damages. The fact that economic imperialism so blatant—and, on the detailed evidence of the original transactions, so indefensible in its historical basis—should have persisted for so long is one small indication that the changing climate of world opinion since 1945 has not entirely erased the values and practices of the pre-1939 Pacific.[14]

Similar indications of the lasting effects of imperialism can be found in the New Hebrides. There the spirit of metropolitan domination which on the French side animated the Convention of 1906 has long remained very much alive. The French seem to have subscribed to a domino theory: if significant political advancement were permitted in the wild New Hebrides, considerably more would have to be allowed in the more sophisticated New Caledonia. In New Hebrides the French resident commissioner has been accustomed to stress the continuance of France's "mission," the length of time that must elapse before that mission can be regarded as fulfilled, and the necessary preeminence of the metropole in policy making. This was reflected until recently in the rudimentary nature of political institutions in the territory, the key feature of which was the Advisory Council established in 1957 with only very limited functions. A perceptive observer has noted about more recent developments, "In late 1971 it was proposed to make it obligatory for the Resident Commissioners to consult the Advisory Council about the Condominium budget, taxes and duties and town-planning, and this alone is ample demonstration of the slowness in any distribution of formal political powers." [15] The New Hebrides have lately received a great inflow of capital, attracted by the tax structure. The territory has been made an international tax haven, but not to the noticeable advantage of the islanders. On Espíritu Santo, the largest island in the group, there have been attempts at settlements by Americans and Europeans seeking an escape and a new start in the South Pacific.

The islanders have protested. On Santo the most active group has been one called Nagriamel, a traditionalist movement with some messianic overtones. Its immediate political object was originally to prevent European expansion into the interior. That expansion had its motivation in the transformation of the island European economy. Turning from cutting copra to running cattle, the Europeans have been moving inland to areas which, though recognized as alienated by the Joint Court, had hitherto remained unworked. The Santo people regarded these lands as their own. With their lands expropriated, the New Hebrideans see themselves increasingly as strangers in their own islands; small wonder that they are attracted to a movement like Nagriamel—all the more since it has now acquired a political sophistication infused by the educated native elite in government and church service.[16] As a result, as one analyst wrote in the early 1970s, "the tone of Advisory Council debates has undergone a sea change, and it seems even possible that in this one Melanesian territory the laggardly hand of metropolitan governments will be forced . . . by the vocal emergence of a xenophobic nationalism." [17] The irony of the New Hebridean situation is that the intensely nationalistic Nagriamel seems to have been captured by a group of French investors in league with American land speculators. They have encouraged Nagriamel to declare Santo independent, their object being to secure an international refuge for the rule of unfettered capitalism.

There is also a nationalist movement among British-educated youth, who formed the New Hebridean National party in 1971.

In 1976 they renamed it the Vanuaaka party as a protest against the colonialist name "New Hebrides." At present, the Vanuaaka party is pressing for immediate independence, flying in the teeth of French-oriented parties like Union des Communautés des Nouvelles-Hébrides and Mouvement de L'Action des Nouvelles-Hébrides, which prefer to contemplate taking that plunge in the 1980s, if it must be taken at all.

A fairly clear, and historically very understandable, gulf seems to exist between the British-educated—some would claim, British-inspired—Vanuaaka party and the older traditionalist elements like Nagriamel, now allied not only with the indigenous elites but also with the established French planters, an alliance facilitated by France's policy of handing back the alienated land.

There is no doubt about the ambition of the Vanuaaka party. Its members paraded placards demanding independence for their islands and for New Caledonia in 1978, for Tahiti in 1979. Having won almost 60 percent of the votes in the first elections to the new Representative Assembly in November 1975, Vanuaaka closed the Assembly by boycott in 1977, when it was robbed of its majority by the creation of special seats for the chamber of commerce. At a conference on Tana in June 1977, the party declined to attend a meeting scheduled in Paris to resolve the impasse, saying that the meeting should be held on the spot. The party demanded immediate independence without fresh elections and promised that under its aegis education would be in English alone, not French. This led *Nabanga*, the French residency's news sheet, to comment that the Vanuaaka party was formed by apprentice sorcerers with strong support from Protestant churches, which, as far as the party's origins go, seems to be accurate enough. And, if the apprentice sorcerers had intended primarily to press Paris to accept at least the principle of independence for the New Hebrides, they seem to have won.

In the case of the Solomon Islands, by contrast, London's instinct to decolonize has had fewer fetters. Metropolitan thinking has been more in step with indigenous aspirations, perhaps even ahead of them. The Solomon Islands are still of doubtful economic viability, even in prospect. Politically they are less fragmented than the New Hebrides, though local differences remain strong. Britain's main anxiety clearly has been to get them off its hands. Until 1969 that desire had been demonstrated conventionally enough; an Advisory Council was established shortly after the war, building upon the earlier District Councils, and Legislative and Executive councils were created in the early 1960s. The indigenous response, however, was disappointing, and a fairly radical—though not novel—solution was now attempted. In 1969 a single Governing Council was established, with seventeen elected and nine official members divided into four overlapping committees, the chairmen of which were virtually ministers. In principle this experiment was directed toward achieving consensus in the Melanesian style. The attempt was no doubt admirable, but it failed. The British then introduced a more conventional ministerial system, reportedly in response to local opinion. Internal self-government was achieved in January 1977, and the islands became independent in July 1978. The expectation is that the Solomon Islands will become a republic on the first anniversary of independence.

As in the Solomon Islands, political development in the Gilbert and Ellice Islands was pressed by London during the 1960s. There, as in other island groups, constitution making has a complexity that seems remote from the people's understanding. Nevertheless, a series of councils was created, leading in 1974 to a Legislative Assembly and a Council of Ministers. With internal self-government achieved in January 1977 and independence just over the horizon, finance is a pressing problem. It is hardly surprising, though perhaps unjust, that on the phosphate question local feeling is decidedly that the displaced Banabans are Gilbertese and that the resources of Ocean Island can fairly be used to finance the entire Gilbert and Ellice group. The problems of the colony—political and financial as well—have been vastly complicated by the decision of the culturally distinct Ellice Islanders, who provide a high proportion of the civil servants, to secede. Rather against London's wishes, they formed their own state, Tuvalu, in order to escape Gilbertese resentment at their ubiquity in government service and to insure their cultural identity. And so the Gilbert and Ellice Islands, two island groups associated together for more than three generations under British rule, will soon come separately to independence. In each case the constitution will be a modified version of the Westminster model. But Westminster itself seems determined to insist that the secessionist principle applied to the Ellice Islanders cannot be extended to the Banabans, who so eagerly want to apply it to Ocean Island, because the Gilbertese do not agree. Here is a curious illustration of the paradox of colonial self-determination. The Ellice Islanders have applied the principle and apparently have won, but where should the line be drawn? Are the claims of the Banabans not equally valid? Apparently the British and the Gilbertese do not think so, because the economic resources of Ocean Island (though not those of the Ellice Islands) are necessary to support the Gilberts. In any case the Ellice Islands have seceded, and the new mini-state of Tuvalu with its seven thousand people and its highly dubious economy is an accomplished fact. It has been called "secession in the defence of identity"[18]—an impulse that manifests itself in many other parts of the Pacific as well.

The same impulse is observable also in Niugini, the largest of the Pacific island territories. There is a burgeoning sense of nationalism among some Papuans which may lead to a demand for an independent state. A nationalist sentiment, more serious in its dimensions, can also be found in copper-rich Bougainville. As one of the Bougainville separatist leaders says plainly: "Our fear is that we will always be a fixed, unchallengeable, hopeless minority in the midst of an overwhelming majority."[19] The black Bougainvillians' sense of ethnicity owes much to the feeling that they are simply exchanging white colonialism for the "red-skinned" Niugini counterpart. Their sense of ethnic identity is heightened by outrage at the changes in landscape and lifestyle caused by copper mining. Doubtless it has also been increased by a recognition that, in good times for copper, royalties would support an independent Bougainville—perhaps in federation with the northern Solomon Islands—whereas now Bougainville copper underpins the dominance of Port Moresby. This is a viewpoint which Banabans might understand, but it is not attractive to the national leaders who are committed to a united Niugini. Nonetheless, those leaders talk of conciliation and consensus rather than of force. The model of provincial government recently established for the northern Solomons may afford a useful compromise, since each side in its own fashion views it as a satisfactory "Melanesian way."

For that matter islanders throughout the Pacific, from Niugini to Tahiti, plead for the Melanesian, or Fijian, or Samoan, or Tahitian way. For instance, an observer, seeing the official cars leaving Government House in Fiji with turtles to distribute to adherents of the Vunivalu of Bau, knows that "change" is often superficial; by no means is it clear that the great chief's outlook has been changed by his metamorphosis into a governor general. The same observer—watching foreign capital pour into the mines of New

Caledonia and Bougainville, seeing the growth of hotels and resorts throughout the whole Pacific area, and noticing the level of Japanese interest in Niugini—may doubt whether constitutional advance has really produced political progress. Regardless of the transfer of formal political power, capital, profits, and actual power seem more than ever in expatriate hands. The Pacific islands have always been economic satellites since the advent of Europeans. Paradoxically they are becoming more, and not less, economically dependent as they achieve nominal political independence.

Island governments seem bent on the course of self-determination. With rising populations and limited resources, however, their leaders may have no alternative to seeking economic help from neighboring capitals like Canberra. The Australian government now recognizes the needs of its island neighbors and is lending assistance to the extent of $6,000,000 in aid over three years. Yet that very assistance means an increasing Australian influence over the island nations whose independence is being so proudly hailed.

There are still further paradoxes. In Fiji for many years, Europeans and even Indians have assured the islanders that their society is "fossilized" or "irrelevant," yet the Fijians have amply and persistently demonstrated a strong political vitality. Nevertheless, they are becoming victims of a creeping urbanization without the corresponding advantages of industrialization. And what holds true for Fiji also holds true for many island groups: villages are becoming deserted, agriculture languishes, and the economy stagnates. This grim condition is the product not only of an uncertain economy but of an educational system that has been inculcating westernized wants and aspirations which may be irrelevant to the true needs of the islanders. At the same time, as the resources of multinational corporations are brought to bear on the Pacific islands world, the islanders' response is both apprehensive and resentful. In a lament that no doubt summarizes the sentiment of many islanders, the deputy leader of the opposition in Niugini complained that his people are strangers in their own country. Since the islanders own only 3 percent of company property and earn only about the same percent of business income, he is clearly not far wrong. In Niugini as elsewhere in the Pacific, the islanders may increasingly question whether they would not do better to remain poor in their own way.

Notes

1 J. W. Davidson, "The Decolonization of Oceania," *The Journal of Pacific History*, vi (1971), 135.

2 Deryck Scarr, *Fragments of Empire: A History of the Western Pacific High Commission, 1877–1914* (Canberra: Australian National University Press, 1967), 252–297.

3 See Barrie Macdonald, "Local Government in the Gilbert and Ellice Islands, Part I," *Journal of Administration Overseas*, x, 4 (October 1971), 280–293, and "Local Government in the Gilbert and Ellice Islands, Part II," *Journal of Administration Overseas*, xi, 1 (January 1972), 11–27. Also A. M. Healy, "Administration in the British Solomon Islands," *Journal of Administration Overseas*, v, 3 (July 1966), 194–204.

4 C. Hartley Grattan, *The Southwest Pacific since 1900: A Modern History* (Ann Arbor: University of Michigan Press, 1963), 490.

5 See, generally, Scarr, *Fragments of Empire*, 219–251.

6 H. C. Brookfield, *Colonialism, Development and Independence: The Case of the Melanesian Islands in the South Pacific* (Cambridge: Cambridge University Press, 1972), 122.

7 William E. Tagupa, "Some Aspects of Modern Politics and Personality in French Polynesia," *The Journal of Pacific History*, ix (1974), 134–145.

8 Jean Guiart, *Journal de la Société des Océanistes*, xxxi, 49 (December 1975), 475.

9 Davidson, op. cit., 145.

10 Ibid., 146.

11 Quoted in ibid., 148, 149.

12 Francis X. Hezel, *Journal de la Société des Océanistes*, xxxii 50 (March 1976), 112.

13 See, generally, Nancy Viviani, *Nauru: Phosphate and Political Progress* (Canberra: Australian National University Press, 1970).

14 The Banaban community is studied in Martin G. Silverman, *Disconcerting Issue: Meaning and Struggle in a Resettled Pacific Community* (Chicago: University of Chicago Press, 1971).

15 A. L. Jackson, "Towards Political Awareness in the New Hebrides," *The Journal of Pacific History*, vii (1972), 156.

16 Ibid., 155–162.

17 Brookfield, op. cit., 121–122.

18 Barrie Macdonald, "Secession in the Defence of Identity: The Making of Tuvalu," *Pacific Viewpoint*, xvi, 1 (May 1975), 26–44.

19 Leo Hannett, "The Case for Bougainville Secession," *Meanjin Quarterly*, xxxiv, 3 (September 1975), 292.

C. HARTLEY GRATTAN

The Southwest Pacific
since the First World War:
A Synthesis

This essay attempts to identify and briefly discuss certain events and responses to events that have transformed the way in which the Southwest Pacific—Australia, New Zealand, and the islands— is perceived by those who live there as well as by overseas observers. As a commentator in whom the historical sense is strong, I shall not imply, I hope, that there are any shattering discontinuities to be noticed but rather that the present is continuous with the past. The future will certainly contain large elements of both.

Although the uncovering of the Southwest Pacific was begun by Spaniards operating from the west coast of South America in the sixteenth century—and though the Dutch operating from Java in the seventeenth century made major discoveries, including Australia (1606) and New Zealand (1643)—it was not until the late eighteenth century that the area can be said to have been perceived with any accuracy by Europeans. The most effective actors in the eighteenth century were French and British explorers, representatives of a deep-seated imperialist rivalry, and the premier actor of all was the British explorer Captain James Cook. Without exhausting all the possibilities, Cook not only defined the area geographically but also made clear its relation to Antarctica to the south and to the North Pacific up to the Arctic. By rediscovering New Zealand and charting its islands with remarkable accuracy and by discovering the east coast of Australia, Cook suggested the places where European colonization was probably feasible. The British acted upon this in 1788, when they established the first European settlement in the area at Sydney in Australia. From that base the British during the nineteenth century established themselves step by step as the paramount power in the Southwest Pacific.

When the situation in the area was tidied up at the end of the nineteenth century in the wake of the Spanish-American War, the British had full sovereignty over, or a protectorate relation with, Australia, New Zealand, Fiji, Papua (passed by Britain to Australia as a colony in 1906), the Solomon Islands, the Gilbert and Ellice Islands, Tonga, the Cook Islands (passed by Britain to New Zealand and made an integral part of New Zealand in 1901), and Pitcairn Island. The French had the Society Islands (including Tahiti), the Tuamotus, the Marquesas, and New Caledonia, as well as several minor groups; they shared the New Hebrides with the British under a condominium. The Germans had Western Samoa, several groups of Micronesian islands north of the equator up to the Philippines, the northeastern quarter of New Guinea, and associated with it several outlying islands, including some that were geographically in the Solomons. The Americans had Eastern Samoa and Hawaii. The First World War changed this situation: the Germans were expelled from their island possessions. German New Guinea passed to Australia as a mandate from the League of Nations, while Western Samoa became a mandate to New Zealand. Ex-German, phosphate-rich Nauru became a joint mandate of Australia, New Zealand, and Britain, Australia administering.

In general, the Southwest Pacific still stood in a colonial relation to the metropolitan European powers, of which the most prestigious was Britain, both worldwide and within the area. The British position was somehow supported by its position as the paramount European imperialist in Asia. It should be noticed that the British march to power in India, the base of their Asian power, effectively began about the same time as they were establishing themselves in the Southwest Pacific. On this reasoning, the decline of British power in Asia, which appears to have begun early in the twentieth century, would directly affect the world position of Australia and New Zealand. The effect was obvious in the years after the First World War and became determining after the Second.

By the end of the First World War, the British had been established in Australia for 132 years, in New Zealand for 80 (from 1840), in Fiji for 45 (from 1875), in New Guinea for 34, and so on. In sum the British position was largely created (or defined) during the nineteenth century, especially if we accept the historians' view that the nineteenth century did not really end until 1914. Australia was of continental dimensions; New Zealand was fundamentally two large islands twelve hundred miles across the

Tasman Sea from Australia; and Fiji was a group of ninety five islands, of which the principal one was Viti Levu.

In economic terms the significant British focuses were Australia, New Zealand, and Fiji. All three were primary producers: Australia in 1920 was chiefly perceived as a producer of fine wool, wheat, and minerals (especially lead and zinc); New Zealand, as a producer of pasture-based products like butter, cheese, meat, and wool; and Fiji, as a producer of cane sugar. The export-import trades were in largest measure concentrated on London, as were financial relations. Differently put, the British possessions in the Southwest Pacific were firmly incorporated into the British imperial trading-financial system. In 1920 the British were resolute to preserve the position, to recover the status quo ante bellum, and to make progress along lines established in the nineteenth century. What that meant was summed up by the prime minister of Australia (1923–1929), Stanley Melbourne Bruce, in three words: men, money, and markets; that is, immigrants, investment capital, and remunerative export markets. Australia, New Zealand, and Fiji had historically sought to build up their production beyond the needs of the domestic markets and to sell the surpluses overseas, chiefly in Britain. Thus they were heavily dependent for national income on the export trade, and the health of the export trade was thus a *sine qua non* of domestic economic health. It was the failure of the British market between the wars to maintain its health—its capacity to absorb ever increasing imports at prices rewarding to the producers—that accounted for the troubles in the colonies and dominions in the period from 1920 to 1939.

Much of the economic story of the Southwest Pacific between the wars is unquestionably related to a failure to understand how deeply wounded Britain had been by the First World War. The colonial story is replete with improvisations to evade the point that "normalcy" was irrecoverable. Only belatedly was it recognized that the whole business needed rethinking, though both thinking and action of a creative kind were more or less unconsciously produced along the way. In Australia the Great Depression underlined the necessity of rethinking without actually causing it. In New Zealand the situation was different. There, in regard to both thought and action, the improvisations to escape the inadequacies of the British market chiefly involved tinkering with the "market" in one way or another. They involved the "syndication" of the producers and the engineering of one price for domes-

tic consumers and the "world price" for surpluses—the two aver-
aged to give remunerative returns to the producers. There was
no disposition to adopt the policy of a "little less" to accommodate
to constricted markets by reducing supplies, since in both Australia and New Zealand the overall emphasis was on development.
When the depression came along and further constricted markets,
the task became to defend the special colonial position in the British market, for which the quid pro quo to Britain was "preference"
for British commodities in the colonial markets. The upshot of
this was the great shift in British trade policy known as "Ottawa"
(1932), which had the effect of tying Australia and New Zealand
more tightly than ever into the imperial trading system. Both
countries were quite complacent about this, New Zealand more so
than Australia. The first obvious line of escape was diversification
of trade outlets, an escape not really feasible in a depressed world
but which came into its own in both countries after the Second
World War. The second line of escape was to effect a structural
change in the domestic economy by elaborating and intensifying
factory industry. In Australia this course was pursued by private
enterprise during the 1920s and 1930s and, by the time of the
Second World War, it was the favored policy for growth among
all political parties. It was much less feasible for New Zealand,
and it was only feasible for island economies like Fiji's insofar
as a limited range of light industries might be set up.

Australia and New Zealand had controlled their domestic affairs
under the forms of "responsible government" from the 1850s, and
for practical purposes both had had the status of "dominion" since
1907. They were both firmly involved, however, in the imperial
financial system. The accumulated balance of funds in London
was the measure of their financial health. The capital they required beyond local accumulations came from London on both
public and private account. Non-British investment was marginal.
They had local currencies in pounds, shillings, and pence, and the
maintenance of their par value with sterling was a sacred dogma.
The illusion was that they were on the gold standard; the reality
was that they were on a sterling standard. Failure to maintain
par with sterling during the depression was a traumatic experience,
especially in New Zealand. Banking was in the hands of private
banks—Australian, New Zealand, and British. Australia did not
have a reserve bank formally until after the Second World War,
but New Zealand established one in the 1930s. One of New Zea-

land's purposes was to gain knowledge and better control of its London balance, for the private banks mixed New Zealand's funds with Australia's funds in London to the confusion of New Zealand's understanding of its true position. But, whatever the particulars of the situation, the gist of the matter was that the British possessions (and mandates) in the Southwest Pacific were securely entangled in the British imperial financial system, the French islands in the French, the American in the American. In finance as in trade, the task after the Second World War was to temper, or escape from, this overinvolvement, particularly for Australia and New Zealand.

Domestically, Australian politics was conducted within a federal system, initiated in 1901, New Zealand politics within a unitary system tempered to some extent by a persistent regionalism. In Australia the fundamental political division was between a social democratic party (Labor) on the one hand and the conservatives on the other. The Australian Labor party had existed continuously since federation, but the majority conservatives had a history of recurring instability. Moreover, the conservatives had been a divided force since the end of the First World War—and to the present day. The majority conservatives were urban-based with some country support, procapitalist, and strongly imperial-minded; while the minority conservatives, gathered into a stable grouping called the Country party, were of course rural-oriented—appealing to moderately well-to-do farmers and graziers and apt to be critical of urban capitalists and their aspirations and doings—but thoroughly proimperial in outlook. On balance, the Country party conservatives were more conservative than the urban-oriented grouping, which normally had a "liberal" wing. Both conservative groups were held together by a strong anti-Labor bias. Between the wars, neither could hope to hold power alone, so the political solution was to form coalition governments, thus compounding the fissiparous character of the conservatives generally.

The Labor party, which had split over the issue of conscription for overseas service in 1916, did not return to office until 1929, and then only briefly. Labor was seen as the party of innovation, while the conservatives were the party of resistance (especially to Labor). The conservative coalition ruled throughout the interwar period except for the years from 1929 to 1931, so for that whole period innovation got short shrift, except when the conservatives could see it as shoring up the status quo—for example, in tinkering with the market. By the end of the 1930s, it looked as though resistance had decisively triumphed over innovation, but in 1941 Labor gained office once again and held it for eight years.

The position in New Zealand was different. There the anti-Labour parties ruled from 1912 up to 1935, when Labour achieved office and power for the first time in history. It retained both until 1949. For legitimization it harked back to the Liberal regime of Richard Seddon, 1839–1906, thus attaching itself to a powerfully appealing New Zealand tradition. New Zealand Labour had arrived at what may be characterized as its left-liberal position after a warm devotion to a doctrinaire socialism for over a dozen years after its founding in 1916. During the depression there had been a fierce struggle within the ruling conservative party between those who recognized the need to innovate to meet the unprecedented conditions and those who proposed to meet them in a stolidly orthodox fashion.

In summary, what Labour set out to do was (1) take into government hands the responsibility for economic and social policy, while interfering as little as possible with the capitalist foundations of the rural-biased economy; (2) redistribute the fruits of the capitalist economy through mechanisms clearly in the control of the government; and (3) insulate the country from the effects of economic fluctuations overseas by taking the control of foreign trade and finance into the hands of government. The effect was to turn New Zealand into a tightly controlled country, well beyond anything hitherto experienced. It was not socialism, since the capitalist base was preserved, but it was a capitalism socialized to a marked degree. It was also an adaptation to the world of the depression that might not survive in a differently constituted world. In New Zealand, as elsewhere, the depression dissolved into the Second World War. Now war itself was a great "socializer," as had been made clear by the First World War, and New Zealand seemed to be on the wave of the future. Thus, as the Second World War approached, Australia was firmly in the hands of its cautious conservatives, while New Zealand was undergoing an innovative reordering even more startling than that of the 1890s.

Both regarded themselves as integral parts of the British Empire, New Zealand even more decisively than Australia. Neither was concerned to act upon the innovations afforded by the Statute of Westminster, 1931. In fact, Australia did not formally accept all the provisions of the statute until 1942, New Zealand not until 1947—both finally acting at the behest of Labor governments. The concern of both was to have a voice as of right in decision making on the imperial foreign policy. Once decided, the policy would be common to all the empire, which would, so to say, speak with a single voice, disregarding local reservations. That was what the Australians and New Zealanders believed was required by "the diplomatic *unity* of the Empire," founded in the dogma (already somewhat eroded) of the "indivisibility of the Crown" (or of sovereignty). In the later 1930s the Australian conservatives consistently supported British policy as it unfolded, including Neville Chamberlain's appeasement policy. New Zealand Labour took an independent tack. It took a strong stand against European dictators and Japan, invoking "collective security" and proclaiming a resolute opposition to disturbers of the peace by violence, both in imperial councils and at the League of Nations. Both countries, however, arrived eventually at the same destination—war. But, as they did so, New Zealand reasserted loyalty to the old formulation, "when Britain is at war, the Empire is at war."

Both nations, however, came to that cataclysmic decision on war with unresolved doubts, both about the probable nature of the war in Europe and about the probable effect of the European war on the situation in the Pacific and Asia—in short, on Japan. There was no question about the compelling imperial logic of supporting Britain in Europe. But what about the position of Australia and New Zealand if Japan, encouraged by the war in Europe, should turn southward and therefore toward them? In defense terms, what should they prepare to defend themselves against? How strongly could they rely upon their traditional defender, Britain, to take care of them in the extreme situation of a Japanese attack? Could they depend upon Singapore, the symbol of British power east of Suez, to keep the Japanese at a safe distance—well north of the equator? And could any useful help be obtained from America, which between the wars was little known and held in low esteem? Australia and New Zealand went into the Second World War with these doubts unresolved, and the actual course of the war intensified them. In 1940 the Australians—with a nice impartiality—established diplomatic relations with the United States, Japan, and China, protesting the while that they were not violating the diplomatic unity of the British Empire. By contrast New Zealand's first minister arrived in Washington only after Pearl Harbor. It was the war with Japan in the western Pacific that propelled Australia and New Zealand into the international arena in their own distinctive national personalities. The imperatives of that new situation led to the gradual transformation of the traditional out-look of both countries on world affairs. The Second World War is thus a decisive turning point in the history of the Southwest Pacific.

There were, however, important continuities, not least the demographic and cultural. Australia, though situated geographical-ly close to the "colored" peoples of Asia and the Pacific islands, per-ceived itself—self-consciously and even stridently—as a "white" country. The Australian "whites" were predominantly of British stock ("98 percent British," the politicians said), including a con-siderable proportion of Irish. The non-British "white" peoples within the resident population—some of them long-established—included Germans, French, Italians, Greeks, Yugoslavs, and Scan-dinavians—all few in number. These "whites" of Australia—British and Europeans alike—seemed to be oddly distributed on a continent replete with empty spaces. In each state there was a single great city, a few small provincial towns, and a scatter of population inland. Although Canberra became the national capital in 1927, it grew to substantial size only after the Second World War. The concentration of population was in the southeastern part of the country—Sydney and Melbourne being the two largest cities.

In New Zealand the concentration of population was in the North Island, which contained the two principal, though small, cities of Auckland and Wellington; the South Island also had two major cities, Christchurch and Dunedin. Taking the towns and cities together, New Zealand was only slightly less urbanized than Australia, although New Zealand as a whole had more provincial towns. At the outbreak of the Second World War, Australia had a population of about 7.5 million, New Zealand about 1.5 million.

In the islands, the indigenous populations everywhere predomi-nated (except in Fiji, where the Indians were overtaking the native Fijians), and in each group the Europeans, while a small minority, were predominant politically and economically. As it happened, the largest single European community in the islands was not in British territory but in French New Caledonia.

Australia's sense of "whiteness" was fortified by its exclusion-ary immigration policy, by its insistence on a historical "British-ness," by the character of its political culture, by the dominance of the British factor in cultural affairs, and by the proempire—more precisely, pro-Britain—orientation of the establishment in its political and other manifestations. The sustaining word was "loyalty," the ultimate disparaging epithet was "disloyal." (To what? Why, to the Empire!) New Zealand was even more "British" and "loyal" than Australia, both in actuality and in the self-conception of its people. Perhaps the New Zealanders were also reacting to Australian nationalism, which though latent after the war began to revive around 1930.

Australian nationalism had first found expression most potently among writers and painters in the 1880s and was vigorous up to 1914, while at the political level it had been given expression by the Labor party. The First World War dealt a heavy blow to cultural and political nationalism alike. While both revived in the 1930s, they noticeably gained strength during the Second World War, when Labor was in power. After the war the position of Australia and the condition of the world required a nationalistic response from whoever was in office. Between the wars Australian patriotism was normally double-barreled: one barrel was for Australia and one for the empire. Which barrel was fired depended upon the issue. It was rare to find anybody carrying a single-barreled gun of either kind. In both Australia and New Zealand, the cultural influence, historically and contemporaneously, was overwhelmingly British; the influences coming from Europe, North America, and Asia were of minimal importance. In a sense that was the "thesis." The second most important factor was the Australian response, figuring as the "antithesis." On this reasoning an Australian culture was bound to emerge as a synthesis. But, in the prevailing circumstances, its emergence was necessarily slow, and its exponents frequently found themselves in an uncomfortable adversary position vis-à-vis the predominantly British tone of the local establishments.

At the governmental level (and in education up to the university level) conservatives were little interested in nationalism in either country. In the 1930s in both countries, there was cultural ferment—in literature, painting, and education—at all levels and on practically all questions. The genesis of this ferment can be found in the 1920s, but its surfacing belongs to the 1930s. It came at a time when Australia was dominated by the conservatives and New Zealand by Labour. In both countries this burgeoning cultural nationalism survived the stresses of war. Thus the origins of the cultural change that came in both countries after the Second World War must be sought in the ferment of the Great Depression.

In the postwar world as in the 1930s, the restrictive immigration policies of both Australia and New Zealand were aimed at Asians. Those immigration policies had always symbolized a sense of psychocultural distance from Asia. Australia and New Zealand perceived themselves as European outposts under the overhang of Asia, and Asia was a menace to them. Their economic relations with Asia were minimal beside the tie to Britain, and their political relations to Asia were via Britain, not direct. It was the tie to Britain that allowed these countries to sustain their distance from Asia since Britain, the paramount power in Asia, was able to prevent any serious challenge by Asians to the Australia–New Zealand position. In regard to the colored peoples of the islands, the position was different. There was no sense of menace or fear of the islanders. Indeed, the situation there was reversed, for in the late nineteenth century the "trade" in kanakas was a scandal in which Australia, through its employment of them on plantations in Queensland, was deeply involved. By the First World War that was a thing of the past. Between the wars it was an unexamined assumption in both countries that the islanders were firmly under the control of their metropolitan masters. Little thought was given to the Asian communities in the islands, of which the most conspicuous was the Indian community in Fiji. There was remarkably little Australian interest in New Guinea between the wars, but the New Zealanders took considerable notice of Western Samoa because of persistent unrest among the Samoans, the most ardent politicians of all island peoples. In general, the new ideas about the proper relations between metropolitan and dependent peoples received little attention in the Southwest Pacific in these years. Only when the whole question of relations with dependent peoples came up for debate in the Second World War did Australia and New Zealand undertake a thorough reappraisal of their attitudes toward the islanders.

In the 1930s the old idea that the islands were a "protective shield" was revived. Australia was assumed to have a special responsibility in this respect in the New Guinea–Solomon Islands area, New Zealand in Fiji and vicinity. In New Zealand the domestic concern was with the indigenous Maoris, a perennial problem since the earliest days. The Polynesian Maoris were a sizable and growing minority, predominantly rural by residence but beginning to move into the towns. By contrast, the Aborigines of Australia were an almost invisible minority of blacks in a "white country," mostly out of sight in the outback and effectively out of mind. In the late 1930s the "abo" problem began to assume a more central position in the repertory of Australian concerns, and after the Second World War it emerged as a social problem of real exigency.

From 1939 to 1941 the Australian preoccupation with the islands was strategic. At that time the British and French dominions and colonies in the Southwest Pacific were at war in Europe. Since the central point of British imperial strategy was "Europe First"—on the argument that, if the center (i.e., Britain) holds, all will hold—Australia and New Zealand had committed their war-making capacities to the British effort in Europe and North Africa. However, the nagging uncertainties about the probable or possible course of Japan in the western Pacific continued. Neither dominion had the resources to deal adequately with war on two fronts; hence the western Pacific was being slighted. Then in 1940 the staggering shift of forces in Europe produced a crisis. Australia and New Zealand were told by the British that, for the time being at least, Britain could not be counted on to reinforce Singapore if Japan turned southward. The Australians questioned whether Singapore was the only key, speculating that Japan might strike them from their mandated islands and proceed via New Guinea down the east coast of the continent to the Australian heartland. Nevertheless, they redeployed their inadequate reserves—chiefly to Singapore and secondarily into the island shield.

When the Australians sent their minister to Washington in 1940, they were not only advertising their own perilous predicament but also attempting to persuade the Americans to support the imperial position in the western Pacific. Even though the United States had assumed greater control of relations with Japan, there had been almost no joint military planning. When the Japanese turned south, the Americans and British had to improvise a resistance. It was strikingly unsuccessful, fundamentally because of a shared underappreciation of Japan's capacity to wage a war to the south. The assault on Pearl Harbor, the fall of Singapore, the collapse of the Philippines, the takeover of the Netherland East Indies, and the arrival of the Japanese in New Guinea—these were great symbolic events as well as military disasters. As the Australian military had anticipated, these defeats left the Australian continent as the sole viable base in the western Pacific from which to mount a campaign against the Japanese. That was also the assessment of the Americans; so, when it became clear that the Pacific war would be primarily an American responsibility, an Australian–New Zealand–American collaboration became inevitable. The collaboration arose out of strategic necessity—not from a diplomatic triumph or any vague sense of kinship. In the fight against the Japanese, not only were Australian and New Zealand bases of fundamental importance, but such islands as Western Samoa, Fiji, New Caledonia, New Hebrides, the Solomons, and New Guinea were involved either as secondary bases or as scenes of fighting. The waters environing the islands were also of primary importance in the war because the Japanese were stopped in the islands, and that naval victory preserved American access to Australia and New Zealand.

Labor was newly in office in Australia when the Japanese struck. In New Zealand Labour had been in office and power for six years. In both countries these governments continued in office throughout the war and beyond, both being displaced by conservatives in 1949. From then on, though there has been some alternation in office, the conservatives have predominated. (For conservative read "anti-Labor.") From 1972 to 1975 both countries were again under Labor governments, but in 1975 both passed once again into conservative hands. Indeed, from the end of the First World War to 1978, Australia has been governed by conservative coalitions for forty-eight of fifty-eight years. This way of putting it sharply understates the influence of Labo(u)r, particularly on general social policy. Rather frequently, the political balance in both countries has been so nearly even as to leave the conservatives only precariously on top. Continuously in both countries, the Labor parties have been, and still are, the recognized official political opposition as well as the established ideological, social, and cultural opposition to the conservatives.

Australian Labor's first duty after the outbreak of war was to guarantee the survival of the country. In the circumstances, that meant swinging the country toward the United States. The great question was whether this was a permanent political reorientation or an accommodation to the circumstances that the U.S. was a surrogate for Britain in this war. It took a long time to answer that question. But it soon became clear that whatever the final answer was to be—and it is not final even yet—the effect of the Second World War, particularly the Pacific war, was to intensify sharply the nationalistic responses of Australia to the challenges confronted. That response was quite consistent with Australian Labor's traditional stance and also with the personal views of Dr. H. V. Evatt, Labor's foreign policy spokesman over the eight years it was in office. On the other hand, the Labor prime ministers during those years—John Curtin and Ben Chifley—were rather more inclined to preserve the traditional political and defense ties with the British Empire Commonwealth. It is not unfair to say that whereas Evatt believed in devolution, up to and including total autonomy, his prime ministers did not. Evatt thought that the war would further diminish imperial power east of Suez and that Australia must of necessity defend its own position in the new situation because while Britain could withdraw, Australia had to remain. Apart from careful accommodation to the new circumstances, Evatt foresaw that the British withdrawal would probably be slow. Since in his view Australia was rising, he thought Australia should assume primary responsibility for British interests east of Suez, with Britain backing Australia as hitherto Australia had backed Britain.

Evatt, however, was no better a prophet than anybody else. Not only did he fail to foresee the shape of the postwar world, he overestimated Australia's power to determine its own international positions. As a marginal power Australia could only realize its own policies by accommodating them to the politics of the great powers. In the final analysis Evatt vaguely understood this. He rejected power politics and embraced the idea of the sovereign equality of all nations. He sought to realize Australia's objectives through a United Nations so organized as to curb the great powers' disposition to power politics and tip the weight in decision making more toward the numerous small powers.

Evatt also had some specific concerns. He was friendly to colonial aspirations to freedom, as can be illustrated by his policy in Indonesia. He was fearful of a militaristic-imperialistic revival in Japan and adamantly opposed the Japanese peace treaty negotiated by the U.S. He promoted a development and welfare policy in the islands, but he did not foresee early independence for any group. He sought to promote the advancement of his own Labor party's position by promoting full employment at the international level. Evatt failed to achieve what he really wanted, namely, a firm American guarantee of Australia's security. To go with that, he also wanted a regional collective security agreement among Australia, New Zealand, and the emerging nations of South and Southeast Asia. He hoped the U.S. would provide an endorsement of that pact and the necessary military strength, but he was reluctant to permit direct American participation in it.

In 1949 Evatt lost his position as foreign minister, but from 1950 to 1960 he was leader of the Labor opposition in the federal Parliament. His general position then was to criticize conservative foreign policy by stressing the United Nations, not least during the Suez crisis of 1954. That criticism was quite consistent with his own policy while in office, but it is also fair to say that his policies represented more an aspiration than a realistic appraisal of world politics. Evatt failed, not because his ideals were ignoble, but because he concerned himself too little with the reality of foreign relations and became obsessed with the ideal as he conceived it.

The war provided the Labor government with both the occasion and the necessity for a fairly comprehensive control by the central government of production, distribution, and exchange—to which it was predisposed by its own ideology. Since the First World War, centralization of power had been the Labor ideal, but it remained unrealized because of constitutional restrictions even more than electoral failures. Labor did not seek control at the center for its own sake but to promote a social democratic polity. In Labor's imagination the central issue was control of finance, with which Labor had become more and more obsessed since 1911. As it happened, the shift of financial predominance to the central government had begun during the First World War, had not been reversed between the wars, and had been resoundingly confirmed during the Second World War. Labor had advanced the cause when in office during both wars, but anti-Labor—ostensibly opposed to federal dominance in finance by conviction and policy—not only had failed to reverse the trend but actually came to accept it and freely exercised that power after 1949. Labor espoused a "mixed" economy but had a built-in bias in favor of the public sector. Threaded through Labor opinion was a highly critical view of capitalism and private enterprise.

The postwar Labor reconstruction program embraced a variety of objectives: centralized decision making, membership in international institutions, economic growth with an emphasis on the public sector, encouragement of white immigration, full employment, expanded welfare policies and educational opportunities, support for the arts and welfare and development policies in New Guinea and the islands. After 1945 Labor set about implementing this program in a somewhat chaotic national and international environment, one characterized by the dollar shortage (Australia was traditionally a dollar-short country), the fear of the return of general depression, the distressing position of the United Kingdom (still to Australia a primary point of reference), and uncertainty about communism at home and overseas. Labor lost office at the end of 1949, ostensibly because of the success of the conservative parties in exploiting the notion that Labor was soft on communism at home, but more perhaps because the anti-Labor forces had decried as "socialism" Labor's effort to nationalize banking. The conservative campaign was seemingly supported by the court decision that nationalization was unconstitutional. Perhaps Australia was feeling the "swing to the right" which had already affected New Zealand and would soon affect Britain and the United States. At any rate the conservatives were back, but nobody, including themselves, had any prevision of how long they would stay in power. To an astonishing extent, Labor had defined an agenda of concerns to which the conservatives would have to provide the answers.

New Zealand Labour at the time of its defeat in 1949 was disheveled and exhausted. Up to the outbreak of the war, it had been fully occupied with installing its system of social management for which the *annus mirabilis* was 1938. The Labour government had assumed the burden of rearmament but was uncertain what to do and unclear as to its purposes. Unlike the conservatives, Labour had never supported the completion of the Singapore base while in opposition and did so only after gaining office. When in 1940 Britain said it could no longer reinforce Singapore if worse came to worst in the Far East, New Zealand's Labour Prime Minister Peter Fraser was outraged, alleging that the foundation of New Zealand's defense had been destroyed. But New Zealand nevertheless continued the war effort, concentrating on Europe. At the end of 1941, when Australia withdrew troops from North Africa and brought them home to be deployed against Japan, New Zealand gave in to Winston Churchill and allowed its troops to remain in North Africa. When in 1944 Australia and New Zealand formally concerted their foreign policy ideas and aspirations in a famous agreement, it was the New Zealanders who insisted that both were British countries and that the language of the agreement should reflect that fact.

When the Americans entered the Southwest Pacific, the New Zealanders fervently hoped the U.S. was merely standing in for the British and held onto that hope much longer than the Australians. New Zealand found the adjustment to new and changing circumstances far harder to make than did the Australians. To the extensive efforts at social reconstruction begun before the war, New Zealand Labour added the exhausting efforts of the wartime struggle. And they labored hard at the San Francisco conference to realize their ideals of international organization, especially in the arrangements about dependent peoples.

The controlled and directed society they had constructed to realize their peacetime ideals had proved, somewhat tightened up and redirected, very serviceable for war. But now the system had to be readjusted to peace while it was under attack from the right by its conservative political opponents and from the left by communists in the labor unions. The Labour leadership began to scold and also to give ground. The syndicates were returned to the producers for operation, as though to say that Labour was no longer sure that the government could carry the entire burden of the economy. The regime appeared no longer sure of its ideology. The conservatives—sensing Labour's tiredness, uncertainty, and willingness to give a little but recognizing too its stubborn disposition to defend essentials—stepped up their attacks and argued for a return to private enterprise. Whether because the voters accepted this proposal or because they felt an exhausted Labour party deserved a rest, they voted Labour out in 1949.

The conservatives did not recreate a free-enterprise economy in New Zealand. They found themselves inextricably involved in a directed economy. They might ease the constrictions here and shift the emphasis there, but they could not systematically dismantle the structure built by Labour. Though they wished to do so for ideological reasons, they were faced by both internal and external economic imperatives that compelled them to retain or restore controls. Consequently, New Zealand since the war has been a classic example of a managed economy, though directed mainly by conservative politicians who felt obligated to protect the welfare of the citizen. This policy was made necessary by the character of New Zealand's export-import trade, on which it had been historically heavily dependent. The British market, still of primary importance, was insecure and uncertain after the war and was increasingly threatened by Britain's movement toward entry into the European Common Market.

New Zealand has, therefore, been required to search for alternative markets for its limited range of traditional exportable commodities, and it has proved hard to make any economically weighty additions to that list. New Zealand's exports today find their way to about 150 different markets, but in most cases the quantities are small. The greatest success has been in Australia, the U.S., and Japan, but no new market has been found that would really replace Britain. The search has required constant efforts to adjust domestic production to the possibilities of external sales—for example, by the reordering and diversification of the still important pasture-based industries, such as dairying. No great new industry has appeared to give New Zealand a major lift, though the exploitation of the forests for pulp, paper, and chips has had useful consequences. The development of the abundant hydroelectric resources for the treatment of Australian raw materials may also be profitable economically, even if costly environmentally. Any wholly satisfactory shift into manufacturing is very unlikely, although factory industry would seem to be well worth cultivating. Nor is there any solution in free trade with Australia—first, because New Zealand's pasture products are competitive with Australian products and, second, because the New Zealand demand for Australian manufactures quickly outruns the Australian demand for New Zealand's remaining exportable commodities, which causes acute balance-of-payment problems. In short, what New Zealand requires is an overseas market comparable under the new circumstances to the British market in the past, and it has yet to be found.

The change in the pattern of production in New Zealand has been accompanied by a considerable shift in the distribution of the population. There has been a continuing movement from the rural areas to the towns, from the South Island to the North, and from the south of the North Island to the north of the North Island—all this along with a slow rise of total population and a gradual diversification by nationality and racial origin. The total "European" population now approaches 3,000,000. About 70 percent of the 200,000 Maoris are concentrated in the North Island and are undergoing constant urbanization. They are still an economically depressed group in the New Zealand community and are undereducated in European terms. There is a powerful disposition to try to preserve the Maori cultural heritage, and the influence of the Maoris on the British culture of New Zealand is greater and more visible than, say, that of the Hawaiian culture on Americanized Hawaii. Nevertheless, the British culture clearly sets the tone of the country.

Since the war the tone of New Zealand nationalism has increased in resonance at the expense of the traditional British influence. The change is visible in literature and painting and also in education, particulary in the reorganized and expanded university system. The cultural influences flowing into New Zealand are today far more cosmopolitan than they used to be, and New Zealand is far more hospitable to them than it used to be—though the New Zealanders are rather less receptive to foreign cultural influences than the Australians. The New Zealanders seem to be determined to establish and defend their own cultural identity against Britain, Australia, or whomever. It is upon this determination that they take their national stand, although the often projected closer orientation toward Australia has changed their economic and foreign policies.

Perhaps one might say that New Zealand has an Australian problem—one that arises as much out of the contrast in size of the two countries as out of definable differences of outlook. Australia tends to assume, consciously or unconsciously, a posture of bigness vis-à-vis the smallness of New Zealand to the exasperation of the New Zealanders. Moreover, Australia tends to its relation to New Zealand rather fitfully. The intimacy of relations proposed in the Australia–New Zealand Agreement of 1944, a sharp deviation from the indifference of the interwar years, has never quite come off in the shape suggested, especially when major issues are under consideration. Australia decides, and New Zealand's agreement is assumed rather than achieved by prior joint discussion of the question. Occasional reiterations of the 1944 concord have not been followed up in practice as conscientiously as is required to keep relations harmonious. The New Zealanders grumble in private but make no scenes in public. The result is that not all observers are aware that there is any tension at all between the two countries.

The difference between their views of foreign policy questions is unquestionably subtle and easily overlooked abroad. From long association the British gained an exceptional sensitivity to this difference, and it is still occasionally useful to New Zealand, as when Britain finally joined the European Common Market. Just as New Zealand's loyalty to Britain was adjudged more intense than that of any other dominion between the wars, so New Zealand's nostalgia about its historical loyalty has been more visibly operative in the postwar years. More obviously even than Australia, New Zealand has sought to preserve the British connection, even while Britain was unquestionably declining in strength. It has done so while accommodating itself to the new reality, ordinarily in association with Australia, but with a visible lack of enthusiasm. The ANZUS treaty of 1951 is a good example. It was undoubtedly realistic of New Zealand to accept the treaty. It was also realistic for it to accept logical concomitants like the wars in Korea and Vietnam, SEATO, and so on, just as it was "realistic" to join the International Monetary Fund and the World Bank.

These policies were no doubt realistic, but a realism that tramples on a cherished tradition cannot be expected to generate enthusiasm. It was a matter of intelligent accommodation—an accommodation made more feasible by the continuing decline of Britain, the real object of New Zealand's affections. Thus New Zealand in its way was forced by history to act more or less nationalistically—to adjust reluctantly to a world it never made and did not much like. Accommodation was the ruling necessity over the crucial twenty years from 1951 to 1971. While alternatives like nonalignment were explored, the ruling conservatives doggedly stuck to a policy of accommodation to the new power alignments.

As for the Pacific islands, both Australia and New Zealand were keenly interested in the reform of the relations between the metropolitan powers and their dependent peoples. They argued for economic and social policies along the lines of Britain's Colonial Development and Welfare Acts of 1929, 1940, and 1945. They espoused the cause of accountability for stewardship to an international body, and they contributed greatly to the success of the principal organization for which they were responsible, the South Pacific Commission, most particularly in public health measures. Neither country foresaw the rapid decolonization that began in the late 1940s. Western Samoa set the pace in the islands in demanding freedom. This it achieved in 1962, leaving New Zealand with a heavy, continuing financial obligation, an intimate advisory position with regard to foreign relations, and a responsibility as principal source of technical assistance.

The Australian relation to New Guinea (the colony of Papua now combined administratively with the trust territory of New Guinea) developed differently. New Guinea was much larger. With regard to population, development, consciousness of national identity (as opposed to tribal loyalty), and acculturation to western values, New Guinea was far more complex than Western Samoa. The sheer magnitude of the task of bringing New Guinea to the point where independence could be contemplated was staggering—even taking into account the strong external pressures from the United Nations to get to that point. Nor was the task facilitated by the assumptions of the Australian government or the attitudes of either the resident whites or the public servants posted to the country. Given the standards of the time, it was quite understandable that the Australians were pessimistic about the prospects of independence—let alone about what might happen after independence. Nevertheless, after an intermediate step of self-government, independence was achieved by the end of 1975. The Australian government was left with an onerous, continuing financial obligation and an ambiguous responsibility for defense, internal order, and technical assistance of various sorts.

The British problems in Fiji were rather different from those faced by New Zealand and Australia. When the wind of decolonization really began to blow, there was no delight in it for the Fijians. They had had a special status in their country since Britain acquired sovereignty in 1874; a special protection was conferred upon them by a governmental system somewhat analogous to the "indirect rule" devised by Lord Lugard in Africa. The Fijians wished to preserve that status all the more intensely as the Indian population moved inexorably to numerical dominance. Anxious to protect their position, the Fijians regarded independence with concern because, if it brought one-man one-vote democracy, they would, in the absence of their protectors, fall under the dominance of the Indians. Even so, after a series of careful negotiations lasting up to 1971, the problem was finally solved to the ostensible satisfaction of both groups.

The only remaining problems for the British were Tonga, the Solomons, and the Gilbert and Ellice Islands. Tonga, a protectorate, resumed independence in 1971. The Solomons achieved a precarious independence in July 1978. Self-government in the Gilbert and Ellice Islands, now separated into the Gilbert Islands and Tuvalu, will be coming soon. That will leave almost all the Australian, New Zealand, and British colonies either in full independence or in something so near it as to make little difference. Whether it is a good thing that the Southwest Pacific has been decolonized is difficult to say. Clearly it was the inevitable consequence of a great shift in the sense of propriety in the world's view of relations between governments and subject peoples that began early in this century and gained force during the Second World War. The change was encouraged, too, by the patronage of the very differently motivated anticolonial powers, America and the Soviet Union, and it rather quickly became a universal imperative after 1945. Along the way, freedom became hypostatized at the expense of any concern for political and economic viability. None of the Southwest Pacific island countries can be said to be economically viable, and few give unequivocal promise of political stability. They are what they are today because of the influence of Europe since the end of the eighteenth century, when the "fatal impact" was first felt and the destabilization of their indigenous cultures began. None has ever been as completely transformed as Hawaii—a cautionary paradigm of the ultimate island fate—and none is likely to become so. But, today in the islands, there is a pervasive anxiety about economic viability and cultural integrity—the former closely related to European conceptions and norms and the latter related to the continuing concern for a solid, unique identity. Material aid can be expected, or at least solicited, from international agencies and from Australia and New Zealand, joint but not coequal leaders of the area. But the islands are a long way from real economic or political self-sufficiency.

To summarize the main themes of this book. It should be apparent that on the turntable of the Second World War the three segments of the Southwest Pacific—Australia, New Zealand, the Pacific islands—have been reoriented from positions of close involvement in the trade, financial, cultural, defense, and foreign policy systems of Great Britain toward positions of autonomy or independence. That is very clearly true of Australia and New Zealand, but it is true as well of those island groups that were formerly within a British Empire that had been the predominant power in the area since the end of the eighteenth century.

The rise and consolidation of British imperial power in Asia had for long years allowed Australians, New Zealanders, and British subjects in the Southwest Pacific to remain effectively isolated from Asia. Although the world position of the Southwest Pacific began to shift after the First World War, there was only an incomplete recognition between the wars of that transformation. Indeed, only after the Second World War has it become entirely apparent—as far as the Southwest Pacific is concerned—that the decline of the British Empire, particularly east of Suez, has been as important as ever was the rise of the empire in the earlier days.

This great change—with the Second World War as the turning point—has thrust the Southwest Pacific squarely into a world from which it had earlier felt apart and has forced it to redefine its relation to Europe, to Britain, to America, to Japan, and to Asia in general. But thus far the world has largely failed to redefine, either in fact or in imagination, the new place of the Southwest Pacific in the world of nations. It will soon have to do so. No longer merely ancillary to British power in the western Pacific and Asia, the three segments—Australia, New Zealand, and the Pacific islands—are today evolving new identities of growing significance and autonomy in the Southwest Pacific. They are motivated by their own imperatives, conscious of their own distinctive character, and governed by a new sense of independence and responsibility for their own destiny.

The Contributors

RODERIC ALLEY—is Senior Lecturer in Political Science at the Victoria University of Wellington. His fields of interest and publication include politics in Fiji, New Zealand foreign policy, and regional cooperation throughout the South Pacific. He is a member of the National Council of the New Zealand Institute of International Affairs.

MARY BOYD—is Reader in History at the Victoria University of Wellington. She is a contributor to *New Zealand's Record in the Pacific Islands in the Twentieth Century* (edited by Angus Ross for the New Zealand Institute of International Affairs) and editor of *Pacific Horizons: A Regional Role for New Zealand*.

C. HARTLEY GRATTAN—(LL.D., Australian National University) is Professor Emeritus of History and Curator of the Grattan Collection of Southwest Pacificana at the Humanities Research Center at the University of Texas. His publications on the Southwest Pacific include *Australian Literature; Introducing Australia; The United States and the Southwest Pacific;* and the two-volume work, *The Southwest Pacific to 1900* and *The Southwest Pacific since 1900*.

NORMAN HARPER—is Professor of American History at the University of Melbourne and a former president of the Australian and New Zealand American Studies Association, as well as of the Australian Institute of International Affairs. He is coeditor and co-author of *Australia and the United Nations*. Other works which he has edited or to which he has contributed include *Australia and the United States: Documents and Readings; Australian Orbit: A History of Australian-American Relations, 1943–1968;* and a four-volume collection, *Pacific Circle: American Studies Down Under*.

JOSEPH JONES—is Professor of English at the University of Texas. He is the author of *The Cradle of Erewhon: Samuel Butler in New Zealand; Terranglia: The Case for English as World Literature;* and, with Johanna Jones, *People and Places in World English Literature*. He has also written several volumes of verse.

WILLIAM S. LIVINGSTON—is Professor of Government at the University of Texas at Austin, specializing in Britain and the Commonwealth and in the comparative study of federalism. He is the author of *Federalism and Constitutional Change* and editor of *Federalism in the Commonwealth: A Bibliographical Commentary*. A former editor in chief of *The Journal of Politics*, he is currently president of the Southwestern Social Science Association.

WM. ROGER LOUIS—is Professor of History and Curator of Historical Collections at the Humanities Research Center, the University of Texas. He is the author of *Ruanda-Urundi, 1884–1919; Germany's Lost Colonies; British Strategy in the Far East;* and, with Jean Stengers, *E. D. Morel's History of the Congo Reform Movement.* With Prosser Gifford, he has edited *Britain and Germany in Africa* and *France and Britain in Africa.* His most recent work is *Imperialism at Bay: The United States and the Decolonization of the British Empire, 1941–1945.* In 1978 he was named Visiting Fellow of All Souls College, Oxford University.

ALLAN MARTIN—is former chairman of the Department of History at La Trobe University and is presently Senior Fellow at the Australian National University. With P. Loveday, he is the author of *Parliament, Factions and Parties: The First Thirty Years of Responsible Government in New South Wales.* He is presently completing a major biography of Sir Henry Parkes.

J. D. B. MILLER—is Professor of International Relations at the Australian National University. His books include *Australian Government and Politics; The Commonwealth in the World; The Politics of the Third World; Britain and the Old Dominions; Australia; Survey of Commonwealth Affairs: Problems of Expansion and Attrition;* and *The E.E.C. and Australia.*

GEOFFREY SAWER—is Professor of Law at the Australian National University, specializing in Australian constitutional and administrative law and in comparative federal studies. He is the author of the two-volume study of *Australian Politics and Law, 1901–1949;* of *Australian Federalism in the Courts;* of *Modern Federalism;* and of *Federation under Strain.*

DERYCK SCARR—is Senior Fellow in Pacific History at the Australian National University. He is joint editor of *The Journal of Pacific History* and the author of *Fragments of Empire: A History of the Western Pacific High Commission, 1877–1914* and *The Majesty of Colour: A Life of Sir John Bates Thurston.*

KEITH SINCLAIR—a poet as well as a historian, is Professor of History at the University of Auckland. He is the author of *The Maori Land League; Imperial Federation; The Origins of the Maori Wars; A History of New Zealand;* and, with W. F. Mandle, *Open*

Account: The Bank of New South Wales in New Zealand. He has also published four volumes of verse and two biographies, *William Pember Reeves* and most recently *Sir Walter Nash*.

M. P. K. SORRENSON—is Professor of History at the University of Auckland. He is the author of *Land Reform in the Kikuyu Country*; *Origins of European Settlement in Kenya*; and *Maori and European since 1870*.

W. E. H. STANNER—C.M.G., is an Honorary Fellow in the Department of Anthropology at the Australian National University and a member of the Australian Council for Aboriginal Affairs. He is the author of *The South Seas in Transition*; *On Aboriginal Religion*; and *After the Dreaming: Black and White Australians, An Anthropologist's View*.

F. L. W. WOOD—is Professor Emeritus of History at the Victoria University of Wellington. He is the author of *New Zealand in the World*; *This New Zealand*; and *The New Zealand People at War*.

Index

Aboriginal Land Fund Commission, 163

Aboriginal Policy and Practice (C. D. Rowley, 3 vols., 1970–1971), 24

Aboriginal Studies, Institute of, 23

Aborigines: despised and ignored by Australians, 5, 152; treatment of, by Australians equated with racism, 22; population of, 23, 150–151, 156; rights of, 23; arrival in Australia, 24; improved position of, 99; as focus of literary interest, 135; writings by, emerge in 1960s, 135–136; damage to, not willful, 148; emerge as public issue, 148; impact of early settlers on, 149–150; European impressions of, in mid-nineteenth century, 150; urbanization of, 151; first scholarly study of, 151; constitutional provisions for, 153, 161; agitation for better treatment of, 155; ignored in favor of non-Australian "natives," 155; political attitudes of, 156–157; 1937 conference on, 155, 157–158; apartheid policy toward, considered, 158; new attitude toward, emerges in early 1950s, 159; 1960s most turbulent decade of relations with Europeans, 160;

1967 constitutional referendum on, 161; Department of Aboriginal Affairs created, 161; policy of McMahon government toward, 162; concern for, in 1970s, 163; emerge as exigent social problem after Second World War, 212

Aborigines Progressive Association, 157

Aickman, Colin, 183

Airey, W. T. G., 36

Airlines of New South Wales case (1965), 117

Alexander, Fred, 12

Alice Springs, 92

Alpers, O. T. J., 34–35

Amato, Renato, 132

American Commonwealth (James Bryce, 1888), 106

Ancient Voyagers in the Pacific (Andrew Sharp, 1956), 43

Anglo-Japanese alliance, 50

ANZAC, 11, 14, 21, 47, 48

ANZUS, 5, 41; creation of, 55, 220; strengths and weaknesses of, 71–72; as historical milestone in Australian-American relations, 89–90; protects Papua–New Guinea, 90–91; role in Vietnam conflict, 92–93; reappraised by Whitlam, 98

Archibald, J. F., 127

Art and Letters in New Zealand (E. H. McCormick, 1940), 35

113; conflicts over income tax, 109; "claimant states" of, 110; as a colonial power, 118; Parliament, double dissolution and joint sitting of, 120–121; political parties to the left of those in the United States, 122; socialism in, 122; literary output in, curtailed by First World War, 125; literary output isolated and limited until 1930s, 126 ff.; literary output much increased, 1935–1960, 131 ff.; literary achievements in 1970s, 134; literary influence on World English, 134; literary self-consciousness, emerging, 129 ff.; expatriation of writers in 1920s and 1930s, 129; reaches literary maturity in 1960s, 133–134, 141; public support for the arts, 130–131; dramatic arts flourishing in, 135; population of, disperses into interior, 148; policy toward Aborigines embarrasses government in London, 154; and cult of "Aboriginality," 164; and South Pacific Commission and Forum, 188; economic aid to Pacific islands, 201; analysis of early discoveries of, 203; and erosion of British power, 204; economic condition in 1920, 205; and the Great Depression, 205–206, 211; party competition in, 207; and the doctrine "when Britain is at war, the Empire is at war," 209; and security against Japan, 209, 213; Second World War decisive turning point, 210; demographic analysis of, 210; culture of, emerges as a synthesis, 211; shows no interest in New Guinea between the wars, 212; and the crisis of 1939–1941;

collaboration with United States during Second World War, 213; alternation of parties in, 214; political reorientation toward United States, 214; swings to right after 1949, 217; more receptive to foreign influences than New Zealand, 219–220; condescension of, annoys New Zealanders, 220; and preparation for independence of New Guinea, 221. *See also* Aborigines

Australia (R. M. Crawford, 1952), 16, 23

Australia (W. K. Hancock, 1930): as watershed in Australian historiography, 9–10; as expression of urgent wish to provide democracy with self-knowledge, 13

Australian Council for the Arts, 131

Australian Dictionary of Biography, 19

Australian Institute of Aboriginal Studies, 161

Australian Labor party: wins election in 1929, 13, 112; loses sense of direction because of depression, 13–14; vital source of creativity in Australian society, 14; postwar reconstruction characterized by heady excitement, 14–15, 216; radical tradition of, 17; wins election of 1952, 58; wins election of 1972, 88, 95, 119; loses election of 1949, 88, 216; attitude toward U.S. base in Western Australia, 91, 98; commitment of, to expanding Commonwealth powers, 105; loses election of 1975, 106, 121; Fisher-Hughes government of 1910–1914, 107; divided over deflationary policies of Loan Council, 113–114; wins

content in, 36; radicalism in,
36–37, 208; universities in,
43–44; provincial histories, 44;
tariffs, 49–50; and Japan, 50–51,
67–68; and the Second World
War, 52–55, 217; and naval defense, 51; and defense cooperation with Australia, 52, 90–91;
and improved communication
with Australia, 54–55; and
formation of NATO, 55; trade
with Australia increases after
Second World War, 56–57; attempts to block nuclear testing
in Pacific, 59; Polynesians given
greater freedom in, 59; differs
from rest of Commonwealth on
autonomy, 62; and Royal Navy,
63; and League of Nations, 64;
asserts independence in foreign
policy, 64–65, 80; and collective
security, 65; establishment of
foreign affairs bureaucracy, 66;
and Australian-New Zealand
Agreement of 1944, 66; and control over own armed forces, 66;
opposes appeasement, 68; and
San Francisco Conference of
1945, 68; and United Nations,
69–70, 72, 80; and postwar policy toward Japan, 70–71; insistence on policy of "universalism," 71; independence in
foreign policy symbolized by
ANZUS, 71; and defense arrangements in Southeast Asia,
72; and China, 72–73; and Suez
crisis of 1956, 73; and Vietnam,
73, 76; and EEC, 73, 75; and
changing trade patterns, 74; and
major changes under Kirk government, 75–76; and South Africa, 77; and nuclear testing, 59,
78–79; and aid to Pacific islands,
78–79; and Southeast Asia,
79–80; as satellite of United

States? 93; and South Pacific
Commission, 101; literary output in, curtailed by First World
War, 125; literary output isolated and limited until 1930s,
126 ff.; literary output much increased, 1935–1960, 131 ff.;
literary achievements in past
decade, 134; literary influence
on World English, 134; literary
self-consciousness, emerging,
129 ff.; expatriation of writers in
1920s and 1930s, 129; reaches
literary maturity in 1960s,
133–134, 141; public support for
the arts, 131–132; surpassing
humility of, unchallenged by
Australians, 140–141; race relations in, thought to be better
than elsewhere, 168; insignificance of non-Polynesian
minorities in, 169; European
preponderance in population decreasing, 169; constitutional
progress in midnineteenth century, 169; and Polynesians other
than Maoris, 182; and Pacific islands, 182–183; and South
Pacific Commission and Forum,
188; grants self-government to
Cook Islands, 194; attitude toward Pacific islands in contrast
with Australia's, 194–195;
analysis of early discoveries of,
203; and erosion of British
power, 204; economic development of, in 1920, 205; and the
Great Depression, 205–206,
211; failure to maintain par with
sterling a traumatic experience,
206; socialism in, with capitalist
base, 208; attitude toward collective security and the League
of Nations, 209; and the doctrine
"when Britain is at war, the Empire is at war," 209; and security